PROCESS MAPPING

How to Reengineer
Your Business Processes

V. DANIEL HUNT

JOHN WILEY & SONS, INC.
New York • Chichester • Brisbane • Toronto • Singapore

To Janet C. Hunt

Contents

Acknowledgments

Process Mapping has been developed based on information from a wide variety of authorities who are specialists in their respective fields. The following publications were used as intellectual resources for this book.

Quality in America, V. Daniel Hunt, Irwin Professional Publishing, Homewood, IL: 1996.

Reengineering—Leveraging the Power of Integrated Product Development, V. Daniel Hunt, Omneo/Oliver Wight, Essex Junction, VT: 1994.

IDEF Architects Manual—IDEF0 Definition Methodology, SofTech, Inc., Report Number 7500-15.

As-Is System Development Methodology, Timothy L. Ramey and Glen R. Mitchell, Report Number 170130001U, April 17, 1983.

An Assessment of Simulation Systems Applicable to Business Process Reengineering at Army Directorates of Public Works, Edgar "Skip" Neely, James H. Johnson, and Mark J. Orth, USACERL Technical Report FF-94/31, September 1994.

Improving Performance—How to Manage the White Space on the Organization Chart, Geary A. Rummler and Alan P. Brache, Jossey-Bass Publishers, San Francisco, CA: 1990.

Integration Definition for Function Modeling (IDEF0), U.S. Department of Commerce, Technology Administration, National Institute of Standards and Technology, Federal Information Processing Standards Publication, Report Number FIPS PUB 183, December 1993.

Modeling Business Processes with Simulation Tools, Bruce Gladwin and Kermin Tumay, PROMODEL Corporation, Orem, UT: 1995.

The preparation of a book of this type is dependent upon an excellent staff and I have been fortunate in this regard. Special thanks to Jasmine Rohani for research assistance for the material in this book. This manuscript was word processed by Mrs. Valerie J. Western. The internal graphic design was provided by Mr. Karl J. Samuels.

Many individuals provided materials, interview comments, and insights regarding how to understand, simplify, and improve performance by mapping business processes. I appreciate their input and help in shaping this book.

I want to acknowledge the special support and assistance of Ms. Mary Ellen Johnston, and all the members of the Society for Enterprise Engineering (formerly known as the IDEF Users Group) for providing product and service information, interview time with the author, and general information that has been synthesized and used in this book.

Special recognition is noted for: *Judy Albert,* Defense Information Systems Agency; *Dan Appleton,* D. Appleton Company Inc.; *Mike Amundsen,* Texas Instruments; *Alan P. Brache,* Rummler-Brache Group; *Simon Carter,* D. Appleton Company Inc.; *Keith Comstock,* Triune Software Inc.; *Kevin Coombe,* Meta Software Corporation; *Thomas P. Cullinane,* Consultant; *Mark Ernest,* IBM; *Rita Feeney,* Wizdom Systems Inc.; *Bruce Gladwin,* PROMODEL Corporation; *Umesh Hari,* Knowledge Based Systems Inc.; *Joseph Harrington,* Ernst and Young; *James H. Johnson,* U. S. Army Corps of Engineers; *Mary Ellen Johnston,* IDEF Users Group; *Jay Karlin,* Viable Systems Inc.; *Steven Loveridge,* ADC; *Jeffrey Mershon,* Logic Works Inc.; *Mike Mondata,* Maxim; *Dennis Murphy,* Wizdom Systems Inc.; *Edgar "Skip" Neely,* U.S. Army Corps of Engineers; *Joe Nesheim,* Hewlett-Packard; *Keith McConnelly,* Defense Information Systems Agency; *Doug McDonald,* Defense Information Systems Agency; *Frances Morawski,* Defense Information Systems Agency; *Mark J. Orth,* U. S. Army Corps of Engineers; *Allen Perper,* D. Appleton Company Inc.; *Rusty Roesch,* CACI International Inc.; *Jack W. Rose,* General Services Administration; *Douglas Ross,* SofTech, Inc.; *Geary A. Rummler,* Rummler-Brache Group; *Robert Seltzer,* Meta Software Corporation; *Vijay Shende,* UES Inc.; *Neil B. Snodgrass,* D. Appleton Company Inc.; *Paul A. Strassman,* Consultant; *Julian Swedish,* J.A. Swedish & Associates; *Ken (Kerim)*

Permissions

Grateful acknowledgment is made to the following for granting permission to reprint portions of their previously published materials. Government funded reports, assessments, or publications are in the public domain. Portions of publications that are used in this book, have been reproduced with the permission to reprint of the respective publisher, copyright holder, or author; and are so noted below.

Portions of "Quality Template" and related material reprinted from *Quality in America: How to Implement a Competitive Quality Program,* by V. Daniel Hunt, Published by Irwin Professional Publishing, 1996. Reprinted with permission of Technology Research Corporation.

Portions of *The Survival Factor: An Action Guide to Improving Your Business Today,* by V. Daniel Hunt, Published by Oliver Wight Publications, 1994, Reprinted with permission of Technology Research Corporation.

Portions of *Reengineering—Leveraging the Power of Integrated Product Development,* by V. Daniel Hunt, Published by Oliver Wight Publications, 1993, Reprinted with permission of Technology Research Corporation.

Portions of *IDEF Architects Manual—IDEF0 Definition Method,* SofTech Inc., Report Number 7500-15. Public Domain Document.

Portions of *An Assessment of Simulation Systems Applicable to Business Process Reengineering at Army Directorates of Public Works,* Edgar "Skip" Neely, James H. Johnson, and Mark J. Orth, USACERL Technical Report FF-94/31, September 1994, Public Domain Document.

Portions of *Integration Definition for Function Modeling (IDEF0),* U.S. Department of Commerce, Technology Administration, National Institute of Standards and Technology, Federal Information Processing Standards Publication, Report Number FIPS PUB 183, December 1993. Public Domain Document.

Portions of *Improving Performance—How to Manage the White Space on the Organization Chart,* Geary A. Rummler and Alan P. Brache, Jossey-Bass Publishers, San Francisco, CA, 1990. This excellent book was used to provide the basic process description material described in Chapter 1. Some of the material from *Improving Performance* was edited to address specifically the process mapping topic.

CHAPTER 1

Do You Need a Roadmap?

This chapter provides a brief introduction to the basic elements of process mapping and describes the rules of the road for implementing process mapping as part of your business process reengineering efforts.

Business process reengineering is still the *hot* management concept for the late 1990s. The problem in implementing business process reengineering is that many business leaders do not recognize that everything their business enterprise does to survive is *process driven*. If you do not know what your existing processes are, or what your new optimum processes should be, you will fail at your reengineering efforts.

Process Mapping provides tools and a proven methodology for identifying your current "As-Is" business processes and can be used to provide a "To-Be" roadmap for reengineering your product and service business-enterprise functions. Process mapping is the critical link that your reengineering team can apply to better understand and significantly improve your business processes and bottom-line performance.

INTRODUCTION TO PROCESS MAPPING

"Process mapping" is a management tool initially developed and implemented by General Electric as part of their integrated "Workout," "Best Practices," and "Process Mapping" strategy to improve significantly their bottom-line business performance. The process

1

mapping concept is used to describe, in workflow diagrams and supporting text, every vital step in your business processes.

Too often we believe that we know our business processes, but in reality most managers do not really understand what their processes are or whether they can be improved, simplified, or eliminated.

Process mapping is a proven analytical and communication tool intended to help you improve your existing processes or to implement a new process-driven structure in order to reengineer your business processes. Process mapping is an excellent process management tool that you can use to better understand your current processes and to eliminate or simplify those requiring change.

The General Electric process mapping approach allowed their process improvement and reengineering teams to gain real understanding of their processes. At the General Electric Louisville appliance facility, process mapping showed that "while a fifth of the parts in any given appliance model were unique, only 5 percent were expensive enough to substantially affect inventory costs. General Electric found that it could speed manufacturing and cut costs by keeping ample stocks of the cheap components while working out just-in-time programs with suppliers to quickly deliver the other parts as needed. The biggest gains came from controlling the sequence in which parts were delivered from a plant's loading dock to its assembly line."[1]

WHAT IS A PROCESS?

Geary A. Rummler and Alan P. Brache, in their excellent book entitled *Improving Performance: How to Manage the White Space on the Organization Chart*,[2] "have found the process level to be the least understood and least managed level" of business enterprise performance. (All quotations not otherwise identified in this chapter are drawn from *Improving Performance*.) "Processes are rolling along (or, frequently, stumbling along) in organizations, whether we attend to them or not. We have two choices—we can ignore processes and hope that they do what we wish, or we can understand them and manage them."

A tremendous amount of learning and improvement can result from the documentation and examination of the input-output (customer-supplier) linkages depicted in a process map.

However, "between every input and every output is a process." Your understanding and improvement are incomplete if you don't peel the onion and examine the processes through which inputs are converted into outputs.

A business "process is a series of steps designed to produce a product or service. Some processes (such as the programming process) may be contained wholly within a function. However, most processes (such as order processing) are cross-functional, spanning the 'white space' between the boxes on the organization chart."

Some "processes result in a product or service that is received by an organization's external customer. We call those customer processes." Other processes "produce products or services that are invisible to the external customer but essential to the effective management of the business. These are referred to as administrative processes." Examples of these types of business processes appear in Table 1.1. Another "category of processes—management processes—includes actions managers should take to support the business processes." Management processes include goal setting, day-to-day planning, performance feedback, rewards, and resource allocation.

A process can be seen as a "value chain." By its contribution to the creation or delivery of a product or service, each step in a process should add value to the preceding step. For example, one step in the product development process may consist of conducting market acceptance tests. This step adds value by ensuring that the product meets the needs of the market before the product or service is finalized.

At the business-enterprise level, you can "peel the onion" to increase your understanding of the customer-supplier relationships among functions. At the product or service business-enterprise level, you "peel the onion" by breaking processes into subprocesses, workflow elements, business service processes, and manufacturing processes.

Mark Youngblood, as shown in Table 1.2, based on his book entitled *Eating the Chocolate Elephant*, lists more than 30 ways to improve your business processes. Most of these suggestions have been applied to process problems for decades. Nevertheless, it is

Table 1.1 Examples of Business Processes

Generic customer processes

- Marketing and sales
- Product/service development and introduction
- Manufacturing
- Distribution
- Billing
- Order processing
- Customer service

Industry-specific customer processes

- Loan processing (banking)
- Claim adjudication (insurance)
- Grant allocation (government)
- Merchandise return (retail)
- Food preparation (restaurants)
- Baggage handling (airline)
- Reservation handling (hotels/airlines)

Generic administrative processes

- Formal strategic and tactical planning
- Budgeting
- Training
- Facilities management
- Purchasing
- Information Technology (IT) management

SOURCE: Figure 5.1, page 46, *Improving Performance*, by Geary A. Rummler & Alan P. Brache.

Table 1.2 Business Process Improvement Possibilities

- Eliminate duplicate activities
- Combine related activities
- Eliminate multiple reviews and approvals
- Eliminate inspections
- Simplify processes
- Reduce batch sizes
- Process in parallel
- Implement demand pull
- Outsource inefficient activities
- Eliminate movement of work
- Organize multifunctional teams
- Design cellular workplaces
- Centralize/decentralize

SOURCE: Based on *Eating the Chocolate Elephant*, by Mark Youngblood.

worthwhile to mention some of them because they highlight why we want to understand, improve, or reengineer our business processes.

WHY SHOULD YOU LOOK AT YOUR PROCESSES?

Your business enterprise is only as effective as its processes. Business goals can be achieved only through development of logical business processes, such as those listed in Table 1.1. For example, one of an automobile manufacturer's goals may be to reduce the time it takes to deliver a car with the options requested by a customer. The company cannot hope to meet this goal if an inefficient ordering process or a convoluted distribution process is used.

To continue our automobile example, salespeople may be thoroughly completing order forms, data-entry clerks may be accurately coding information, and dock crews may be efficiently loading cars onto trucks. However, the effectiveness of any improvement in their performance could be limited by the logic (or illogic) of the total distribution process, made up of the order entry, production scheduling, and transportation subprocesses.

People in jobs such as these can certainly influence the effectiveness and efficiency of the processes to which they contribute. However, individual and team problem solving seldom focuses properly on total system process improvement. Actions taken in a single organizational unit often lead to the reinforcement of functional silos and system suboptimization. The clear message is that, over the long haul, neither strong people nor process improvement teams can compensate for a weak systemic process. All too often, "management relies on individual or team heroics to overcome fundamentally flawed processes. Why not fix the processes and enlist our heroes in the battle against the competition?"

Finally, the process level is important because process effectiveness efficiency should drive a multitude of business decisions. For example, a reorganization or downsizing of your business enterprise serves no purpose if it doesn't first improve process performance. Many reengineered or downsized organizations have failed because management has "cut 10 percent across the organization" rather than simplify, eliminate, or reengineer their basic processes. Process mapping provides a proven tool with which to understand and change your processes to help improve your bottom-line and competitive position.

The pivotal link between business enterprise performance and individual performance can be established through the three process-based variables: (1) process goals, (2) process design, and (3) process management. Each of these process-based variables is described next:

Process Goals

Each customer process and each administrative process exists to make a contribution to one or more business enterprise goals. Therefore, each process should also be measured against process goals that reflect the contribution that the process is expected to make to one or more business enterprise goals. "In our experience, most processes do not have goals. While functions (departments) usually have goals, most key processes cross functional boundaries. If we are working in an organization in which billing is a key process, and if we ask for the goals of the billing process, the response usually is, Oh, you mean the goals of the Billing Department. When we reply that we really do mean the billing process—including those steps accomplished outside the Billing Department—we frequently get blank stares."

Performance measurement is most effective if it is done in relation to strategic or tactical business enterprise targets, or goals. Process goals are derived from three sources: (1) business enterprise goals, (2) customers' requirements, and (3) benchmarking information. Process benchmarking—comparing a process to the same process in an exemplary organization—is very useful. Often the business enterprise that is best in its class for a given process is not a competitor and is therefore easy to study. Business enterprises have learned a lot by benchmarking their order-handling and distribution processes of companies such as L.L. Bean; the product development processes to those of 3M; and their customer service processes of IBM.

Process goals are linked both to business enterprise goals and to customers' requirements. Note that they are not merely goals for the product development department. These process goals also reflect the performance expected of product development's partners in the process of product development and introduction, including marketing, sales, and field operations. By meeting these goals, this process will make a significant contribution to the realization of the business enterprise's strategic vision.

A software company's business goal may be to reduce the software package's order-cycle time response to an average of 72 hours by the end of next year. To meet this software business goal the order-filling process becomes strategically critical. The goals for this process might include:

- No products will be shipped to incorrect addresses because of errors.

- We will meet our 72-hour goal without increasing the cost of order filling.

- We will provide our customers with a single point of contact for order questions and feedback.

To meet these business goals your managers should also establish process goals for the customer support process. In all cases, the key process mapping goal is for the key processes to be linked to customer and organization requirements.

Process Design

After you have established goals for your critical processes, your managers need to ensure that the processes are designed to achieve those goals efficiently. To determine whether each process and subprocess is appropriately structured, you should create a cross-functional team to build your process map that shows input-output relationships among process-dependent operations and departments and that documents in a step-by-step process sequence the activities that are required to convert inputs to outputs for the specific process. "Too often, a process mapping team finds that there isn't an established process; the work just somehow gets done."

Figure 1.1 illustrates an "As-Is" (current state) process map of an order-filling process, as developed by a process mapping team representing all functions that contribute to the process. The process mapping team (made up of representatives from all the process activity functions—including even the customer) traces the process of converting the input (orders) through all the intervening steps until the final required output (payment) is produced. The map shows how all functions are involved as the order is processed. This process mapping structure allows the team to identify all the critical interfaces, overlay the time to complete various subprocesses on the map, start to define the opportunities for process simulation, apply activity-based costing methods, and identify "disconnects" (illogical, missing, or extraneous steps) in the processes.

As your team documents and analyzes the current "As-Is" process for filling an order, it may identify a number of disconnects, such as:

- Sales representatives take too long to submit orders.
- There are too many process steps.
- Sales administration slows down the process by batch-processing orders.
- Credit checking is done for both old and new customers.
- Credit checking holds up the process because it is done before (rather than concurrently with) order picking.

Figure 1.1 Current Process "As-Is" Process Map

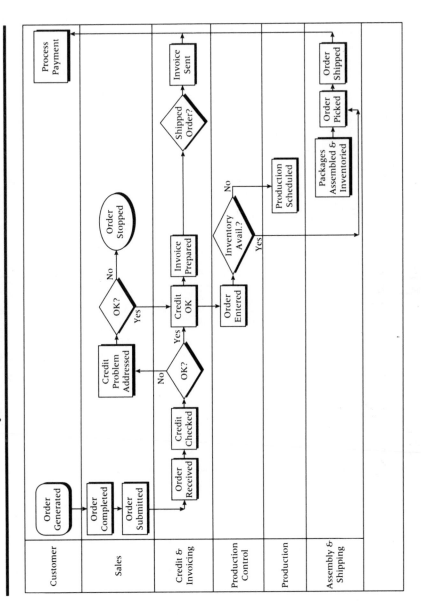

The team then created a "To-Be" Process Map, which reflects a disconnect-free order-filling process. That process map is shown in Figure 1.2.

As Figure 1.2 shows, the major changes in the "To-Be" map are:

- Direct order entry by sales, eliminating sales administration

- Parallel order processing and credit checking

- Elimination of multiple order-entry and order-logging steps

Another possible "To-Be" process would include a just-in-time production system, in which packages are assembled to order and not inventoried.

"As-Is" and "To-Be" process mapping are the central steps in process improvement projects. However, do not get mired down in excessive "As-Is" detail; the objective is to aggressively eliminate, simplify, or improve your "To-Be" processes.

A successful process improvement effort results in a positive answer to the key process design or improvement question: Is this the most efficient and effective process for accomplishing the process goals?

Process Management

Unfortunately, even the most logical, goal-directed processes don't manage themselves. These are the "four components of effective process management":

1. *Process Goal Management:* The overall process goals should serve as the basis for the establishment of subgoals throughout the process. If we managed a water pipeline, we would want to measure pressure and purity, not only at the end but also at various critical junctures along the pipeline. Similarly, we need to establish process subgoals after each step that has an especially critical impact on the ultimate customer-driven process goals.

   Once process subgoals have been established, functional goals can be developed. Any functional activity goals established at the business enterprise level should be modified,

Figure 1.2 Reengineered "To-Be" Process Map

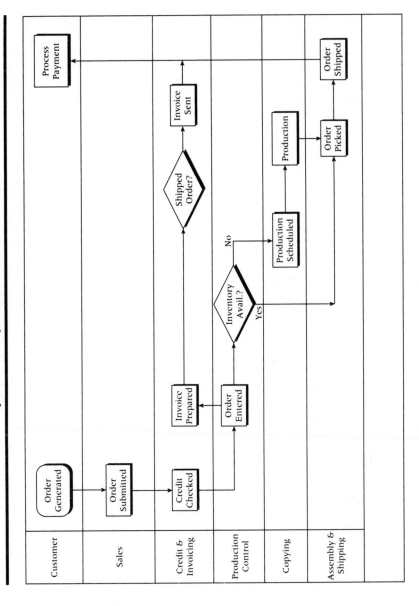

if necessary, to reflect maximum functional contributions to the process goals and subgoals. Since the purpose of a function is to support processes, it should be measured by the degree to which it serves those processes. When we establish functional goals that bolster processes, we ensure that your team meets the needs of your internal and external customers.

Your first step should be to identify each activity function's contribution to the process. For example, order entry is the first segment (subprocess) of the order-filling process. Three specific activity functions contribute to this process element:

- Sales, which enters the order via telephone

- Finance, which determines the customer's credit status

- Production control, which determines the inventory status and, if necessary, triggers production of additional product

2. *Performance Management:* After you have established a workable process and a set of goals and subgoals for its performance, its managers should establish systems for obtaining internal and external customer feedback on the process outputs, tracking process performance against the goals and subgoals, feeding back process performance information to the functions that play a role, establishing mechanisms to solve process problems and continuously improve process performance, and adjusting goals to meet new customer requirements.

During the last few years, a lot "has been learned about managing process performance (which is, in effect, managing the horizontal organization). We have learned that if processes are to be managed on an ongoing basis (and not just fixed when they break), then managers must establish an infrastructure, which many organizations are beginning to call process management."

You could take several process management actions to ensure that the order-filling process is continuously managed, such as noted here:

- Rate the performance of the process, giving it a grade in

such areas as customer satisfaction, cost, clarity and thoroughness of documentation, and quality and quantity of product or service performance measures. Each activity function's contribution to the process could also be rated.

- Designate a process owner to oversee the entire process.

- Identify a permanent process team, which will meet monthly to review and improve process performance.

- Hold monthly operations reviews, in which process performance will be reviewed first.

- Reward people within a function only if process goals are met and if the process function's contribution goals are met.

Understanding process improvement is such a pivotal element of process mapping that all of Chapter 4 is devoted to that single subject.

3. *Resource Management:* Managers have always understood that resource allocation is a major part of their responsibility. However, "process-focused resource allocation tends to be different from the usual function-oriented approach. Functional resource allocation usually results from a series of one-to-one meetings between a senior manager and his or her departmental or subdepartmental managers. In these meetings, each manager makes a case for a bigger slice of the pie, and the most persuasive presentations are rewarded with the largest budgets and headcount allocations."

Process-driven resource allocation is the result of a determination of the dollars and people required for the process to achieve its goals. After that is done, each function is allocated its share of the resources, according to its contribution to the process. If activity-based process management is institutionalized throughout your business enterprise, each function's budget is the sum total of its portion of each process budget.

4. *Process Interface Management:* A process map clearly displays the points at which one process activity function provides a product or service to another process activity. At each of these points, there is a customer-supplier interface. These interfaces often

represent the greatest opportunity for performance improvement. A process-oriented manager closely monitors interfaces and removes any barriers to effectiveness and efficiency.

The key process management questions are:

- Do you understand your processes?
- Have appropriate process subgoals been set?
- Is process performance managed?
- Are sufficient resources allocated to each process?
- Are the interfaces between process steps being managed?

THE PROCESS MAPPING CONCEPT

The fundamental concepts of process mapping are based on the idea of structured analysis, which has produced significant payoffs in diverse business enterprise applications such as banking, insurance, manufacturing (auto and aerospace industries), pharmaceuticals, and service enterprises.

The benefits of process mapping include reductions in product and service development costs, fewer system integration failures, uniformly better process understanding, and improvement in overall business enterprise operations and performance. The basic process mapping concepts can be summarized by the following key points:

1. Understand a process or system by creating a "process map" that graphically shows things (objects or information) and activities (performed by men or machines). The process map is designed to properly relate both things and activities.

2. Distinguish what functions a system should perform from how the system is built to accomplish those functions. The distinction must be clearly evident in the process map.

3. Structure the process map as a hierarchy with major functions at the top and successive process map levels revealing well-bounded details. Each process map should be internally consistent.

4. Establish an informal process map review cycle to "proofread" the developing map and record all decisions in writing. This ensures that the process map reflects the best efforts of a committed team.

For new or reengineered systems, projects, or processes, process mapping may be used to specify the needs, requirements, and functions and then may be used to improve the process that meets the customer's requirements and performs the required functions. For existing processes, process mapping can be used to analyze the purposes that the application serves and the functions it performs, and in addition, to record the mechanisms by which these are done.

A process map consists of graphic hierarchical diagrams, supporting text, and a glossary of common terms and process definitions, all cross-referenced to one another. The major output of the process map is a workflow diagram drafted on either conventional paper drawing or created by computer graphic process mapping techniques.

The process map is shown in the form of a graphic language designed to:

- Expose process detail gradually and in a controlled manner

- Encourage conciseness and accuracy in describing the process map

- Focus attention on the process map interfaces

- Provide a powerful process analysis and consistent design vocabulary

A process map considers activities, information, and interface constraints simultaneously. However, in any one process map, the emphasis will always be on one of these constraint aspects. For example, a process map typically shows activities as boxes and uses arrows to represent data and interfaces. Thus a representation— whether it be current operations, functional specification, or design—always consists of an activity element, an information element, and a user interface element in the process map.

Process mapping usually begins with a functional process representation of "WHAT" the process problem is, carefully separated from the design of "HOW" the process problem will be solved or implemented. This approach ensures that the process is fully and clearly understood before the details of a process solution are decided. The process map shows HOW the WHAT is to be realized.

Process mapping provides a notation to express how a function in the process map is carried out by a process mechanism, including how a single process mechanism can perform related functions at several different places in the functional process map.

Process mapping starts by representing the whole system process as a single modular unit—a box with arrow interfaces, as shown in Figure 1.3. Since the single box represents the system process as a whole, the descriptive name written in the process map box must be general, rather abstract, and lacking in detail. The same is true of the interface arrows, since they also represent the complete set of external interfaces to the system process.

The process map box that represents the system process as a single module is then expanded in more detail on another diagram with several boxes connected by interface arrows, as shown in Figure 1.4. These interconnections make the process map boxes represent major process submodules of the parent process module.

Each succeeding process map sublevel reveals a complete set of submodules, each represented as a box whose boundaries are defined by the interface arrows. Each of these submodule process

Figure 1.3 Process Map Top-Level Graphic Description

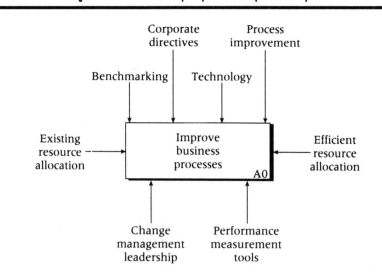

Figure 1.4. Next Process Map Sublevel Graphic Description

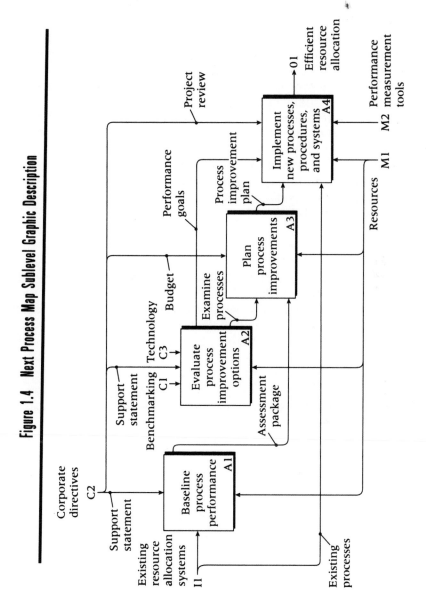

17

map boxes may be similarly decomposed to expose even more process detail.

Process mapping provides consistent rules for gradually introducing further detail during process map decomposition. An upper limit of six process map boxes forces the use of a hierarchy to describe complex process subjects. The lower limit of three process map boxes is usually chosen to ensure that enough detail is introduced to make the process map valuable.

Each diagram in a process map is shown in precise relationship to other process diagrams by means of interconnecting arrows. When a process module is broken down into process submodules, the interfaces between the submodules are shown as arrows. The name of each submodule box plus its labeled interfaces define a context for detailing that process submodule.

In all cases, every submodule is restricted, containing only those elements that lie within the scope of its parent module. Further, the module cannot omit any elements. The parent box and its interfaces provide a context. Nothing should be added or removed from this precise boundary.

The creation of a process map is carried out by process "authors." It is a dynamic process that usually requires the participation of more than one person, and team action is preferred. Throughout a project, the draft versions of the process map diagrams are each distributed to one or more other project members for review and comment. The discipline requires that each person make comments about a process map diagram, make them in writing, and submit them to the "author" of the diagram. This cycle continues until the process map diagrams, and eventually, the entire process map, are accepted by the process analysis team. During the process, incorrect or unacceptable analysis and design results are usually spotted early, and oversights and errors are detected before they can cause major disruptions.

The end effect of this approach to organized process understanding and process improvement is a high assurance that the final process maps are valid. The process map diagrams are changed to reflect corrections and valid comments. More detail is added by the creation of more process map diagrams. More comments are made. More changes are included. The final process map represents the agreement of the process map analysts on a representation of the system or process that is being improved or reengineered.

PROCESS-DRIVEN REENGINEERING

The increasing competitive pressure to minimize the "time" it takes to service customers, increase profits, and develop new products promises a broad range of applications for process-driven business process reengineering.

All service processes and processes that support production (e.g., order management, integrated product design and development, engineering changes, purchasing, marketing support, and payroll) can be considered business processes, and thus subject to improvement or reengineering.

Some typical examples of business process reengineering opportunities are listed here:

- *Order Management Processes:* Purchasing, contracts, receiving, shipping, storage, and materials management

- *Financial Management Processes:* Payroll, ledger control, taxes, accounts receivable, and accounts payable

- *Information Management Processes:* Database management, networking, and client-server applications

- *Product Development Processes:* Product design, testing, configuration, and documentation processes

- *Human Resource Processes:* Hiring, placement, personnel services, and training

Reengineering often begins with an assumption that the hierarchical, non–value added, departmentalized structure of most businesses enterprises today is fundamentally flawed. And only through a radical reinvention of the value-added process stream required to produce a product or service can your business enterprise hope to survive the intense competition of the future. For your reengineering effort to be successful you must actively involve all of your people, processes, and technology.

Reengineering gurus Dr. Michael Hammer and James Champy note in their book *Reengineering the Corporation* that only about 30 percent of the reengineering projects that they have seen were successful. For reengineering to be successful, as noted in

Chapter 2, you need top-down active leadership that facilitates real reengineering change; and a bottom-up quality management improvement-driven process to see real, sustainable, bottom-line results.

PROCESS MAPPING TOOLS

When asked the question, "If you were to rebuild or reengineer your business enterprise from ground zero, what would you do differently," the answer can usually best take the form of a process map. Whether the answer is a narrative, a flow diagram, or a process map simulation, you need to define the processes that take inputs such as raw materials or potential customers and turn them into outputs such as products or services.

Over the past few years, several new software tools have been developed specifically for mapping business processes and work-flows. Chapter 8 describes a variety of these tools and provides a "Best Buy" suggestion for you to start your process mapping tool-selection process. Most of these tools define business processes using graphical symbols or objects, with individual process activities depicted as a series of boxes and arrows. Special characteristics of each process or activity may then be attached as attributes of the process. Many of these tools also allow for some type of activity-based costing (ABC) or simulation analysis depending on the so-phistication of the underlying methodology of the tool.

These process mapping tools can be divided into three general categories:

- *Flow Diagramming Tools:* At the most basic level are flow dia-gramming and drawing tools that help define processes and workflows by linking text descriptions of processes to symbols. Typically, flow chart models provide limited analysis capability. Examples of flow-charting tools are ABC Flowcharter from Micrografx, EasyFlow from Haventree Software, and Flow-Charting 3 from Patton & Patton.

- *CASE Tools:* These tools provide a conceptual framework for modeling hierarchies and process definitions. They are typically built on relational databases and include functions that provide linear, static, and deterministic analysis capability. Examples of CASE tools include Meta Software's Design/IDEF and Workflow Analyzer, TI's Business Design Facility, and Action Technology's Action Workflow.

- *Simulation Tools:* Simulation tools provide continuous or discrete-event, dynamic, and more sophisticated analysis capability. Simulation tools typically provide animation capabilities that allow the process designer to see how customers and/or work objects flow through the system. Examples of simulation modeling tools for business process mapping include Service-Model from PROMODEL Corporation, SimProcess from CACI, and Extend+BPR from Imagine That.

SIMULATION FOR PROCESS MAPPING

A process map simulation is an analysis that focuses on changes that occur over time. Generally, process map simulation addresses the dynamic properties that are often of greatest interest to process improvement. Today process map simulation provides a relatively low-cost means to examine process improvements before substantial funds are invested in a new product or process improvement effort. Simulation of your processes is important[3] for three specific reasons:

- Process map simulation also provides a means of measuring overall changes in the value (output) of an organization or system caused by the specific changes you make to your processes.

- Process map simulation's graphic capabilities help decision makers understand complex operations through a relatively simple graphic representation.

- Process map simulation identifies utilization rates of activities (money, time, people), revealing bottlenecks or underutilized activities. Bottlenecks tell you where to apply resources or suggest a redesign of your systems. Underutilized activities tell you where waste exists and identify resources for reallocation and activities that can be discontinued for a cost savings without degrading overall productivity.

Process map simulation can also be integrated with Activity-Based Costing analysis in that it increases the possible dimensions of your cost/benefit analysis.

Proponents of any version of sophisticated structured-process map analysis say that process activity maps first require the establishment of purpose, goals, context, and viewpoint. A complete viewpoint may be difficult, if not impossible, to establish using only fixed-process map descriptions. Process map simulation provides a suitable means of addressing this difficulty given that the functions represented by a process map do not perform dynamically.

There are three structural cases (see footnote 3) in a process map that imply a need to simulate process interaction changes, as noted here:

- [First] when a process is structured so that an output from one process map activity provides input to *two or more activities*, organizational processes may jam because sequencing requirements are not met. Process mapping will not reveal this deficiency, but process map simulation will. Effective process sequencing of process activities can have a dramatic impact on the overall effectiveness of your business processes.
- Second, when a process is structured so that an input to two or more activities comes from *only one activity*, organizational processes may jam over resource conflict, particularly consumable resources. If different activities are placing demands on a common pool of resources and the balance of those resources reaches zero, one or more activities will stall until the resources are resupplied. The system wide impact of this process change can be marginal or substantial. Only through process map simulation can these impacts be effectively quantified.
- Finally, when outputs of two or more activities are inputs to each other, then parallelism (also known as concurrency) occurs. This structural phenomenon represents coordina-

tion. Coordination is a prerequisite for process success when activities must exchange information or other resources with other activities at the same time. The efficiency of information exchange between concurrent or parallel activities can have counter-intuitive, yet profound, effects on the length of time necessary to produce a product or process.

—Modeling Business Processes
with Simulation Tools, p. 6

Process map simulation addresses aspects of processes for which static activity and data modeling are inadequately suited, because they cannot cope with the impact of resource flow. Process map simulation is an excellent method for this purpose and, as a result, can provide insight that may be a more truthful representation of reality. In the context of other process improvement methodologies, there are two general areas to which simulation may contribute uniquely. These areas are dynamically measuring "activity utilization" and "system workload."

Activity Utilization Analysis

In an unchanging environment, activity utilization can be measured using static process mapping techniques. Activity-Based Costing (ABC) is an effective, relatively new accounting technique that involves measuring both the cost and value of activities. It may be possible to identify the resources supporting each activity and their sunk costs in dynamic processes but difficult to measure the proportion of such resources actually devoted to one activity. Process map simulation can provide these measures. Process map simulation can identify bottlenecks and underutilization of activities or equipment, enabling management to redistribute resources or restructure processes to enhance overall efficiency.

System Workload Analysis

Another capability of process map simulation is to provide a linking of process local changes to global process changes. One aspect of process mapping that we have already described is the development of a "To-Be" process map. The options for projecting a "To-Be" map can be unlimited. Many different relationships can be redefined between activities, and the application of resources used by activities can be varied in many different ways. When two or more "To-Be" process maps are under consideration, how does one choose the best alternative? Process map simulation provides a means of measuring anticipated global enterprise or subset process performance when changes are made locally.

Process map simulation provides a disciplined way of describing the detailed structure of your processes and how they relate. Since understanding process hierarchy is important in understanding large, complex systems, process mapping is particularly useful, since it includes hierarchy as an element of its basic capability. Process mapping provides the structure that exists between processes for effective simulation, analysis, and process improvement.

DO YOU NEED A PROCESS ROADMAP?

YES! Most of us do not understand how our business enterprise really works. It is process driven, and we do not really know the processes that drive our operations. Process mapping helps you understand and improve your processes and your bottom-line performance. YES—you do need a process roadmap.

Work gets done in your business enterprise through its customer and administrative processes. If you want to understand the way your processes really work, to apply a proven methodology to improve the way work gets done, and to manage the way work gets done, process mapping should be the focus of your attention and actions.

Who needs to apply process mapping?

- Executives, who can use the process perspective and tools to link business enterprise goals to individual performance, measure what's really going on in the business, benchmark performance against other companies, establish competitive advantages, assess the impact of mergers and acquisitions, and evaluate alternative organization structures.

- Managers, who can use the process perspective and process mapping tools to identify and close quality, cost, and cycle time gaps; manage the interfaces with other departments and the interfaces within their own departments; implement change; and effectively allocate resources.

■ Analysts, who can use the process perspective and process mapping tools to diagnose business needs and recommend improvements that will have a significant impact on business enterprise performance, to evaluate actions they are asked to take, and to facilitate improvement teams.
        —*Improving Performance*, p. 63

In summary, process mapping can provide a disciplined way of describing the detailed structure of your processes and how they relate. Since understanding your process is critical to understanding and changing process-driven systems, process mapping and process map simulation are particularly useful. Process mapping provides a proven methodology that can be used in your business enterprise for effective simulation, cost and schedule analysis, and significant process improvement.

ABOUT THE REST OF THIS BOOK

The balance of this book describes a proven process mapping approach that you can apply to your business enterprise—today! The 11 key process mapping steps are:

Step 1: Determine if you need a process roadmap.

Step 2: Chapter 2 can be used to help you assess your need to improve or reengineer your business processes.

Step 3: Chapter 3 can be used to help you define the role of process mapping in your reengineering strategy.

Step 4: Chapter 4 helps you determine if you really understand your business processes.

Step 5: Chapter 5 illustrates the value of process mapping by illustrating success stories from a broad variety of process map users.

Step 6: The process mapping methodology is described in Chapter 6 in sufficient detail to help you learn how to apply it in your own business.

Step 7: Chapter 7 shows how to create your own process mapping team.

Step 8: Chapter 8 describes how you can find the right process mapping tools and provides a comparative assessment; "Best Buy" suggestions are given for process mapping tools.

Step 9: How to collect process map information and process details via focused interviews is discussed in Chapter 9.

Step 10: Chapter 10 provides specific steps for implementation of process mapping.

Step 11: Simply encourages you to just "Change it!"and concludes this user-friendly, easy-to-understand, hands-on book.

CHAPTER 2

Reengineer Your Business Processes

"Reengineering" symbolizes radical change in the 1990s. Do you wonder why your business should go through such a change—one that is turning many businesses upside down? Although downsizing is causing great disruption in business, and downsizing and reengineering are often linked or addressed as one and the same process, this chapter considers reengineering in a more positive light. The focus is a description of the potential for reengineering your business enterprise processes.

Reengineering can be used to help simplify your processes, improve productivity, and, in an evolutionary manner, provide an opportunity for your employees to take on entirely new job responsibilities as your business is turned around and begins to grow again.

WHY REENGINEER?

In order to satisfy your customers, you must develop new products cheaper, better, and faster then you did last year. You should examine the possibility of reengineering your processes to assure that your competitors, by significantly changing the way they do business, won't surprise you in the competitive game of global survival.

Table 2.1 Motivations To Reengineer

MOTIVATOR	PERCENT
Reduce costs	84
Improve quality	79
Increase speed (throughput)	62
Overcome a competitive threat	50
Change the organizational structure	35
Other	9

SOURCE: Grant Thornton, *Motivations to Reengineer*, NCMS Focus, September, 1994.

Businesses do not reengineer their processes just to cut costs, according to a Grant Thornton study noted in Table 2.1. This survey of chief executive officers uncovered several additional reasons to reengineer your business.

In response to these motivational interests, business organizations are implementing various functional changes by mapping their business processes, improving process flows, investing in automation, organizing operations by customer or product line, and bringing the management communication levels closer together.

Reengineering is a state-of-the-practice management approach that applies the "best practices," process understanding, process simplification principles, computer-aided analytical tools, and management techniques to help assure survival in this very competitive global marketplace. Reengineering concentrates on examining the ways you can significantly improve your business by understanding, replacing, deleting, or improving processes.

Quality-based reengineering is a management approach where system defects are avoided rather than corrected later in the process. The potential of reengineering is tremendous, if properly conceived and implemented.

Reengineering provides an optimum application of people and technology to (1) produce new products, (2) provide new or better services, (3) enhance existing processes, (4) improve your business enterprise, and (5) administrate support processes. The significance of reengineering is that it can create a better way of satisfying your customers' needs.

As shown Figure 2.1 the greatest opportunities for reengineering lie in the following areas:

- Functional "process" reengineering—65 percent
- "Product" reengineering—23 percent
- Corporation-wide "business process reengineering" (BPR)—12 percent

Many consulting companies are trying to sell the idea that every business must be totally reexamined and reengineered. Based on Technology Research Corporation's "cultural change" management experience we can only identify a small number of companies that will totally reengineer their business enterprise. The problems with radical corporation-wide business process reengineering recommendations are as follows:[1]

- Companies will only take the radical enterprise-wide business process reengineering path if they are *forced to change.*
- The culture change requires too much time and commitment for top management to stay the course. Often consultants sell "reengineering" as a quick fix for business success or survival, but significant bottom-line performance improvements take at least 18 months.

Figure 2.1   Potential Reengineering Opportunities

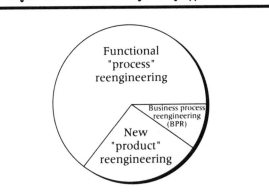

- If your business has a history of not being able to implement any new business management system, it is unlikely that you will be able to adopt radical corporation-wide BPR without major disruption.

- Executives often rely on "peer experience" with new management systems before they will take the risk of change. They are unwilling to risk massive change unless they either know that it has worked or their path to survival has no other alternative approach.

- Very few companies have adopted radical business BPR for all of their corporation's products and processes.

The good news is that the basic principles of reengineering (asking why we are developing products or processes the way we have been) are very useful for "new product" reengineering, service business process improvement, and functional "process" reengineering. The potential to reengineer your processes, wherein you reexamine the product or process with a new vision of the type and extent of alternate approaches, has been clearly demonstrated. Pilot demonstrations of process mapping reengineering efforts can help convince your team that it will benefit your business.

Present reality is, in a word, change. The world has never changed so fast as in the present century and change will escalate in the future. Present reality demands quality, value, reliability, and consumer satisfaction; and your customers want all of these goals achieved at a lower cost.

Top management leaders, co-workers, suppliers, information system wizards, product design specialists, resource managers, service providers, marketers, and every one of your employees must play an active role in your reengineering effort if it is to be really successful.

The only way to succeed is to understand, map, and change (where needed) your strategic processes so they can be improved from end to end to significantly improve your business. The reengineering process shown in Figure 2.2 identifies an optimum management systems approach that can produce the desired product or service, that has the required level of quality, and that is delivered in a predetermined time within a preset cost.

Figure 2.2 Process-Driven Improvement

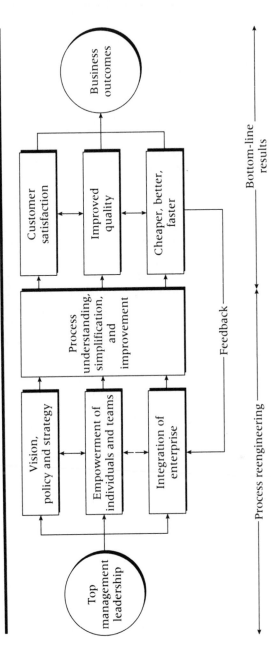

American business leaders, faced with the need to survive in a changing market, are beginning to recognize the advantages of reengineering. The concept of reengineering as used in this book is a shorthand way of stressing two fundamental beliefs:

- Reengineering of products and service "processes" should become part of your business survival strategy. Reengineering takes considerable top management attention and persistence. If you have world-class quality products, services, and people, you will also generate world-class profits and prosper in this rapidly changing market.

- Your business's reengineering program must address your own unique needs. Off-the-shelf, "just add water," canned reengineering solutions cannot generate the level of human commitment within your business that is needed for you to succeed. In fact, you may substitute your business's reengineering initiative name (Business Process Redesign, Inspire, Team Zebra, or Rapid Product Realization) in place of the term "reengineering" when thinking about some of the concepts presented in this book.

WHAT IS REENGINEERING?

Reengineering is a fundamentally new way of looking at how product and service processes are changed from conception to customer delivery and satisfaction.

Process development has often been described as a sequential process. Traditional process development has been characterized by separate functional units (such as marketing, order processing, product or service design, and production) that pass their new products or service efforts "over the wall" to the next isolated functional area in your business enterprise process. Communication among functional units is very formal and interdepartment boundaries limit effective communication. Each functional group sees the new product or service only after the preceding group is finished with its own functional efforts.

The traditional sequential product and service development process becomes progressively less efficient as product or service complexity, organization complexity, and global market demands increase. Reengineering can be used to reflect the synthesis and application of the best management methods available today in America.

Figure 2.3 illustrates the basic elements of reengineering your product and services processes. It is focused on outcomes (continuous value improvement, profit improvement, defect reduction, faster product development cycles, etc.) that directly affect the competitiveness of your business.

The fundamental elements of business process reengineering stress:

1. *Customer Satisfaction:* Reengineering requires you and your associates to understand what your customers want and helps you define product or service requirements that will satisfy your customers.

2. *Process Understanding:* Most new process improvement efforts are hindered because your business management, product engineers, service creators, production staff, and business teams do not understand all the process elements from product or service conception to end-user customer support. Before reengineering your processes, you need to benchmark and identify your product and service process strengths and weaknesses. To arbitrarily throw "the baby out with the bathwater" does not solve your near-term business growth needs. If reengineering of your products and services is done without understanding your businesses processes, you might reinvent your original organizational process problems. Process mapping is a critical tool in helping you understand your "As-Is" process and helps you formulate effective new "To-Be" processes to improve your performance.

3. *Radical Reengineering:* According to Dr. Michael Hammer and James Champy in their book *Reengineering the Corporation,* from 50 to 75 percent of the organizations that undertake radical business process reengineering do not achieve the dramatic results they expected.[2] Some consultants recommend "radical" change in terms of questioning everything that is done and trying to determine if it should have been done. Business process reengineering efforts often question the total enterprise-wide and individual processes involved in satisfy-

Figure 2.3   Elements of Product and Service Process Reengineering

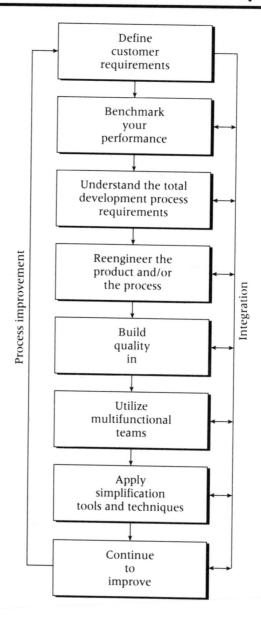

ing the development of new products or services for your customers. However, for all the management books and press hype, few corporations will turn their business over to an outside consultant to radically change the way you do your business.

4. *Quality Goals:* One concept that you should also focus on is quality-driven "bottoms-up" team participation in your business process reengineering effort. The vision for your business should include quality stretch goals, such as Motorola's Six Sigma approach, or more specific product and service customer satisfaction-driven quality metrics. Today's quality goals concentrate on reducing variation in processes and application of effective measurement systems. Your reengineering effort should be characterized as focusing on process mapping, product and process elimination, process simplification and integration, process improvement, teamwork, and your active leadership and participation in change.

5. *Adoption of Multifunctional Teams:* The only way to unleash the power of reengineering is to create multifunctional process mapping and process change teams that include, rather than exclude, all of the relevant process owners within your business enterprise. New products or services that satisfy the cheaper, better, faster requirements of your customers are "good business." New product and service efforts should include all the "product" and "process" owners, from purchasing through customer service to assure customer satisfaction.

   Teamwork is important for successful business process reengineering implementation. The process improvements from each project contribute total process improvement. Both management and the organizational structure must promote team activities. No longer can you effectively dictate all activities within your business. Your management system should be changing to focus more on participative management and teamwork.

   In these quality-based approaches, the organizational structure flattens. Strict functional alignments found in vertically structured organizations are removed and the organization becomes more unified. Flatter organizational structures promote cross-functional teamwork to address process issues and processes that impact the entire organization. Less restrictive communication results from removing bureaucratic barriers between process work areas. Employees can work together to improve the supplier-customer process relationships. A flatter organizational structure also improves communication through the organizational hierarchy; management listens to what the teams are saying rather than telling them to "listen up" during one-way, downward-directed communications.

Reengineering requires a team approach to new "product" and "service" creation and delivery. Technology is useful in efficiently analyzing increasingly complex systems; but technology is not the total answer to improving your process. Without any computer or special software, you can, today, with pencil and paper, identify your business's major process problems and the critical "bottleneck" problems that you need to begin to address.

Early conceptual or "systems" process thinking involves many issues. Thus it requires a multidisciplined team gathered from across the entire organization and chartered to address issues impacting the overall system life cycle. While early details may often preclude detailed decision making due to risk and uncertainty in the eventual system characteristics, issues such as customer requirements, support services, maintenance policy, manpower utilization and trends, personnel policy, and training needs should be considered early to avoid later conflicts as your new process evolves and the system characteristics become more defined. This reengineering team approach requires a process improvement organizational structure characterized by open communication among team members, access to evolving conceptual information, clear and concise reporting channels to management, and commitment to the project versus commitment to the functional "home" office.

The reengineering multifunctional team concepts can also be applied to contract-subcontractor relationship as organizations work together to improve their product and service processes.

6. *Software Tools and Techniques:* Knowledge about individual reengineering tools such as process mapping does not by itself constitute understanding of, nor create the management leadership that facilitates, substantive process change. Each soft-

ware tool must be viewed in terms of the synergistic benefit possible when it is combined, integrated, or uniquely applied to improve your processes. Software tools and techniques are process mapping aids that can help you to facilitate change.

Because every business is unique, you will have to be the change agent; you will have to understand these new software tools and process mapping techniques (see Chapter 8) and then select and apply them to your own processes.

7. *Continue to Improve the Process:* Management must recognize that all reengineering efforts are made up of process understanding, process mapping, process simplification, and effective change management intended to significantly improve the way you have done business. Process improvement is not a one-time task. You must continuously examine your processes and continue to improve.

Any organization, whether a manufacturing firm, a service organization, or a consulting firm, accomplishes its mission via processes. Within these business processes are the "hidden operational processes." These "hidden operational processes" cost your business money without generating income or adding any value. Reducing the unrecognized costs of your "hidden operational processes" by eliminating, simplifying, or improving your work processes clearly increases profits. A climate of process improvement evolves through an ongoing focus on mapping your actual work processes. All workers should be knowledgeable in their work process and those input-output processes that affect their own process. This will provide them the ability to ask and address the question: "Is there a better way?" Management must allow workers to openly question the current standards and form teams to examine and improve the work processes. With the increased emphasis on satisfying your customers by addressing the cheaper, better, and faster (CBF) factors must also come the realization that significant increases in performance can also result from eliminating the need for the process. Furthermore, by continuing to improve the work processes, management can build flexibility into the organization—flexibility needed to cope with rapid change caused by increasing systems complexity and changing technology.

Reengineering is also characterized by focus on the customer's requirements and priorities, a conviction that quality is the result of improving the product and service processes, and a philosophy that improvement (radical, revolutionary, or evolutionary) of all the business enterprise processes is the never-ending responsibility of the entire team.

The building blocks of reengineering are not new. The terms *system engineering, enterprise engineering, simultaneous engineering, concurrent engineering, continuous value improvement,* and *process value engineering* have long been used to describe portions of reengineering.

The integrated examination of your processes is the key to reengineering. Reengineering seeks to improve the total business processes by the functional integration of your processes.

Your business is capable of fully implementing some level of process reengineering now! Implementation can be based on a simple reengineering strategy, which is summarized here:

- Eliminate, simplify, or integrate organizations, products, processes, and activities based on reengineering principles, eliminating "stove-piping" and "over-the-wall" transactions through the use of multifunctional teams.

- Encourage active top management leadership and participation to facilitate enterprise-wide business process reengineering.

- Rethink how your business addresses gaining a better understanding of both co-worker and customer needs.

- Implement a process that will lead to the use of appropriate process mapping tools and techniques to improve process integration and efficiency.

UNIQUE CHARACTERISTICS OF REENGINEERING

Table 2.2 provides a generic delineation of the unique characteristics of reengineering.

Figure 2.4 illustrates reengineering's unique emphasis on people, process, and technology. People are the critical mass in terms of reengineering implementation. More than 50 percent of your reengineering effort is tied to your management leadership and to team member and co-worker understanding of how you can implement

Table 2.2 Unique Reengineering Characteristics

Focuses on understanding, eliminating, simplifying, and bundling business processes to improve your productivity and significantly reduce operational costs

Optimizes the suite of product and service processes in a systematic, integrated, comprehensive, phased, and practical manner

Establishes product and service process customer satisfaction criteria based upon customer needs and continuous value improvement competitive requirements

Provides better understanding of your internal and external support requirements, and their examination as part of your total business enterprise needs

multifunctional process assessment teams and emphasize quality management to effect change in your business. Approximately 45 percent of your reengineering effort is process mapping, process understanding, process elimination, and process simplification driven. The balance of 5 percent is applied to the use of new or better process analysis information technology.

Figure 2.4 Reengineering Emphasis on People, Process, and Technology

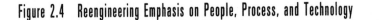

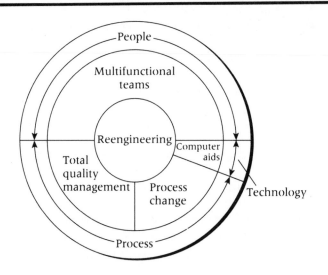

Beware of the technology salesmen! We do not require any new technology today to gain significant benefits from reengineering. As Figure 2.4 shows, the two key implementation elements are applying multifunctional process assessment teams (5 percent) and adopting quality management (25 percent) principles from the bottom up to evaluate and significantly change your business processes.

PITFALLS OF REENGINEERING

The benefits of reengineering, if properly implemented, are substantial, but they are not easily achieved. Some of the most important lessons learned in the implementation of reengineering are noted below.

Top management commitment in the form of learning, understanding, and leading your reengineering efforts with unwavering direction and constant management involvement is absolutely vital to your success. The many process improvement and cost savings that result from reengineering are due mostly to the application of multifunctional process examination teams, to willingness to manage change, and to the use of quality improvement techniques.

But the really impressive savings (potentially hundreds of thousands of dollars—depending on the size of your business) remain largely unrecognized because they result only from reengineering improvements of the larger "management systems" and "operational choices" over which only top management has control. These larger systems include strategic policies of your business such as eliminating whole marginal business entities, reducing marginally profitable product lines, establishing corporate willingness to foster better working relationships with your suppliers, improving the adversarial relationships with employees or unions, providing for pay-for-performance or lifelong learning of new skills, adopting new compensation policies to reward performance, reducing turf battles between other elements of your corporate world, and presenting a constant message to all your change agents. To date, those reengineering efforts that have failed have been due to the failure of top management to really comprehend the scope of change that is associated with successful reengineering efforts—to their failure to actively participate and oversee their reengineering initiative. Their verbal "support" for reengineering is simply not enough!

Your reengineering effort must be led. One corporation's lack of reengineering leadership resulted in a "new" effort without any clear direction or guidance within division and between the divisions. This fosters the widespread perception that reengineering is a fad that will eventually go away. In contrast, the efforts underway at Chrysler, Ford Motor Co., Motorola, Hallmark, Xerox, United Parcel Service, Capital Holding, Bell Atlantic, and other companies are well directed and guided because of top management leadership, starting with the chairman of the board.

Most companies place too much emphasis on the techniques of reengineering and not enough emphasis on the critical management system philosophy underlying the application of reengineering techniques. This partly explains the lack of top management understanding and involvement. Some top managers view reengineering as something the corporate strategic planners can conceive and implement on their own. Reengineering is more a management system than just a "quick fix" bag of tools and techniques.

Some businesses have ushered in continuous "waves" of new management techniques over the past several years, fueling the perception that reengineering is a coming-and-going fad. These techniques have included quality circles, value engineering, zero-base budgeting, management by objectives, and many others. Your people are confused about what they ought to be doing today to help assure the survival of their company and their jobs.

As the pace of global change increases, we all need to recognize that we can expect a continuing proliferation of new management techniques and buzzwords. Our task regarding these "new" initiatives, such as total quality management, Activity-Based Costing, or reengineering, is to examine and apply to our own unique enterprise those management techniques that work for our business. We should recognize that continued learning of new state-of-the-practice management techniques will permit you to blend the best of the management tools and techniques into the next suite of new management techniques; so stop worrying about fads of the month and encourage continuous improvement of your business processes.

Management should focus more on the reengineering management system integration concepts in their initial roll-out and then follow through with the tools and techniques. This would provide a sound baseline for guiding your reengineering team's effort. Because they did not do this, some people still view reengineering as a bunch of techniques that may or may not apply in the "same old way" management environment. So far, the fact that these techniques are powerful and profitable is not sufficient to ensure their successful proliferation.

Many enterprises facing financial destruction begin implementing reengineering without having a workable plan of attack. They "just want to do it now!" Consequently the reengineering staff tries to apply the techniques with little upper management understanding and guidance. Upper management does not know how to support the efforts. What was their responsibility? What questions should they ask? The end result was that many attempts sputtered along, then stopped, leaving a bad taste with everyone.

If they were to start completely over again, the best approach would be to have top management take whatever time necessary to understand the impact of such massive change on their organization; to talk with their executive peers in other companies that have gone through the painful process of reengineering their business; to try to better understand their responsibility; to develop purpose, vision, strategic direction, and a realistic plan to implement the effort business wide; and then execute and continuously communicate the plan.

Some of the most common reengineering pitfalls[3] are described below:

Pitfall 1: Failing to Focus on Strategic Business Needs

Business enterprises sometimes start business process reengineering without really knowing if they are focusing on the things most important to the business enterprise's strategic business needs. Priorities are often vague and mandates for change may call for individual, uncoordinated process improvement actions. Process improvement efforts may be based on picking processes to improve based upon whether they have willing process owners, not because they are the most important process "bottlenecks" or problems facing the business. Often, multifunctional dependencies across process improvement efforts are not identified or fully taken advantage of. The bottom line: Businesses must focus their reengineering efforts on those critical things that are important to their strategic needs, as limited resources and the need for quick action require that their team not waste their efforts.

Pitfall 2: Senior Leaders Misunderstand or Abdicate Their Responsibility

While senior leaders often voice their commitment to reengineering, many fail to take the "hands-on" role that is required to achieve successful business process reengineering.

In addition, they may force a top-down reengineering strategy on the organization that fails to mobilize employees to want to be involved in the change efforts. As senior leaders play the key role in managing business process performance improvement, often through reengineering executive councils and steering committees they must understand their role—that is, to take a "hands-on" approach to communicate the need for real change and to continuously encourage reengineering throughout the organization.

Pitfall 3: Acceptance of Shortsighted Solutions

Managers often settle for traditional, shortsighted solutions because they find it hard to "think outside-of-the-box," as described by Dr. Michael Hammer. In some cases, business leaders embrace "meat-ax" layoff programs (today called downsizing), playing "musical chairs" with the organizational structure boxes or restructuring operational functions "stovepipe mergers"—before they have even analyzed their business processes.

Unfortunately, some business leaders, in their frustrated efforts to quickly improve their business, begin to implement business process reengineering to "shake up the troops." This urge to "do something" wastes valuable human and strategic resources that could have been better invested in specific improvement actions to help the business survive. The pressure to "just do it!" may be causing more problems for a business in the long run. Unfortunately, these solutions from old management paradigms are shortsighted and fail to address the real systemic process problems within a business.

Pitfall 4: Failure to Recognize the Unique Strategic Nature of Business Process Reengineering

Many quality management consulting organizations try to sell business process reengineering as a simple derivation of total quality management that can be performed through existing quality departments, training departments, organizational development, human resource departments, or total quality management continuous process improvement teams. When this extension of quality management approach is put into practice, business process reengineering becomes a collection of a large number of nonrelated elements of your business enterprise process problems. Project-based strategies never seem to interface with the other processes that are integrally involved with the process being reengineered. The bottom line: If you are using a piecemeal approach to reengineering that is not tied to your strategic business process reengineering needs, you may not obtain the level of performance improvement that you expect. In some cases, depending on your unique strategic needs, you may need to reexamine your approach to reengineering and start over again so you can better address the true scope and impact of reengineering as part of managing your business needs.

Pitfall 5: Reengineering Is Not Technology Driven

Many business make the mistake of believing that strong doses of information technology or sophisticated business process simulation models are all that is needed for major process improvement gains. These businesses place too much emphasis on elaborate process modeling to a fault, believing that once an "As-Is" model of your business process is completed, reengineering is automatic. There are too many examples of information technology product salesmen overselling the utility and need for their products. The typical "As-Is" process mapping problem is the never-ending search for the last sub-sub-sub-sub-process step, which is not relevant to your need to wipe out or simplify the total process involved. Many businesses that are in love with consultants' process mapping models exhaust their energy, interest, and resources before they can identify the "To-Be" process improvement opportunities. In the application of information technology, business technology advocates often fail to develop an understanding of their strategic business needs before designing new information technology applications. Business leaders must understand that information technology and business process reengineering computer-aided modeling are merely components of the larger effort that is reengineering.

Pitfall 6: Lack of Experience Before Starting Your Reengineering Efforts

Some business leaders attempt to reengineer their whole business enterprise in their first reengineering effort. This is a mistake. Successful business leaders recognize that your staff needs to have a great deal of experience in reengineering before embarking upon larger efforts. Successful organizations learn to use reengineering to their advantage by starting with a key functional process or "bottleneck" or a new product that is to be developed prior to embarking on an enterprise-wide significant change program. Only those companies that have not planned ahead to meet the adoption of reengineering by their competitors or those that are forced to change due to financial problems will wade into the swamp of total enterprise reengineering as their first reengineering effort. There is no substitute for experience and building reengineering capabilities over time.

Pitfall 7: Believing That Reengineering Is a "Quick Fix"

One of the greatest myths sold to American business leaders is that reengineering is a "quick fix" to turn around their business. On average, depending on the size and scope of your reengineering effort you can expect to devote nine to 18 months for your nominal reengineering efforts—this is not the instant success that many consultants are selling to business leaders. Due to inaccurate promotion of the "quick fix" solution many executives mandate short reengineering project time frames.

Managers also often feel constrained by existing business performance delivery schedules, bottom-line constraints, and limited additional resources to implement reengineering. This often causes them to withhold their "best and brightest" personnel from their reengineering teams or to ensure that such teams have a wide, cross-functional team representation. Managers need to understand that reengineering is a long-term effort with both long- and short-term bottom-line benefits.

Pitfall 8: Believing Performance Measurement Is Unnecessary

Business enterprises often make the mistake of beginning reengineering without developing performance measurement systems, believing it is more important to put a new process in place before designing performance measures. But this approach can be detrimental to your business process reengineering effort because it leaves business enterprises without the means to compare your old process baseline measures to new reengineered process performance. In addition, most businesses do not have the direct means to link business process reengineering improvements to bottom-line performance outcomes. Therefore, continuation of reengineering efforts cannot be justified on a cost/benefit basis.

Pitfall 9: Forgetting Change Management

Many organizations learn a hard lesson when they forget that change management is a fundamental and critical element of business process reengineering. Failure to develop strong bureaucracy-elimination change initiatives and communication improvement and training programs and to act on the rhetoric of "empowerment" and "teamwork" to fully implement the new reengineering behavior sends mixed signals to employees.

In addition, traditional personnel policies (responsibility and authority expectations), traditional job classifications (shift to broadbanding), and flatter organizational structures emphasize a narrow functional role rather than an enterprise-wide process role when change management is neglected.

Pitfall 10: Failing to Stay the Course

Sustaining continuous change is difficult. Business leaders have to overcome their own past histories, which may include episodes of unsuccessful reform, strong resistance to change, and traditional barriers to change. Too many business leaders view reengineering as a "one-shot" quick fix to their business problems. Business leaders need to realize that reengineering is a long-term effort and that their effort, as painful, time consuming, and personally difficult as it is, must be sustained almost solely by the leadership of the management team if meaningful change is to take place.

These are some of the pitfalls your peers have recognized. Try to fully understand the culture change, cost, personal effort, and bottom-line outcomes before you commit your enterprise to business process reengineering.

CHAPTER 3

Role of Process Mapping in Reengineering

All too often business leaders do not really understand the concept of "process" and the fundamental relationship between process thinking, process mapping, and reengineering. In order to improve your business processes you need to understand and adopt a process management approach.

There is a great gap in "process" thinking between different reengineering applications. For example, product designers and manufacturing managers already have "process" thinking embedded in their daily work practices due to their need for specific drawings and manufacturing process specifications to define and communicate their work product. On the other hand, if you are in the service sector many of your team members do not have an understanding of or recognition that what they do on a day-to-day basis is really a "process." Reengineering of your business is fundamentally driven by the simplification, elimination, or improvement of your business processes. Therefore you must adopt a process management approach.

ADOPT A PROCESS MANAGEMENT APPROACH

You need to consider developing your own unique process management approach[1] based on the following key procedures:

- Set strategic directions and goals that are communicated consistently down through your entire organization that define process-specific goals and decision making for the subunit and team levels.

- Define your processes, map these processes, and prioritize the core business processes important for your business success and survival.

- Practice "hands-on" senior management ownership of process improvement through personal responsibility, constant involvement, continuous communication of your strategic process goals, and decision making that is consistent with process thinking.

- Change your business organizational structures by compressing the communication links and organizational bureaucracy in order to better support process mapping management initiatives.

What is your business's strategic direction? What are your core processes for achieving your business strategy? Who is responsible for each of these core processes? Which of your core processes are most in need of improvement? In successful businesses, leaders define their strategic directions and goals as part of a process management approach. They manage performance through business processes—in "process or value streams"—as opposed to linking together functional activities—"functional stovepipes or silos." To succeed in your reengineering efforts your process mapping and process improvement efforts must be developed based on an overarching process management approach. This process management approach creates a sense of common purpose in process improvement activities that can have a significant impact upon strategic business performance results. Successful business leaders identify which processes are critical and in need of priority reengineering attention. They also make senior managers responsible for process improvement and performance improvement.

DEVELOP STRATEGIC REENGINEERING GOALS

Setting strategic directions and goals both across and within your business processes is crucial. In successful business organizations, senior managers set strategic directions and goals for strategic business performance improvements that cascade to process-specific goals and push decision making, wherever possible, down to the individual process team member. Specific business directions and goals tied to providing your products and services cheaper, better, and faster are required to effectively reengineer. They are the glue that can help hold your reengineering effort together and get everyone thinking outside of "the box" (as recommended by Dr. Michael Hammer). The strategic directions and goals will also provide an enterprise-wide perspective for your process improvement team members that will help propel your reengineering and process improvement efforts.

Large business organizations generally establish a vision of the business, then set strategic directions for overall business performance, and then set specific strategic directions for the different "lines of business" carried out by departments, divisions, and offices. At each level, the strategic directions are usually five to ten goals the business is attempting to achieve. In large businesses, where complex five-year strategic plans have failed to address true business survival needs and frequent changes in direction are not unusual, extremely detailed strategic plans are a true departure from the status quo.

But large businesses have to ensure that their strategic plans are realistic and usable in the management of their day-to-day operations. Business leaders from one large corporation recalled how their organization once had a strategic plan with 69 critical success factors. The plan's size made it unmanageable and planning itself was not valued in the company. When the business realized that it had never really focused on what its objectives and business strategies should be, critical success factors were reduced to what people could understand and support. The result was a master business plan that brought together strategic change management needs, operations requirements, process improvement requirements, information technology, and team member considerations for the first time. Today, the business planning products in that company are valued, read, and understood by their team members. More importantly, these strategic and operational planning products serve as the cornerstone for their business process reengineering efforts.

Strategic direction and goal setting for business process reengineering efforts are also useful in situations where there are changes in top leadership or key process owners. Sometimes new management leaders come in and negate your past efforts. This work and rework cycle wastes your already-scarce resources. If your business strategic directions are well thought out and provide a method to facilitate change, it makes it more difficult for a new head or process owner to drastically change your active reengineering efforts. If accepted by the business and its stakeholders, strategic directions and goals can also offer a stability to reengineering that constantly changing top and senior management cannot.

BUSINESS PROCESS DEFINITION, PROCESS MAPPING, AND PRIORITIZATION

Successful businesses that have implemented process management have formulated their own unique approach by defining critical process management needs, applying the appropriate level of process mapping tools and techniques to meet their needs, and prioritizing the process improvement needs that directly drive organization-wide business performance improvement.

To help develop your own unique process management approach, several basic process improvement elements—such as defining your business processes; establishing the level of process mapping; selecting processes to reengineer; and identifying the role of management leadership, the role of process owners, the structure for executive management leadership, and new business enterprise structures—are described below.

Defining Your Business Processes

In an effort to define your business processes, successful businesses have started by identifying five to 10 core processes that are absolutely vital to your business survival and bottom-line performance across the business enterprise. Some organizations hire expensive consultants to come in and talk with your people to identify the problem areas. However most "process owners" and managers know in their hearts what the problems are; they are just not willing to take the risk of changing the status quo. This is where business process reengineering reveals one of its greatest benefits: It encourages your people to map your processes and present a better way to do it. This step is often the most difficult part of process management, as most managers and staff have little experience with business process mapping and process thinking approaches. Defining business processes can take several weeks, or months, as managers and staff rethink their initial definitions and process improvement and process mapping concepts over time.

The Level of Process Mapping

After defining their core business processes, businesses embark upon multiple process mapping stages as described in this book. Initially, businesses do high-level process mapping to further define and understand key business processes and examine how they work together. With high-level process mapping, the intent is to obtain a manageable overall picture of the key processes, showing the complete chain of related activities within the business.

The high-level process mapping stage (see Figure 3.1) enables organizations to (1) determine where their process starts and ends, (2) identify what is included in the process, (3) name the process, (4) state the purpose of the process—along with its inputs and outputs, (5) create several process map-flow charts of the process at a high level, and (6) identify products and services of the process. More detailed lower-level process mapping is then performed to help your business managers to examine specific process steps— their individual values, the beliefs and assumptions behind them, and the resources required for each process step.

Process maps serve a variety of functions. High-level process maps can serve as surrogate business plans to define your business strategy and examine how that strategy can be accomplished. Lower-level maps of your processes can create visual displays of both problems and opportunities. Process maps can be used to define your processes to support quality certification documenta-

Figure 3.1   Example of High-Level Process Map

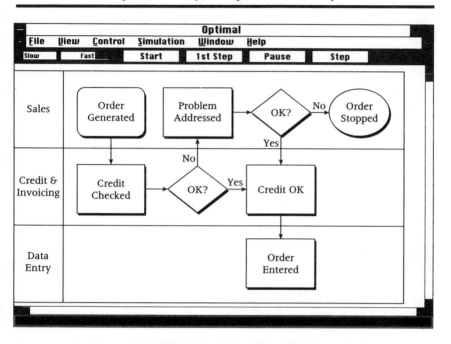

SOURCE: Created with OPTIMA by AdvanEdge Technologies, Inc.

tion requirements for standards such as ISO 9000. Process maps are very useful for identifying your business process "bottlenecks" or "white space" where little or no value is added by the process step. Process maps serve as integrative tools when processes cross functional internal boundaries. Process maps can aid business decision makers in prioritizing improvement actions and resource allocation decisions. Process maps can also be very effective communication tools that facilitate, across internal and external organizational boundaries, in a very simple visual format, transmission of ideas concerning what is actually happening in your business and ways to improve your business.

In spite of these benefits, process maps are sometimes not wisely used by some reengineering managers. In some cases, high-level and detailed process maps are misused by failure to implement change. In the government world of reengineering there is more talk than action. In many cases government organizations study to death the finer-and-finer-level details of their "As-Is" process without ever addressing the changes identified in terms of process elimination, simplification, or significant downsizing. In these instances, process mapping may even fail to cover the real process(es) that should be reengineered. This process mapping problem is often due to employees feeling uncomfortable in mapping their own processes so they reach out to their suppliers or external customers or an organization that clearly will not impact their own position in the organization. Artificial boundaries that limit implementation of process mapping should be avoided if you are serious about change.

Defining processes at a high level can help create enterprise-focused process maps. These process maps can reflect processes across the entire business enterprise. It is important to look at the whole business process so business leaders can see the interconnections when they want to make hard decisions on reengineering priorities.

Selecting Processes to Reengineer

Business process reengineering can be focused on an entire business enterprise, an entire delivery system, one product or service, one functional process, or one subprocess that crosses several functions. For the most part business process reengineering zeroes in on business processes that are absolutely vital to carrying out the strategic business requirements and related business performance objectives of your business. These are the business processes that mean the most to your business customers. Generally, the selection process focuses on core critical processes in need of repair and strives to obtain the greatest impact from reengineering, both for the customer and for better bottom-line business performance.

However, other factors can influence the selection of a process or subprocess for reengineering. Businesses with little or no experience with reengineering may select a process to reengineer based upon how much reengineering experience the organization can gather from the episode. Experiences from the early reengineering projects can then sometimes be transferred to larger projects which address major business processes. Business capacity can also be a factor. If your business management team feels unable to handle the reengineering of an entire process, parts of the process may be selected for reengineering.

The Role of Management Leadership. Reengineering will fail if your management team does not actively lead the effort. Significant change does not happen without top management commitment and support. Businesses that have survived significant change initiatives, such as General Electric, Xerox, and Motorola, have demonstrated executive or senior leadership commitment to initiate and sustain change. Your senior leaders and change agents must continually emphasize the importance of reengineering through their behavior and in *all* their communications to their reengineering and process mapping teams. Successful businesses require and practice "hands-on" senior management ownership of reengineering and process-mapping-related process improvement through personal responsibility, involvement, and decision making. Senior management in successful businesses understand the need to understand the actual processes and are committed to reengineering the processes. In many cases the organizational management systems had to change to support reengineering. At one level you need changes in planning, budgeting, and procurement to add flexibility. At another level you have to change the culture to encourage rapid change.

Frequently senior managers and process owners set the tone for improvement within your business. Reengineering managers and process owners keep up with current management literature, bring in expert speakers, and have their people attend conferences on process management or related developments in their field. Overall, they promote curiosity and experimentation as an overall philosophy. Many business leaders encourage communication of their shared vision and behavior common among top managers who devote their valuable resources to change and effective process improvement.

In one business, setting up a waiting room for customers, replacing old furniture, and dealing with chronic problems in simple things such as mail delivery set a new professional standard for managers and employees alike. Managers in another business stress making changes in people, processes, and structure to bring about fundamental change. This approach ensures cultural change, not just a change in program or project orientation.

The Role of the Process Owner. While one of the success factors for creating your reengineering strategy is based on recognition of the critical role of management leadership, the need for senior leadership is fundamental to initiating and sustaining reengineering. Successful business reengineering programs usually also have another operational leader or process owner in place to serve as the day-to-day "point person" for the process mapping and process improvement efforts. If the business is only conducting one or two reengineering projects, this process owner can provide a leadership umbrella for several process changes within the business. In some instances, the process owner may be the business leader who provided the executive commitment to reengineering.

Considering the crucial role that management leadership and process owners play in the context of reengineering, business leaders should take the utmost care in selecting process owners. In successful businesses, process owners are viewed as people who get things done. They are considered visionary; have credibility within the business; are in charge of, or closely associated with, the process or subprocess to be reengineered; have a strong grounding in contemporary management techniques; are willing to devote extensive amounts of time to the reengineering project; and have excellent communication skills. They also maintain excellent relations with top managers in other elements of your businesses.

In most successful businesses, the management leadership and process owners are the key point of contact for specific reengineering projects, spending anywhere from 20 to 60 percent of his or her time on process-mapping-based improvement. The process owner usually has the following responsibilities:

- Help determine the critical strategic processes for reengineering
- Select and support process mapping improvement teams
- Provide specific charter and accountability for teams
- Manage process mapping team implementation efforts
- Support management process steering groups
- Map the designated "As-Is" processes
- Define "To-Be" process improvement changes
- Improve the identified processes

- Ensure that a cross-functional, cross-boundary focus is maintained and system integration issues are resolved

Since reengineering projects often have the life cycle of their mentors, a process owner's attention to reengineering projects is crucial. In one business we studied, a process owner's behavior across several teams served as a constant reinforcement of ownership. The owner came to meetings (even if he couldn't attend he read the minutes and responded), provided tools and approaches, picked the right people for the teams, and acted as a bridge between the team and management. The process owner also assured team members that their product would be something management would use. In another business, several team members summed up general ownership behavior on the part of process owners as "constantly paying attention and getting people to think outside the box." In this business, process improvement teams are named after their process owners (e.g., Ben's Bandits, Team Xerox) to further demonstrate ownership.

In many successful businesses, process owners or lead managers are also formally assigned responsibility for a process. As part of their performance appraisals, they have to work toward continual improvement of their process and are held accountable to senior executive committees.

The Structure for Executive-Level Management

The leadership forums of executive committees and process improvement steering groups are another important piece of senior management leadership and demonstration of their ownership. The executive committee of the business enterprise—the business leader and those managers on his or her executive team—provides overall leadership and approves business-wide process management and reengineering projects. Process improvement steering groups handle the more direct leadership for specific reengineering efforts. Senior manager steering groups are cross-functional, working around managers remaining in their own "functional foxholes." Taken individually or together, these leadership forums have the following responsibilities:

- Demonstrate visible ownership and commitment to process improvement

- Identify and prioritize key business-wide processes
- Establish performance improvement goals and performance measures
- Develop and reexamine process maps on an ongoing basis
- Provide process sponsorship and resource support
- Provide guidance to process improvement projects
- Coordinate various process improvement projects
- Provide a channel for strategic change issues
- Mediate unresolved turf issues/disagreements

Through it all, senior management must continually assure process improvement teams that their commitment to reengineering is unwavering. If individual process improvement teams see a deterioration of process ownership or executive steering group support, they will frequently lose their direction, tinker on the margins of change, or, in some cases, simply stop. The support of senior management can also help secure the involvement and support of midlevel managers. In businesses that have had problems with reengineering, much of the difficulty originated with midlevel managers. To overcome their resistance, most successful businesses try to encourage these midlevel managers to participate in their reengineering efforts. Experience shows that midlevel managers have a better chance of survival if they are part of the reengineering team rather than an opponent of change.

The Structure for New Organizational Designs

Many successful businesses are adjusting their formal business organizational structures and reporting relationships to better support reengineering process management initiatives. These adjustments range from process-related organizational structures to informal process management forums and special process teams. Such adjustments change traditional organizational structures designed around functions, product or service lines, or geography.

In making these adjustments, successful businesses address the inherent tensions between a traditional functional orientation and an orientation based on process and cross-functional integration. But many businesses fail to do this. In the words of one consultant: "Traditional organizations support program areas, not processes." It is difficult to just add process management to the old business. No one wants to realign the old responsibilities or functions so they keep the old structure.

Several of the success-story businesses have structures that support process management initiatives. One office in an organization established process improvement teams as their formal organizational structure. In another business, a core business system management approach pulls together activities and functions that appear to be related. While management is exploring these interdependencies, they are still unsure of how they can change the organizational structure to match up to business processes. In this case, an organizational structure matrix approach was used. But obstacles often stand in the way of structural change. In this business, similar to many others, making organizational-structure changes requires union agreements which can take months or even years of concentrated negotiation efforts.

Some question whether organizational structure has any bearing on process mapping and improvement initiatives. As one manager asked: "What does structure do for you in process management? We need to think through the relationships between structure and process." In some businesses, management and process groups and teams provide *the* integration of process improvement efforts in place of a formal organizational change. Frequently, such businesses will assign an ongoing team to be responsible for their individual process mapping and process improvement efforts to assure continuous process examination and improvement.

CHAPTER 4

Do You Really Understand Your Processes?

Most business managers and process leaders believe they understand their business processes until a problem occurs in their operations or they begin to examine how they can eliminate, simplify, or improve their business processes, to provide better, cheaper, or faster products or services for their customers. This chapter describes a methodology for process improvement.

Both radical business process reengineering improvement and continuous process improvement address the creation of positive change in the way your business functions. This chapter describes what you can do to better understand, simplify, and improve your processes.

DO YOU UNDERSTAND YOUR BUSINESS PROCESSES?

Unfortunately most managers do not really understand their operational processes. All too often managers believe they have the documentation or seat-of-the-pants experience that defines their business activity and really know their operational processes. However, when they sit down to describe or map their own process flow many process owners discover problems, surprises, bottlenecks, and unneeded processes that are reducing their competitive position by adding time delays or excessive costs to their business operations.

The benefits of process examination include:

- Simplification of process work flows

- Elimination of whole steps in your processes

- Improved cross-functional communication

- Enhancement of the integration of your supplier's role in your process improvement effort

- Elimination of non-value-added costs throughout your corporate-wide business process

- Reduction of variation that can improve your quality

A MODEL FOR PROCESS IMPROVEMENT

The process improvement model shown in Figure 4.1 is a four-step cycle that begins with the activities needed to create an environment conducive to process understanding by anticipating and planning for change, implementing change, checking your performance improvements, and continuing to improve your process activities. This improvement model is often referred to as the Plan-Do-Check-Act (PDCA) cycle for process improvement.

STEPS TO IMPROVE YOUR PROCESSES

The process improvement steps described below are based on *An Introduction to the Continuous Improvement Process—Principles and Practices.*[1] These seven basic process improvement steps are delineated in Table 4.1.

Each of these seven steps is described in more detail below:

Figure 4.1   The Plan-Do-Check-Act Process Improvement Model

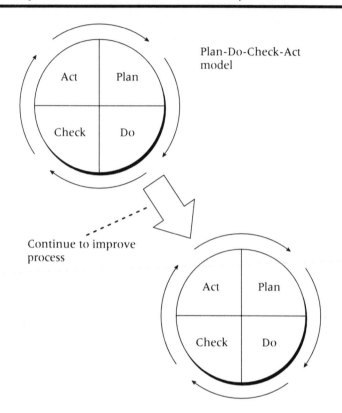

Plan-Do-Check-Act model

Continue to improve process

Step 1: Set the Stage for Process Change

At the organizational level, setting the stage for process change involves everything your business does to become aware of the need for significant change and to establish a commitment to actually follow-through by changing your processes. It includes goal setting, barrier reduction, training, and leadership. Setting the stage means that you must create an environment in which business process improvement is encouraged and nourished. Management must have a clear vision of what it wants to accomplish and where it wants to go, and it must put in place support systems to help your employees implement process understanding and change.

Table 4.1 Process Improvement Steps

Step 1	Set the stage for process change
Step 2	Select candidate product or process for improvement
Step 3	Understand and map the process
Step 4	Standardize the process
Step 5	Change the process
Step 6	Continue to improve the process
Step 7	Assess process improvement performance

At the team and the individual levels, setting the stage involves selecting the process improvement teams. It requires additional training in process simplification concepts; new work flow and process mapping analytical tools, and techniques that you will need for the contemplated process improvement effort. The business process mapping and improvement teams need to learn how to function in the changing overall organizational environment and to support the individuals involved so they can accomplish their task.

Step 2: Select Candidate Product or Process for Improvement

The business process reengineering leadership and team members select the product and/or processes on which the team will focus its process improvement effort. Selecting the process target involves identifying known problem areas that require immediate action, benchmarking industry process improvement opportunities, setting priorities, and choosing those process improvement efforts that present the most serious competitive problem or offer the most significant opportunity for business survival or improvement. Once the process improvement targets are selected, the process improvement teams must identify the major problems to be addressed and the level of change required (radical Business Process Reengineering or incremental Continuous Process Improvement). The process improvement team may, based on new data, revise their plan for improvement, building on the team's objectives. Identifying performance measurement points, such as defects per million parts, cost targets, market share, or profit goals, is necessary before beginning the business process improvement effort.

Step 3: Understand and Map the Process

Once the specific process effort has been targeted for improvement, the team should define the planned effort as clearly and completely as possible. Process improvement is based on determining your customers' needs, documenting how the process is currently performed, determining the type of change that is required, and identifying measures of process improvement performance. Documentation should be sufficient for the task and consistent among all organizational processes. A sound process definition provides a consistent base from which to begin change; without knowing where you are at a given moment, it is hard to determine how to get to your destination. A roadmap (process map) is needed to assure that vital steps have not been missed and to help you understand your real business processes and formulate a logical basis for process change.

Step 4: Standardize the Process

By defining or standardizing the new improvement process, the team institutionalizes the current best way to perform the process. This also creates a tool for instructing people in their jobs within a consistent performance definition, provides a framework for evaluating performance consistently, and provides a basis for evaluating the success of the process improvement efforts. Process improvement team leaders ensure that their team members are trained to the new process standard, and they help adopt its use. Once the new process standard is in force, teams can measure performance against that standard and respond appropriately to deviations from it to meet the new goals. The process standard should continue to reflect the "best practices" way of performing the process for the business.

Step 5: Change the Process

Once a team has defined the process standard, it should optimize the process and continue to significantly improve it. This effort should ensure that the process meets its stated and perceived requirements; adopts state-of-the-practice tools and techniques; encourages significant product and process simplification; eliminates unnecessary equipment and facilities; and establishes reliable, adequate data-collection systems to improve your processes.

Step 6: Continue to Improve the Process

Continue your efforts to improve the process by following the Plan-Do-Check-Act (PDCA) cycle. Your process improvement effort should assure that your business process reengineering teams implement solutions, check for improvement, and act to institutionalize and continue the process improvements. The team's effort involves developing ongoing solutions that address your requirements and improvement goals. Data collection and performance measurement methodologies must support your process improvement actions. The process improvement team needs to be trained in the techniques necessary to carry out the plan.

Step 7: Assess Process Improvement Performance

As the team succeeds in its process improvement efforts, you should reassess their data to determine how well actual performance matches their performance improvement goals. Successful improvement should be institutionalized; less-than-successful efforts require another pass through the business process reengineering improvement cycle.

After process improvement has been implemented, the process improvement team should document the improved performance. That documentation allows others to benefit from the lessons the process improvement team has learned and brings recognition for the team's efforts. Documentation also provides a roadmap for replicating successful process improvement techniques. Documenting the improved process also requires the team to update its process definition; it requires that process goals be redefined to reflect a new standard of performance. Recommending follow-up actions or subsequent process improvement actions is also useful.

No single correct formula or "canned" solution can be used to achieve process improvement in all situations or all businesses. A core set of values or competencies, however, is evident in most successful business process improvement efforts, and they can be applied to your own business.

Your process improvement effort will be unique in its details, but in general it should move your business toward satisfying the six criteria listed below.

- Exceed your customer's requirements and expectations and be a high-quality supplier

- Support significant state-of-the-practice change-oriented management systems. Encourage process improvement change in every facet of your business

- Work to eliminate barriers that prevent people from having pride in their work and involve everyone in your process improvement efforts

- Tap the power of individuals, multiplying that power through training and teamwork, and focus that power on process understanding and process improvement

- Make decisions based on data rather than on opinions or emotions; stimulate creative system thinking; and seek process improvement in products, processes, and services

- Adopt appropriate state-of-the-practice work flow analysis tools and techniques that meet your level of need

SIMPLIFY YOUR SYSTEM PROCESSES

Simplification of your business processes, development of accurate process documentation, reengineering of existing processes, creation of new system processes, reconfiguration of flow of materials, efforts to focus on the quickest path for action, and very careful analysis of design strategies produce significant benefits in terms of increased productivity, business profitability, and business survival.

To simplify your product and process systems designs, the process improvement team must first understand the customer's real requirements and priorities. When resolving and placing priorities on requirements, the customer and your management team must define and evaluate trade-offs. For example, what are the operational environments and performance levels which are an absolute necessity for this product or service?

There are an interminable number of questions relating to the system trade-offs between product performance/reliability, cost, and timing/schedule. In the ideal scenario, there would be an open and active dialog between customer and supplier. This dialog would transform a fairly vague set of requirements into the best specific set of time/cost/performance values available at the time.

To achieve the necessary understanding between the customer and the supplier, the customer must include both those who are "buyers" and those who are "users," including those responsible for the installation, operation, and maintenance of the systems. The vendor must include those responsible for the design, manufacture, and service/repair of the systems. Through the involvement of all these, the process improvement team can identify the various required and desired characteristics that will form the basis of the trade-offs for the system process improvements.

In the ideal environment, the needs of the customer would be translated into increasingly more specific characteristics and features of the product. These, in turn, would be related directly to the process operations and capabilities that affect those specific product features. In this way, the "voice of the customer" would remain consistent and be heard by all those defining the product and process, and at all stages of the design process. To accomplish this, there must be both feed-forward and feed-back of information among various functional organizations (for example, the business management team, the product-design team, the manufacturing-engineering team, the production-planning team, the service providing team, etc.) and feed-forward between the various time phases of your process.

Similarly, there must exist a process whereby the customer and vendor can verify that the service, product, process, and support processes meet their requirements. Like the transmission and translation of these requirements just described, this must first occur at a "macro" level with evaluations which incorporate a significant degree of estimation and uncertainty. As the service, product, and processes become further defined, the level of certainty and exactness of this verification will increase.

Requirements should be translated concurrently and in an integrated fashion into optimal service or product processes. Here the key elements of improved operations relate to the simplification and integration of the creation of service, product and process definition, and the concurrent consideration of all phases of the life cycle. The system simplification process must allow, encourage, and ensure that:

- All requirements of the life cycle are considered and evaluated

- The cross-impacts of various functional decisions are understood and evaluated (with appropriate trade-off analysis)

- Critical risks of various options are identified and addressed early in the process

- Those responsible for the various functional areas within the business enterprise participate with appropriate levels of responsibility and authority

To achieve these integrated service, product, and process development simplification objectives, four specific functions[2] are delineated below:

First, there must be an integrated and continuing participation of multifunctional process mapping and improvement teams in the simplification of your products and processes. In a fully operational process improvement system the information system should have automatic access to the current capabilities and capacities of the corporate operations.

Second, this process of integrating multiple service, overhead, engineering, manufacturing, and management functions must provide for efficient iteration and closure of process improvement. Each change iteration should involve each of the relevant functional process improvement teams for review of the impact of the changes made. This may be done manually through a "marked-up blueline" process, digitally through a process of automatic "flag raising" which notifies affected functions, through exercise of process graphical flow charts, or through computer-aided simulation tools that can project the impact of changes on the adequacy and/or projected performance and cost of the various life-cycle elements (service performance, product capability, manufacturing process, customer support, reliability, etc.).

Third, the process improvement system must identify conflicting requirements and support their resolution through an objective choice of process options based upon a comparison of trade-offs. Any one change can increase product performance, but also can increase cost and cycle time, and simultaneously can decrease reliability. It is very important that your process improvement approach identify, record, and analyze such conflicts and the resulting trade-offs.

Finally, the system process must incorporate an optimization of the process design. This process optimization can be based on either empirical or analytical knowledge. Empirical knowledge can be derived from experts in the field who call upon their experience to project the impact of process change alternatives. Also, empirical knowledge can be systematically derived from data collected and statistically analyzed from current processes which are in some ways similar to those being changed. Analysis of theoretical knowledge and scientific/engineering analysis can also be applied to the evaluation of alternatives. These objectives will be met only when their application is assured and achieved with speed and ease.

You really need to understand your business processes to maintain your competitive position and provide services and products better, cheaper, and faster for your customers.

CHAPTER 5

Process Mapping Success Stories

This chapter provides an array of process mapping (flow charts, workflow process maps, Integrated DEFinition Language [IDEF] government process maps, simulation, and Activity-Based Costing [ABC] process mapping integration) success stories and lessons learned for service, manufacturing, and government organizations based on the experience of AEG Schneider, Allen-Bradley, Bristol-Myers Squibb, Centerbank, Fluor Daniels, Hughes Network Systems, IBM, KPMG Peat Marwick, Litton Industries, Mobil Oil, Morton International, NASA, Shawmut National Bank, and Tandy Electronics. This chapter focuses on each organization's use of process mapping and provides highlights of the lessons learned.

The concept behind process mapping and reengineering your business processes is to remove the non-value-added process activities, thereby lowering your process cost(s). In order to achieve this, you need to be able to identify where the non-value-added process elements are located—which is not a trivial task. This is because the non-value-added elements are often hidden in the form of overhead, unrelated process task impacts, or pooled overhead resources. In order to be able to isolate these non-value-added processes from among the other processes, you need to decompose the overall top-level process into lower layers of subprocesses. Process mapping is a tool that has proven helpful in this process of decomposing into the key value-added element. Once the basic "As-Is" process map attributes are defined simulation software tools can be applied to facilitate "What-If" and "To-Be" scenarios. In addition, process costing data can be assigned to each subprocess along with the value the subprocess adds to the final product by using Activity Based Costing (ABC) software tools.

Process mapping tools facilitate this functional process decomposition and understanding through detailed structured process analysis.

The success stories that illustrate state-of-the-practice process mapping are described below.

BRISTOL-MYERS SQUIBB PRESCRIBES
PROCESS MAPPING

With the health care field in the midst of transition, Bristol-Myers Squibb has initiated several corporation-wide business process reengineering improvement initiatives to prepare for the anticipated changes ahead. Bernie Palowitch, director of Business Process Reengineering, worked with the operating divisions on reengineering projects, using process mapping software tools such as Meta Software's Design/IDEF tool to support their process mapping and improvement effort.

One of the first projects involved the Mead Johnson Nutritional Group, one of Bristol-Myers Squibb's four large operating divisions. The group, which makes infant formula and other nutritional products, was chosen primarily because of its readiness for change. The formula market has shifted dramatically, from medical to consumer channels. "Ten years ago, a doctor said to a new mother, "I recommend this product," says Palowitch. "Now doctors are hesitant to recommend a specific brand and consumers are less likely to look to their pediatricians for this kind of information." Instead they may look for the best buy at food retailers and discount stores. Mead Johnson needs to make sure that it is responding appropriately to these market changes so it can remain competitive.

The project began with a high-level effort Palowitch calls a "business diagnostic." The goals of this effort were to gain a clear understanding of how the group operates now, to identify the key business processes that truly add value, and to develop a plan for reengineering based on the company's strategic goals. An experienced practitioner of process improvement who was formerly a consultant in the field, Mr. Palowitch points out the importance of beginning with this high-level view. "When you make sure that the reengineering project supports business strategies, the final results of the effort will make direct improvements to the bottom-line financial performance of the company. If you rush too hastily into selecting processes to reengineer, you run the risk that the project will have a negligible impact on bottom-line performance."

Palowitch worked with a cross-functional team of Mead Johnson executives at the director and vice president level, including the Chief Financial Officer (CFO) and individuals from R&D, manufacturing, information management, and marketing. The reengineering process mapping team was selected to provide enough perspective to look at organization-level goals and trade-offs in order to prioritize processes for their business process reengineering efforts.

In order to prioritize processes for their reengineering efforts, the team first turned to business strategy, because where and how a company chooses to compete will dictate the importance of specific reengineering projects. For example, for a business strategy of providing products at a low price, one operational goal would be to reduce the cost of goods sold. This would suggest reengineering to reduce the costs of procurement, distribution, and/or manufacturing. A business strategy of broadening market presence with a number of new products would suggest a focus on market research and its links with new product development.

Competitive benchmarking was also incorporated in prioritizing business processes. For example, if a competitor can process a customer order and deliver it in 24 hours and your company takes several days, this could clearly drive priorities as well. But, cautions Palowitch, the benchmarks must be selected to support the company's strategic goals.

The result of this first diagnostic phase was a set of recommendations to senior management on the number and scope of business process reengineering projects to launch.

Process mapping (Meta Software Design/IDEF) software was used to capture material and information flows in the current business, and these maps were used as the starting point for the redesign efforts. "The combination of powerful and user-friendly software and the responsive consulting help allowed us to quickly get through the documentation step," says Palowitch, "and move on to address the more important issues regarding the value of reengineering and its impact on the company's bottom line."

CENTERBANK IMPROVES OPERATIONAL EFFICIENCY

A key indicator in banking is the operational efficiency ratio, which measures what it costs to make a dollar of income. A few of the premier banks in this country have achieved 50 percent, that is, they spend 50 cents to earn each dollar. "Centerbank is cutting costs to bring their ratio in line with industry leaders so they can continue to compete," relates Lou Bonaiuto, who heads a Centerbank process mapping and improvement team that is integral to that effort, the Management Services Division.

Centerbank is a $3 billion 45-branch savings bank based in Waterbury, Connecticut. Management Services provides assistance to managers of the bank in their efforts to improve productivity and reduce costs. The group purchased Meta Software's WorkFlow Analyzer and has used the software process mapping tool in several process improvement efforts for their operations division, including check encoding and the legal research group.

In the legal research group, the process mapping workflow challenge included making better use of the bank's on-line report distribution system. This system stores information on optical disks and allows reports and records to be searched by date or dollar amount, making it easy to find, say, a certain check. The research group's high-volume use of this system created a resource contention problem. The Meta Software WorkFlow Analyzer was used to solve this problem as well as to improve overall productivity.

The first step was to map the existing processes. Then potential improvements were considered and the WorkFlow Analyzer was used to simulate the most promising process scenarios. The simulation runs showed that one of the scenarios considered promising would have made the problem worse—an indication of the value of simulating before redesign. Two of the scenarios were proven to be worthwhile and the processes were redesigned accordingly.

The results of the business process reengineering effort in this one area are a savings of $150,000 yearly in reduced costs and additional revenue. "The WorkFlow Analyzer allows many scenarios to be explored," says Bonaiuto, "And the ability to do simulation lets you perform predictive analysis, which makes a big difference in the results that can be achieved."

SHAWMUT NATIONAL BANK USES PROCESS MAPPING TO CUT COSTS

Cutting costs is still the rage in today's austere banking business environment. In many cases, however, indiscriminate slashing can end up costing money rather than saving it. Like many of its peers, Shawmut National Bank of Hartford, Connecticut, continually looks for ways to cut expenses.

Back-office administration and overhead cost reductions are one aspect of the bank's efforts to sustain profitability. Among the ideas on the table was a consolidation of courier routes connecting bank branches and check processing sites. The plan seemed straightforward enough—fewer daily deliveries would allow the $25-billion-asset institution to reduce its staff and motor pool. But before such a plan could be implemented, the bank needed to make sure it wouldn't have an adverse effect on productivity in other areas. "We had some questions about workflow in our processing areas," said Louis C. Fischer, senior vice president of commercial operations. "We had an idea that cutting back on courier routes was a good solution, but we didn't have the confidence to jump right in and do it."

The primary concern was that any slowdown in the flow of documents would idle workers at the processing sites. Rather than risking failure and creating a potential cost center, Shawmut tested its theory using the WorkFlow Analyzer. Workflow process simulation is an area of mathematics and operations research that predates computers, but it has been greatly enhanced by the use of technology that is less expensive to procure and easier to use. Its underlying theory maintains that workflows and behaviors can be represented by mathematical models. Computers make it possible to develop more sophisticated models and project them in graphic, animated simulation presentations similar to those used in video games. Today's process mapping simulation software makes it easier for bankers to use than the older, complex, and very expensive military simulation products that seemed to enjoy unnecessary complexity and long training times.

Mr. Fischer and his team of workflow specialists entered process mapping information into an Apple Macintosh computer. By doing process mapping, Shawmut National Bank could identify process improvements before trial-and-error implementation, thereby saving time and resources. Then they exported their process maps from Meta Software's WorkFlow Analyzer to their Design/CPN software for simulation and system analysis. "It's difficult to find where the glitches in your operations are. We found the software did it for us," Mr. Fischer said. As it turned out, consolidating courier routes did the job, saving the bank about $60,000 in six months.

Any "production environment that requires people to handle paper, file things, or handle any kind of back-office service support function could use a tool like this," said John W. Stone, a partner at KPMG Peat Marwick in Chicago. On the corporate side, Mr. Stone expects process mapping and simulation software to be used even more often in the area of loan origination. "It can help banks find out how to issue loans quicker and with less risk," he said.

Mr. Fischer and his team prefer to visualize their analytical results. The graphic workflow presentation tools, integrated with the process mapping and simulation tools, create a high-level representation of the problem and its solution.

This sort of process mapping and simulation lets Shawmut analyze performance of the proposed systems, providing the bank with the data to assist in the decision-making process.

Broad use of simulation of business processes came a bit slower to Shawmut. Process-based procedural improvements, Mr. Fischer noted, create new cost reductions and savings but also permit expansion of back-office activities without additional investments in either technology or personnel. "We can now run all kinds of simulation tests to see if certain departments are doing all they can," he said. So far, Shawmut has used process mapping to analyze mostly low-level tasks, such as the movement of paper through back-office operations. But the stage is set for testing in other areas, focusing on finding hidden problems that may be hampering the bank's productivity.

"We're currently benchmarking tasks in other processing areas to map our processes as they exist today," said John W. Dyer, a

Shawmut workflow analyst. Eventually, he added, the bank can plug in the details of different tasks and find out whether or not changes need to be made. If the simulation time matches the amount of time it takes to actually complete the task, no changes are needed. "We may find out after running a simulation that a process is in fact efficient and doesn't need to be reengineered," said Mr. Dyer. "That does happen occasionally."

Shawmut also plans to use process mapping in its corporate banking area. Process mapping analytical teams at the bank are using the simulation software to revamp its wholesale lockbox business, both to save money and to woo customers with a higher level of service. "We've found that the software is helping us increase efficiency in that area and figure out what its potential is," Mr. Fischer said. Process mapping and simulation analysis has provided the bank with a new perspective. Results of task simulations now tell the bank to what degree changes need to be made in operations, from incremental process improvement changes to major business process reengineering shifts. "If a change is needed, we can get an idea of whether we just need to change the resources or if a full reengineering needs to take place," Mr. Fischer said.

ACTIVITY-BASED COSTING AND PROCESS MAPPING PAY OFF AT NASA

In order to manage processes effectively and to make appropriate decisions about changing them, a detailed and accurate set of metrics is essential. Pooled resources tend to distort the actual cost of a process. When a resource is shared, the traditional method for assigning cost to a project is to use the average cost of past missions, instead of assigning a cost that is tailored to the true needs of the project. With the new NASA approach of tailoring the system to each mission's needs, a comparable costing method was needed so that actual mission requirements could be individually costed, thus yielding a more accurate overall project.

Activity-Based Costing (ABC) is a method devised to model the cost of any process that has first been decomposed through process mapping into basic functional process activities that serve as its building blocks. Once the functional process activities have been identified, costs can be assigned to those activities. Then optimization of the general process can be performed in forums such as reengineering and continuous process improvement team committees.

IDEF is a Federal Information Processing Standard (FIPS) that can be used as a tool to support ABC. IDEF actually consists of an integrated pair of tools: the process mapping activity modeler (IDEF0) and the data modeler. IDEF0 is used to model the activities that occur to produce a product or service and therefore shows the interrelationships of work being done in different groups. The data modeler helps show what is being passed between processes by defining a template (i.e., a data structure) for each item. This provides for more accurate, rapid, and meaningful insight into interactions among groups. An example of this might be a form sent to request a service from another group. IDEF process mapping therefore acts as an intergroup coordination tool by providing the overall blueprint or map for the entire process. The best way to use this tool to coordinate different groups is to put IDEF on a distributed network that is accessible on-line to all participants in the process.

IDEF process mapping with ABC allows one to continuously assess the implementation of an overall process and thereby determine the point at which the implementation needs to be changed in order to reduce costs

What happens when your organization chooses to solve problems with the same old processes without considering cost impacts of increasing complexity? Without examining the functional process activities within processes and removing old non-value-added activities, unneeded constraints are carried along like deadwood at extra expense. For example, it may be necessary to derive the system requirements, but it may not always be necessary to have a formal system requirements review whether there is a high degree of reusability.

Since technology changes so quickly, your process mapping analysis has to focus on Continuous Value Improvement (CVI) by constantly monitoring your functional process ABC breakdown. Together, IDEF process mapping and ABC allow large organizations to understand, communicate, and coordinate their business processes and to create a living blueprint for changing and improving their business practices. These tools also provide a forum for each individual to identify his or her viewpoint and to comment on these processes from such a perspective. For the business entity and its organization to remain viable, and since the primary cost savings potential is in the process and not the product or product architecture, these types of management methods should be instituted. Finally, without these type of tools, large organizations find themselves in the situation of making decisions without the necessary metrics.

IBM'S INFORMATION TECHNOLOGY GENERIC PROCESS MAP

When consultants in the IBM Consulting Group needed a process mapping tool powerful enough to capture and express the complexity of IBM's Information Technology Process—the framework that underlies the company's state-of-the-art information technology business process reengineering methodology—they began to use Meta Software's Design/IDEF process mapping product. They have used process maps to increase the productivity of some of the leading technology-based corporations in the world, including IBM itself.

The IBM Consulting Group provides management and information technology consulting to large and medium-sized businesses. This typically involves two separate projects. One is reengineering the actual business process, which frequently causes a reexamination of how technology is used within the business process.

A parallel project involves managing the information technology itself. For example, distributing laptops to 10,000 customer service representatives around the country introduces problems such as keeping track of software upgrades and repairing broken modems. To develop strategies to address these problems, the IBM Consulting Group uses a generalized process map of how large organizations manage information technology.

According to Mark Ernest, a principal consultant with the IBM Consulting Group, one of the major reasons for using process maps is ease of use. If someone understands basic process mapping, using process mapping software is straightforward. In half a day you can build process maps of real customer processes.

In particular, process mapping's simple visual vocabulary lets Mark Ernest and other members of his team describe complex information technology management processes in enough detail to answer meaningful business process reengineering questions without having to master a laborious computer software modeling language.

"We're business analysts!" says Ernest. "We want to be able to focus one hundred percent of our intellectual energy on understanding and solving our clients' problems. Process mapping lets us get the ideas out of our heads and into the process map fairly effortlessly, without having to think our way around the artificial formulations you normally deal with when you're programming."

Another valuable process mapping feature is its tunneling capability, which allows process analysts to create process flows without having high-level sources. When Ernest and his colleagues developed their generic process maps, they could break down their processes into several unrelated process groups. Tunneling lets them introduce process flows that could eventually come from another process group but that did not exist at the time of initial process map design.

"When you're building a process map to manage an information technology operation," explains Ernest, "you deal with everything from the business strategy down to actually operating computers. Tunneling allowed us to bring in subject matter experts for each process and have them work independently of the others. It's a key feature for us—we simply couldn't have created our generic information system model any other way."

Ernest and his colleagues have already used their process map to understand how IBM manages technology and to help a large utility company client streamline its business operations.

LITTON INDUSTRIES USES IDEF PROCESS MAPPING

Several divisions at Litton Industries use process mapping software products for their reengineering projects with the help of a corporate group called Standards and Resource Management. Process mapping tools and methods are among the many disciplines the Standards Group provides in support of the efforts of their 24 operational divisions. By providing support and information on process mapping and reengineering techniques, the Standards Group helps ensure that divisions interested in pursuing process mapping learn as much as possible from the experiences of their associates.

Mark Thompson and Russell Sweeney, members of the Litton Industries Standard Group team, have researched a variety of process mapping tools and methods. Their group has "evaluated many process mapping tools on the market," says Thompson. "Our requirements were for a tool that was inexpensive, simple to use, required minimum training, and enhanced our team's ability to articulate what they do in their daily work life. Meta Software's Design/IDEF software product provided us with those capabilities."

Before adopting IDEF-based process mapping, traditional graphic workflow charting was used. "Flowcharting was never very efficient for capturing large amounts of information." says Thompson. "You would end up with a huge chart on the wall that was difficult to follow. With the Design/IDEF process mapping tool, we were able to look at our business processes in hierarchical layers, so as to gain a high-level conceptual understanding of the processes, and then look at the details only when we were ready to assimilate that level of information. The use of process mapping allows us to increase the descriptive power of our process maps."

Teaching people the IDEF process mapping method and creation of pilot reengineering efforts at Litton divisions are part of Thompson and Sweeney's role. They have found process mapping to be a tremendous help in structuring team communication toward "systems thinking" and facilitating the negotiations required to rationalize process workflow. Process mapping allowed them to "effectively map enterprise-wide processes, identify system problems, and brainstorm alternative processes," says Sweeney. "Once people have a grasp of the IDEF process mapping method, it changes the way they talk about how they do business. Process mapping provided us with a common vocabulary for describing processes. It has enabled people to understand their tasks from a business enterprise perspective and learn to appreciate the interdependent nature of their tasks."

The reengineering process maps will play a continuing role at Litton. The process maps at Litton Industries "will be living models," says Sweeney. "They will be used as a teaching tool to navigate people through the organization, and as a baseline for renegotiating departmental rules and responsibilities, for future enhancement efforts, and for understanding the enterprise-wide impact that future reengineering efforts could have on our business processes."

One of the many goals of their Standards Group is to help the divisions reduce the cycle time for the reengineering effort itself. The group aims to complete process improvement projects in approximately 12 months, from concept to implementation. One pilot project that is on track for this fast cycle time is the reengineering of a financial and manufacturing system at one of their independent divisions. "This goal of this reengineering effort was to enhance this group's ability to manage product costs," explains Thompson.

KPMG PEAT MARWICK HELPS CUT LOAN PROCESSING TIME

The consulting firm KPMG Peat Marwick uses process mapping software such as Meta Software's WorkFlow Analyzer as part of its business reengineering practice. Recently the firm helped a large financial services company to slash costs and improve productivity in its Manufactured Housing Finance Division. Turnaround time for a loan approval was reduced by half, using 40 percent fewer staff members.

Simulation helped the team analyze the complex aspects of the project. "In parts of the loan origination process a lot of things happen in a short period of time," according to team leader Bob Karrick of KPMG. "During data capture, information is pulled from a number of different sources, and the person doing the risk assessment has to make judgment calls at different points throughout the process. There's often a need to stop, raise questions, make follow-up calls, and so on and then continue with the process mapping effort. Simulation allows us to do a thorough analysis that takes into account all these decision points and variables."

TANDY ELECTRONICS ELIMINATES BOTTLENECKS

Tandy Electronics is the division that develops Tandy Corporation's (Radio Shack) consumer products: radios, telephones, wireless microphones, and other hot new product ideas. The division handles 60 to 70 new product designs a year, and each project involves 200 to 300 action items—such as developing packaging or creating the list of materials needed—from start to finish.

Mike Lonergan of Tandy Electronics never considered himself a bottleneck. Hardworking, knowledgeable, conscientious, and responsible, Lonergan was the director of planning and administration at Tandy Electronics Design in Fort Worth, Texas. Lonergan was responsible for tracking and reviewing the company's various research and development efforts.

Tandy Electronics relies on groupware tools to help speed up product development. But a workflow analysis of the process revealed that Lonergan's office was a bottleneck, which contributed to the company's failure to close the communications loop on works in progress. Lonergan said, "Things just ended up piled on my desk," creating significant delays.

The process of developing new products involves ideas: generating them, responding to them, selecting particular ones to act on, and assigning the selected one to a manager, who establishes and manages the development team.

Initially the organization used Lotus Development Corp.'s Lotus Agenda database to track new product development, but it wasn't adequate for their job. "There were so many action items, and we were experiencing all kinds of communications delays," Lonergan recalls. Lotus Notes seemed to offer a better solution. Lonergan noted that they could put all action items into a virtual real-time project database and network everybody into it. Tandy turned to WorkFlow Designs Inc., a Dallas-based Notes reseller, to install Notes—which would eventually tie together all 120 active product development personnel in the United States and Asia—and build the company's first Notes application. But WorkFlow Designs Inc., which specializes in workflow reengineering, suggested that Notes alone would not solve Tandy's problem with delays. Rubi Dodge, WorkFlow Designs Inc. chief executive officer, said that "Just tracking the status of all these projects in a Notes database misses the point. The idea is to look at the whole process of developing new products."

WorkFlow Designs Inc. suggested the use of Action Technologies Inc.'s Action Workflow process reengineering tools and methodology for Tandy's communications bottleneck. Mike Lonergan said, "The new system really alleviated a lot of my workload and freed me and my department head to spend our time on program management."

The Action Technologies' process mapping methodology focuses on the series of implicit and explicit requests and commitments that people make to get work done. Action Technologies' methodology is based on the belief that only by changing the way people communicate can significant improvements to the business occur.

Action Technologies' methodology divides each business process into four phases (each phase may spawn numerous subprocesses, which can be divided in the same way):

- *Preparation:* When someone, such as a product line manager, requests or proposes a project

- *Negotiations:* When the person requesting the work and the workers who will do it reach agreement about the work to be performed

- *Performance:* When the work is carried out

- *Acceptance:* When the customer (the product line manager in this case) evaluates the work and indicates satisfaction or dissatisfaction

Every phase requires very specific communication between the parties involved. If the communications don't take place, the process starts to fall apart and bottlenecks develop.

By contrast, many process reengineering efforts focus on material process analysis, which looks at how materials are moved through a series of steps. Another method is information systems analysis, which focuses on the flow of information. While reengineering these processes is useful, an organization shouldn't stop there, according to Action Technologies officials, because communications between workers is where the biggest problems, or inefficiencies, occur.

People usually think the problem with their process is that they don't have enough information, Dodge says. But in fact the problem is they don't have enough communication between people.

Such was the case at Tandy. For example, there was no formal mechanism by which people worked out agreement on the specifications, conditions, and scope of a given project before it was turned over to a project manager. The process was so informal that the necessary communications often never took place, Dodge explains.

Using Action Technologies' analyst tool, WorkFlow Designs mapped the existing process taking place within Tandy's research and development department and then used the same tool to create new processes.

The company then used Action Technologies' automated work-flow builder tool to convert the process map into forms and views for a Lotus Notes application.

Under the new process, decision making is pushed down into the project team and the communications loops are closed before the project gets to Lonergan. Now all the people who participate in the new development process at Tandy communicate among themselves. "The old way wasn't efficient, with everyone coming to me," Lonergan said.

To facilitate communication, WorkFlow Designs developed a Lotus Notes application that provides a database for every new product development program, as well as views for each member of the new product development group. Each person is required to log on to the system first thing every morning, review all the pertinent action items, and update the status.

Workers at Tandy's Tokyo design facilities update their projects daily, while their Texas counterparts, 14 hours behind, are sleeping, and vice versa. Each group arrives in the morning to freshly updated activity lists.

Lonergan can log on to the system and view only those programs that report problems or that have fallen behind schedule.

In contrast to some reengineering projects that cost a fortune, employ an army of management consultants, and take many months to implement, the Tandy project took about two months. This included process mapping, system process analysis, redesign, and the generation of the Lotus application. Lonergan expects the investment to pay for itself in three months. It is also expected to deliver a 10 percent productivity gain. By closing the information loops and removing the bottleneck around Lonergan's desk, the group should experience shorter development cycles and, there-fore, turn out more products each year.

Dodge says she believes the key to successful business workflow redesign is to focus on the interaction between the people. "Infor-mation system people tend to focus on information," Dodge says. "They start with input and output when they really need to go right to the business process—the requests and commitments between people." That's how work really gets done.

HUGHES SIMULATES SURFACE-MOUNTED TECHNOLOGY (SMT) PROCESS

This use of process mapping and simulation software in the planning, design, and implementation of a new Surface Mount Technology (SMT) production line took place at Hughes Network Systems, where a high mix of products at low volumes are produced. Now bottleneck, capacity, layout, and machine downtime analyses may be performed using menu-driven process mapping and simulation software packages. The surface mount line replaced a job shop-like production environment in response to increased demand and an overall need to change to a continuous-flow environment with a high level of system integration. The equipment chosen is state of the art including high-speed component-placement machines, which required a high initial investment. To ensure a proper design and efficient operation of the line, process simulation was chosen as the design and analysis tool.

Simulation is a tool that can describe real-world operations in a compressed time mode. The objective is to identify the optimum line design and to determine the following performance characteristics: line bottlenecks, re-work, work-in-process and flow-through times, the effects of changing buffer locations, and the optimum number of assembly stations.

The process mapping simulation tool had to be user-friendly, not computer code-intensive, and PC-based. The software selected by Hughes Network Systems was "PROMODEL PC," a menu-driven, flexible program that provided a graphic animation simulation feature, which was useful throughout the project. The process mapping task was performed in two stages: A basic process line configuration was developed to address initial design issues, followed by fine-tuning and optimization in the second stage. The entire process mapping and simulation project took just four months.

With basic information on the machines and material handling equipment provided by the vendors, the process map is able to include all important details of the proposed line. The primary entry data focused on the operating time of each machine, their connecting conveyers, and the hand assembly process operations.

The secondary focus was on the two proposed product family options and the production quantities.

The operations of the proposed process line can be summarized as follows:

- Bare boards enter the line at the load station. After the first sides are paste printed and epoxy is deposited, the boards pass through a component placement machine and are then placed into an infrared oven. This completes operations on one side of the board.

- If the secondary side must be handled, the boards are inverted at this point to face another solder paste printer. The component and fine-pitch placement machines are next, followed by solder flow via an infrared oven.

- The boards may still go through a number of manual assembly operations, wave soldering and cleaning machines, and a manual assembly for the heat-sensitive components.

The machines are of two categories: component placement or paste and epoxy application, and basic conveyor-type machines such as infrared ovens, wave solder, and cleaning machines. Component placement machine process times are based on the insertion rates and associated derating factors for both movements between each placement. The paste and epoxy application machines have specific operating times based on the screen wipe and size of the board and on the number of placements required. The conveyor-type machines are treated as basic transfer units and are simulated in terms of machine length and belt speed. Special conditions such as incline, invert, and so on, are taken into account. Each section is either a transfer or an accumulation conveyor. (There are two buffers on the line; one located before the board inverter and the other between the last infrared oven and the plated through-hole, hand insertion area.) The hand and manual assembly stations are defined according to the number of components to be assembled and on standard assembly times.

The process simulations were run for two product families, which are similar except that one features approximately 45 percent fewer components. The initial warm-up and steady-state simulation run times are determined by checking the system characteristics at hourly intervals. This shows that an initial warm-up time of four hours and a steady-state run time of 40 hours are required. For statistical accuracy, each simulation is run 20 times.

In order to study different output scenarios, the basic model is modified and run to test system performance under different downtime assumptions. During actual production, downtimes typically are attributed to machine malfunction, maintenance, or replenishment of components. The simulation is modified to include different assumptions regarding downtimes using partial data from vendors and those from a sister company running similar component placement machines.

The main issue at this stage is the steady-state production rates. The line is designed to complete a certain number of boards of each type during a specific time period subject to delays imposed by unforeseen "bottlenecks." Thus, a "bottleneck analysis" of the original line design indicates their locations and the expected effect on production speeds for both product families.

The conclusions of their initial process simulation indicate that their process could be fine-tuned and optimized with respect to production rates, buffer locations, and sizes.

AEG SCHNEIDER'S QUEST FOR PROCESS QUALITY

A quest for process quality improvement enabled AEG Schneider (Formerly Modicon, Inc.) of North Andover, Massachusetts, a manufacturer of programmable logic controllers (PLCs) and motion controllers, to cut the time needed to take a product from a concept on the drawing board to a finished piece rolling off the assembly line by 20 months by using a process mapping technique to help track new product development and shorten time to market. This reduction in cycle time was achieved by using a process mapping technique initially recommended by Motorola, Inc. One of the application consultants from Motorola University (MU) taught a cross-functional team at AEG how to implement the process, and AEG's management provided full support.

As a result, AEG was able to bring to market a series of low-end microcontrollers in one-third the time expected, a move that improved their competitiveness. AEG cut their development time and costs by more than half and brought a series of products to market one-and-a-half years sooner than ever before by changing their old processes.

Roger L. Lohn, Motorola University senior corporate applications consultant working with the AEG team, says, "We're challenging the old paradigm that process quality improvement costs more and takes more time. Today we know that quality costs less and takes less time. We used to say, Do it faster. Now we're analyzing the process to understand what's value-added and eliminating all non-value-added activities. As the number of steps in the process is reduced, the number of opportunities to generate defects also goes down."

Modicon invested more than $1 million in approaches and programs to improve their process quality. Results included a 60-percent drop in warranty return rates. When Modicon started to focus on improving strategic business processes such as product development, it turned to Motorola.

At his first meeting with Modicon's managers, Lohn made it clear that in six months, provided that the managers did their jobs well, those same jobs would be different. "You won't measure yourself by profits, return on net assets, or market share—these are lagging indicators. Focus on cycle time and correcting process errors will automatically improve profits and market share. Are you ready to make the change?" he asked the group. They were ready.

Then Lohn worked with a cross-functional process mapping team whose members were selected by managers of each department, including sales, service, accounting, finance, shipping, production, scheduling, manufacturing, and process and test engineering. With Lohn and others from the Motorola application team, the Modicon team developed an "As-Is" process map, outlining their product development process in detail. The map extended around a 25-by-40-foot room, and then some. It revealed several problems with Modicon's product development. "When you map out the 'As-Is' process, you discover there are activities that take up time yet don't add value," says Lohn. "Modicon was duplicating tests in different departments, because each was wary of leaving the job to someone else. There also was a lack of communication between engineering and manufacturing, resulting in misunderstandings about processes and manufacturing capabilities."

According to Lohn, like most other companies, they had functional "silos"—that is, departments working side by side but with "white space" separating them. In this type of arrangement, employees don't understand the significance of interactions occurring between departments. However, such interactions represent the real processes of your business.

"If I measure only profit and manage functional silos by budget, I never look at the true cost of anything being done." says Lohn. "That's managing vertically and nobody is managing horizontally, looking at other parts of the business."

After completing the "As-Is" process map, the team spent time building a "Should-Be" process map, cutting out all unnecessary activities in the product development cycle. "We knew there were extra delays and inefficiencies. But I don't think we expected to be able to cut the process to one-third of what it was. We were very surprised at that," says James K. Robertson, Modicon manager of program management, project planning, and control, and cross-functional team leader.

The team decided to apply the "Should Be" process to developing the Modicon Micro, a family of low-end controllers with functionality comparable to but less extensive than Modicon's other controllers. Managers knew the company needed to get the products to market quickly to remain competitive, but they hadn't been designed.

The team developed a contract book that included a business plan, product requirements document, and product specifications. The business plan detailed what the team agreed to do by way of performance and timing and what management agreed to support by way of capital and other resources. Before product development began, both managers and team members consented to the contract's terms.

The team met regularly to check on the progress of process improvement action items and brought in experts as required to discuss issues that could affect the product's process quality. Their first new microcontroller rolled off the production line 10 months after development began and on schedule.

Successful implementation of the streamlined development process has made a dramatic change in how they work. It sparked an excitement in the company that didn't exist before. "I think this is the greatest thing that's happened to us since I've been here," says Robertson. "It's certainly going to keep us competitive" if people continue to learn how to understand, simplify, and communicate, the real processes by staying open to new ideas. "Middle management has to be prepared to work in a matrix-like, line-management structure, and upper management has to remain supportive. But I think we've done a good job going through this, and we're educating people coming through behind us."

FLUOR DANIELS USES SIMPLE SOFTWARE FOR ISO 9000 DOCUMENTATION

Fluor Daniels has adopted simple flow chart graphic software to document their processes as part of their effort to obtain ISO 9000 quality certification. Fluor Daniels selected *VISIO* as their simple flow-charting process mapping tool because "it's the only product that all employees could use to meet all their everyday drawing and diagraming needs," said Ken Cain, director of Information Services. Fluor Daniels is the principal subsidiary of $8.5 billion Fluor Corporation and is a global engineering, construction, and diversified services company with more than 50 offices worldwide. It manages large international construction projects such as dams and oil refineries.

As part of Fluor Daniels process mapping efforts they established a goal "to have every department document their work process both visually and verbally," explained Cain. He wanted to choose a software program that they all could use to exchange process data and information among the Fluor Daniels global offices. The information might include project plans and drawings of process flow charts. The company's process drawings often included unique engineering graphic representations and many different kinds of shapes and symbols, in addition to the process diagrams. Fluor Daniels began realizing a number of benefits of using *VISIO,* a process mapping and documentation tool, including (1) lower training costs because the company is now training their more than 7,000 users on one process mapping tool rather than several different graphic or workflow products, and (2) increased productivity since their international staff is now better able to exchange data more easily. As Fluor Daniels concentrates its initial implementation of process mapping on using the *VISIO* product to document their processes to facilitate ISO 9000 certification, they have found new uses in their geological engineering department that allow them to even replace some computer-aided-design software products.

A PICTURE IS WORTH A THOUSAND WORDS AT MOBIL OIL

A picture *is* worth a thousand words. Just ask Wayne Kendrick, a system analyst for Mobil Oil Corporation in Dallas, Texas. Kendrick, whose work involves planning and designing complex processes, was scheduled to make a presentation to familiarize top management with a number of different projects his group was working on. And he was not allotted a lot of time to describe his processes. "I was given ten minutes for my presentation, and I had twenty to thirty pages of detailed documentation to present," he says. "Obviously, I could not get through it all in the time allocated." So Kendrick turned to *VISIO* software to solve his communication problem. He says that the decision to use *VISIO* was a natural one. "I think people can relate to pictures better than words." Kendrick applied his thinking to his presentation by using *VISIO* to create process flow maps, and graphs, to represent the original 30 pages of text. "It was an effective way to get them interested in my projects." The visuals provided a way for these top managers "to quickly see the importance of the projects"—and he got approval to proceed with his improvement efforts on the spot. "I think a graphic representation of what you're talking about tends to stick with people better."

Kendrick says he appreciates *VISIO's* unique combination of usability and depth. "When I need to do a process flow chart, I use *VISIO* because it allows me to get my thoughts down quickly," he says. "Yet I still get very detailed process maps. One of the main reasons that *VISIO* has caught on at Mobil is that it is so easy to learn and use. You don't have to be a computer whiz to use it. You just have to be able to use a mouse and drag and drop the process boxes where you want them, and add your supporting text. And when you are ready to make changes, it's very easy to move things around." Kendrick believes that process mapping tools can help anyone make better decisions faster by conveying their ideas and processes visually.

MORTON INTERNATIONAL USES SIMULATION AND ANIMATION

A modern, high-technology manufacturing facility can be an intimidating place. Many are computer-driven, use robotics, and manufacture several products simultaneously. This environment challenges even the best managers charged with finding the lowest-cost, most-efficient solutions to a variety of manufacturing problems.

For example, how does the manufacturing process change when a cost-conscious company wants to substitute parts or introduce a new product? Automobile air-bag manufacturer Morton International says it has found a tool that can help address these sort of problems. They have now begun to apply process mapping simulation and animation software products, such as PROMODEL, to help solve their problems. These simulation software tools allow managers and designers to play "What-If" games and try a number of different solutions to their process problems without leaving their desks.

Morton International, located in Ogden, Utah, uses PROMODEL simulation process mapping software tools for all their automated and manual production lines, said Robert Duke, Morton's manager of continuous improvement. The computer simulation can "quickly find bottlenecks in the line," he said. With PROMODEL simulation a typical manager or engineer can sit down and create your process map and run the simulation with little training. Mr. Duke said their employees picked up the use of the PROMODEL software in less than a day.

SIMULATION ENHANCES PRODUCTIVITY AT ALLEN-BRADLEY PLANTS

Process simulation software has been used to boost productivity at four Allen-Bradley plants: those in Twinsburg and Highland Heights, Ohio; Dublin, Georgia; and Milwaukee, Wisconsin. Process simulation software is used by Allen-Bradley for the design of new manufacturing cells and in evaluating existing processes at these plants.

The particular simulation package used by Allen-Bradley is WIT-NESS Simulation Software from AT&T ISTEL. "In our industrialization process, we build our products in a pilot facility during the period of time from product design to manufacturing, then we work all the bugs out of the manufacturing process here at Highland Heights," explains Tim Portik, senior industrialization engineer in the operations group for Allen-Bradley Co. in Highland Heights. The WITNESS Simulation Software "is a tool that I find particularly helpful in the development of these pilot labs. Before we spend any money on capital equipment, we can determine the real capacity of manufacturing cells, justify new equipment, develop acceptance-testing parameters for new equipment, and see the operation run right on the screen. Process simulation helps in determining process scheduling and identifying bottlenecks in our continuous flow manufacturing process. Simulation enables us to model the newly developed manufacturing process so that we have a fairly good idea as what to expect from the actual process before we buy the equipment and put it all together."

Portik points out two distinct steps in the manufacturing process at Allen-Bradley. In the first step, components are inserted in printed circuit boards in the Electronic Manufacturing Strategies (EMS) lines to create completed modules. The final production cells manufacture the finished products, including assembly, test, and packaging during the second stage.

"We started using process simulation software for development of new manufacturing processes, which dealt mainly with the final assembly and test areas," says Portik. "But we soon discovered that the software was also a useful tool to enhance existing processes, so it quickly worked its way into the manufacturing areas."

Brian McCaffrey, senior industrial engineer in the Allen-Bradley operations group, describes the assembly process this way: Raw printed circuit boards are first populated by a topside, surface mount component operation. Then they go through a reflow solder process, followed by an automated through-hole assembly process. In the reflow solder step of the process, the boards go through three machines: a Dual In-Line Process (DIP) inserter, an axial leaded part inserter, and a radial lead inserter. After this, the boards are prepared for bottom-side surface-mount components by means of adhesive application. The next step is a UV curing oven, which is then followed by manual assembly prior to wave soldering. The boards are then ready for inspection.

At this point, other parts are added after wave soldering. A subsequent step is Thermal Stress Screening (TSS). The boards are now ready for an in-circuit test, after which they are de-panelized using a router, which cuts the circuit boards out of their card. Surface-mount assembly is virtually identical in both the Twinsburg and Dublin plants. Testing and final assembly also follow very similar patterns.

At the Allen-Bradley plant in Dublin, Georgia, process simulation software was used to model the startup of a full-blown production line. "About 18 months ago, we began to install a board assembly line and a model was built to simulate the assembly of printed circuit boards through the different stations," explains Tim Finn, senior manufacturing engineer at Allen-Bradley's Dublin, Georgia, plant. "Process simulation helps us to enhance our production, because we were able to correctly establish the parameters and find out the impact of conveyors and buffers on the overall process. We subsequently used the simulation software as a tool in the rearrangement of our facility, which helped identify bottlenecks and allowed us to eliminate potential production problems. This, in turn, helped us to streamline the flow of product through the plant."

Specifically, Finn says, process simulation was used to optimize the production of through-hole board products in a continuous-flow assembly. The software helped Finn determine expenditures for capital equipment needed to achieve a desired level of production capacity. This was, in turn, instrumental in justifying equipment purchase, such as conveyors and robotics.

"By increasing our productivity, we reduced cycle time by almost half, which helped us to be more responsive to customer orders," comments Finn. "We were actually able to cut cycle time by forty-four percent for through-hole operations."

Allen-Bradley was able to achieve these results because the software represents real-world operations by creating an animated color view of the flow of objects through a process. The software package uses templates from which it builds a process map and simulation model and simple forms, which describe those objects. The familiar Windows environment, tool bars, and pull-down menus speed model building, freeing time for the value-added activities of experimentation and business process reengineering analysis. The user is able to interact with the simulation and see the effect of his or her decision in order to predict outcomes, improve processes, analyze problems, and formulate solutions.

Process simulation has also been used to help design new manufacturing cells, one of which is for a generic control product at the Twinsburg facility. "In this cell, populated boards go through a dynamic burn-in test, after which they are assembled onto a cover, labeled, and packaged," explains McCaffrey. "We broke production records during the first week of operation, cutting cycle times by sixty percent. In this cell, process simulation software has helped us to evaluate future changes of products and processes, determine real capacity, and increase cell capacity by twenty-five percent.

We're currently using it to help evaluate future equipment up-grades."

Another area of enhanced productivity was in the surface-mount operation of the EMS line in Twinsburg. "We were concerned that we might need a second TSS tester in our EMS line," comments McCaffrey. "This is essentially a static tester which accepts modules on racks, where they are exposed to very high and then very low temperatures. The simulation program showed us that we could avoid the purchase of an additional TSS chamber by proving that existing TSS chambers could handle the mix."

Allen-Bradley's headquarters plant in Milwaukee has achieved dramatic reductions in cycle time with simulation software. "Here we're the initial manufacturing pilot for new products and are setting up our final pilot assembly areas," comments Greg Gaberino, senior industrialization engineer. "Our major effort here is to re-duce cycle time from days to minutes."

Future activity in process simulation includes the development of an internal list of standard inputs for building models, and some standardization for outputs from the simulation models. Portik and McCaffrey intend to create a database for storing logic and icons to further increase commonality between models used at Allen-Bradley. This will help in the communication of model concepts throughout Allen-Bradley.

THE LESSONS LEARNED

As noted in each of the previous success stories, it is clear that process mapping linked with simulation and Activity-Based Costing are very powerful tools to help you provide your products and services cheaper, better, and faster. By applying either the military-oriented IDEF0 process mapping techniques or the new non-IDEF process mapping and business process reengineering concepts to your own unique business needs you will be able to be more competitive and help assure your business survival in very competi-tive times.

CHAPTER 6

IDEF Process Mapping Methodology

An IDEF process map (In this chapter we address only the IDEF0 functional process map) is a representation of a set of components of a functional system or functional process area. The process map or "model" as it is referred to in IDEF, is developed to facilitate process understanding, analysis, improvement, or replacement of your processes. Processes are composed of interfacing or interdependent parts that work together to perform a useful process function. Process parts can be any combination of things, including people, information, software, processes, equipment, products, or raw materials. The process map can be used to describe what a process does, what controls it, what things it works on, what means it uses to perform its functions, and what it produces.

IDEF is a process mapping technique based on combining graphics and text that are then presented in an organized and systematic graphic presentation to gain understanding, support analysis, provide logic for potential changes, specify requirements, or support systems-level design and integration activities. An IDEF process map is composed of a hierarchical series of diagrams that gradually display increasing levels of detail describing functions and their interfaces in the context of your process.

IDEF is a process mapping technique for performing and managing needs analysis, benefits analysis, cost trade-offs, requirements definition, functional analysis, systems design, maintenance, and baseline documentation for business process reengineering. IDEF process maps provide a "blueprint" of functions and their interfaces that must be captured and understood in order to make reengineering decisions that are logical, affordable, integrated, and achievable. The IDEF process map reflects how process functions interrelate and operate just as the blueprint of a product reflects how the different pieces of a product fit together. When used in a systematic way, IDEF process mapping provides a systems engineering approach to:

1. Performing systems analysis, process identification, and improvement, and design at all process levels. It can be applied to systems composed of people, machines, materials, computers, and information of all varieties across the entire business enterprise, a specific product or service, or even a single functional process

2. Producing reference documentation concurrent with process development and change efforts, to serve as a basis for integrating new processes or improving existing processes

3. Communicating among process improvement analysts, performance improvement teams, product designers, users, and managers

4. Allowing coalition team consensus to be achieved by shared understanding of your actual business processes

5. Managing large and complex projects using qualitative performance measures for process improvement

6. Providing a reference architecture for business process reengineering, enterprise analysis, information system engineering, and resource management

This chapter describes the basic elements of the IDEF process mapping methodology, it identifies the basic components of syntax (graphical component) and semantics (meaning), it identifies the rules that govern the use of the IDEF process mapping methodology, and it describes the types of process map diagrams that are commonly used. Although the components of syntax and semantics are interrelated, each one is discussed separately without regard for the actual sequence of process map construction.

This chapter is based on portions of the *Integration Definition for Function Modeling (IDEF0)* report prepared by the U. S. Department of Commerce, Technology Administration, National Institute of Standards and Technology, Federal Information Processing Standards Publication, Report Number FIPS PUB 183, dated December 1993.

THE CREATION OF IDEF

In order to help reduce product and process development costs and cycle time the U.S. Air Force sponsored the early process mapping efforts through their Integrated Computer Aided Manufacturing (ICAM) Program. The goal was to develop "generic subsystems" which could be used by a large number of companies to provide support for common process functions such as management of information, shop-floor scheduling, and materials handling.

This ambitious goal needed a common "baseline" communication tool around which to plan, develop, and implement the process subsystems. The baseline was called the "Architecture of Manufacturing" since it was to provide an industry-wide functional processing "architecture."

To develop the architecture, a "language" was also needed to express and document current business process operations. At the outset of ICAM, the Air Force issued a Request for Proposal to build the architecture. A process mapping activity modeling technique was specified as the language for this new architecture. To be successful, this process mapping language had to satisfy the following criteria:

- It had to be able to express process operations in a natural and straightforward way.

- It had to be concise and provide a straightforward means of locating details of interest easily and quickly.

- It had to be able to communicate the process to a wide variety of different levels and types of business personnel.

- Since it was to serve as a baseline for generic subsystem process planning, development, and implementation, it had to permit sufficient rigor and precision to ensure orderly and correct results.

- Since the baseline was to be developed through the cooperative effort of a large number of industry partners, it had to include a methodology (rules and procedures) for its use that would permit many diverse groups to develop architecture pieces that would permit widespread review, critique, and approval.

- Since the baseline was to represent many different businesses rather than just one company or industry segment, the process mapping technique had to include a means of separating "organization" from "function"; that is, a common agreement could not be achieved unless the individual companies' organizational differences were separated out and only the common functional process thread was captured.

The SADT (Structured Analysis and Design Technique) originally developed in 1972 by Douglas T. Ross, of SofTech, was selected as "The Architecture Method" for use in the Air Force ICAM Project. The major elements of this functional process mapping technique initially used by the ICAM Program were later renamed "IDEF0."

THE IDEF0 PROCESS MAPPING CONCEPTS

The original IDEF0 methodology incorporated basic process mapping concepts that address each of the needs listed above. These basic IDEF0 process mapping concepts are:

1. *Process Activity Graphic Representation:* The "box and arrow" graphics of an IDEF0 process mapping diagram, as shown in Figure 6.1, illustrate the process operation as the box and the interfaces to and from the process operation as the arrows entering or leaving the box. In order to be able to express real-life process operations, boxes may be interpreted as operating with other boxes, with the interface arrows providing "con-

Figure 6.1   Process Activity Graphic Representation

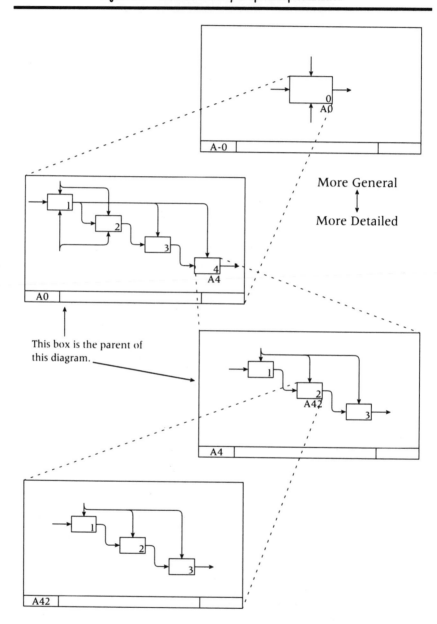

More General

More Detailed

This box is the parent of
this diagram.

straints" as to when and how process operations are triggered and controlled.

2. *Conciseness:* The documentation of a process architecture must be concise to permit encompassing the subject matter. The linear, verbose characteristic of ordinary language text is clearly insufficient. The two-dimensional form provided by a blueprintlike graphic process map has the desired conciseness without losing the ability to express relationships such as interfaces, feedback, and error paths.

3. *Communication:* There are several IDEF process map concepts which are designed to enhance communications:

   - Diagrams based upon very simple box and arrow graphics
   - Plain text to specify box (function) and arrow (data or objects) meanings
   - Gradual exposition of process detail, featuring a hierarchy with major functions at the top and successive levels of subfunction processes revealing well-bounded detail process breakout
   - A node index for locating process details within the hierarchic structure of diagrams
   - Limitation of detail on each successive process mapping diagram to not more than six subfunction processes for ease of reader comprehension and use
   - Process map diagrams supported with text and glossary to increase the preciseness of the graphic representation

4. *Rigor and Precision:* The rules of IDEF0 process mapping provide sufficient rigor and precision to satisfy the architecture needs without overly constraining the process analyst. IDEF0 process mapping rules include:

   - Detail exposition control at each level of the process
   - Bounded context (no omissions or additional out-of-scope detail)
   - Syntax rules for graphics (boxes and arrows)
   - Uniqueness of names and labels on a process mapping diagram
   - Diagram connectivity provided by detail reference expressions

- Data/object connectivity (Input, Control, Output, Mechanism [ICOM] codes and tunneled arrows)
- Input versus control separation (rule for determining role of data or objects)
- Minimum control of function (all functions require at least one control)
- Arrow branch (fork or join) constraint (labels for arrow segments)
- Arrow label requirements (minimum labeling rules)
- Purpose and viewpoint (all process maps shall have a purpose and viewpoint statement)

5. *Consistent Methodology:* Step-by-step procedures are provided for process mapping, review, and interview tasks
6. *Organization versus Function:* The separation of organization from function is included in the purpose of the process map and carried out by the selection of functions and arrow labels during process map development. Continual review during process map development ensures that narrow organizational viewpoints are avoided.

IDEF PROCESS MAPPING INFORMATION

IDEF process maps are composed of three types of information: graphic diagrams, text, and glossary descriptions.

Types of Diagrams

These graphic diagrams, text, and glossary descriptions are cross-referenced to each other. The graphic diagram is the major component of an IDEF process map, containing boxes, arrows, box/arrow interconnections, and associated relationships. Boxes represent each major function of a subject. These functions are broken down or decomposed into more detailed diagrams, until the subject is described at a level necessary to support the goals of a particular process. The top-level or higher-level diagram in the process map provides the most general or abstract description of the process. This diagram is followed by a series of child diagrams providing more detail about the process.

Top-Level Context Diagram

Each process map should have a top-level context diagram, on which the subject of the process map is represented by a single box with its bounding arrows. This is called the A-0 diagram (pronounced "A minus zero"). The arrows on this process diagram interface with process functions outside the process area to establish a focal point for your process map. Since a single box can represent a whole process, the descriptive name written in the box is general. The same is true of the interface arrows since they also represent the complete set of external interfaces to the process. The A-0 diagram also sets the process map scope or boundary and orientation. An example A-0 diagram is shown in Figure 6.2.

The A-0 context diagram also should present brief statements specifying the process map's viewpoint and purpose, which help

Figure 6.2   An Example of an A-0 Diagram

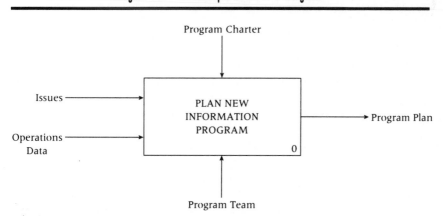

to guide and constrain the creation of your process map. The viewpoint determines what can be "seen" within the process map context and from what perspective or "slant." Depending on the audience, different statements of viewpoint may be adopted that emphasize different aspects of the process. Things that are important in one viewpoint may not even appear in a process map presented from another viewpoint of the same process.

The statement of purpose expresses the reason why the process map is created and actually determines the structure of the process map. The most important features come first in the hierarchy, as the whole top-level function is decomposed into subfunction parts that compose it, and those parts, in turn, are further decomposed until all of the relevant detail of the whole viewpoint is adequately exposed. Each subfunction is mapped individually by a box, with parent boxes detailed by child diagrams at the next lower level. All child diagrams must be within the scope of the top-level context diagram.

THE MODEL FOR THE IDEF PROCESS MAP

One of the most important features of IDEF as a process mapping concept is that it gradually introduces greater and greater levels of detail through the process mapping diagram structure comprising the process map. In this way, communication is enhanced by providing the reader with a well-bounded topic with a manageable amount of detail to learn from each process map diagram.

We have noted that the IDEF process map model starts by presenting the whole subject as a single unit—a box with external-arrow boundary conditions connecting it to functions and resources outside the subject. The single box is called the "top box" of the model. (This top box has node number A0.) Since the single top box of an IDEF model represents the subject as a whole, the descriptive name in the box is general. The same is true of the external arrows of the model, since they represent the complete set of external boundary conditions of the subject as a whole, including access to mechanism support that supplies additional means of performance.

Context Diagrams

The process diagram in which the A0 top box appears represents the context of the process map and is called a context diagram. The minimum context for a process map is the special context diagram with the node number A-0. The A-0 context diagram has only the single-named A0 top box, with its labeled external arrows, and also textual definitions of the viewpoint and purpose of the process map. (The A-0 diagram has no ICOM codes or tunneling at unconnected arrow ends.)

Sometimes, in order to provide a more complete description of the environmental context of the process map, an optional A-1 context diagram is also presented. In the A-1 context diagram, the A0 box takes the place of one of the three-to-six numbered boxes (the other boxes retaining their expected box number), so the effect is to provide a complete parent diagram (with three to six boxes) for the process maps top level—the A1 through A6 nodes still being the first-generation children. In the case where an A-1 context diagram is used, an A-0 context diagram is still presented. This A-0 process diagram still has only the single-named A0 top box, with its labeled external arrows and also textual definitions of the viewpoint and purpose of the process map.

Context diagrams are process map diagrams that have node numbers of the form "A-n" (with a minus sign included), where n is greater than or equal to zero. Ordinary, noncontext diagrams lack the minus sign in their node numbers. The box number of the top box of the process map (representing the whole of the mapped process) is always 0. Box number 0 should appear on the required A-0 context diagram of the process map, and should also appear on the optional A-1 context diagram (if any) where it takes the place of one of the boxes (one to at most six) of that A-1 (map-wide) parent diagram. Thus A0 always is the (shared) node number of the parent box and child diagram for the whole process map and always is detailed by boxes with node numbers A1, A2, A3, to at most A6.

With only one box, A-0 is a proper context process diagram but is not a (proper) parent diagram. Proper diagrams have three to six boxes. The parental context is that which provides or names the context for a diagram in the place of a proper parent diagram. The parental context of the A0 diagram is the required A-0, if there is no A-1 context diagram. If there is an A-1 context diagram, A-1 is the proper parent of the A0 diagram. The parental context of the A-0 context diagram always is "TOP."

High-Level Context Diagrams

High-level context process map diagrams have node numbers of the form A-n for n greater than one. Thus A-1 is a context diagram, is a proper parent (of A0), but is not a high-level context diagram. For a given process map presentation, the highest-level context diagram (largest n) has parental context "NONE," unless the highest-level context diagram is A-0.

Each high-level context diagram, A-n, is an ordinary detail process diagram except that one of its three to six boxes has its box number replaced by "minus sign n-1," so that, for A-1, that box is the A0 top box of the model, and the model as a whole (that A0 box itself, the parent of the children) appears to have parent A-1, grandparent A-2, and so on.

By providing a more complete description of the process map's environmental context, context process mapping (characterized by negative node numbering) provides more-constraining specifications on the boundary conditions of the A0 diagram of the IDEF process map.

Context process mapping proceeds just as ordinary detail process mapping, the only difference being the negative numbering (and the nondefinitive but normative interpretation) that preserves A0 as the "origin" of the node-number-based coordinate system for all process map references.

All the negative-node-number process mapping merely provides more and more details about the sources and uses of the external boundary conditions. That detail may not precisely be matched by any particular specific environment, completely. These context diagrams describe the "typical" context.

Figure 6.3 provides an illustration in node-tree form to show how rich high-level context process maps might appear.

FEOs, Text, and Glossary

The node-numbering scheme provides the basis for coordinating For Exposition Only (FEO), text, and glossary terms. During process

Figure 6.3   Negative Node-Numbered Context

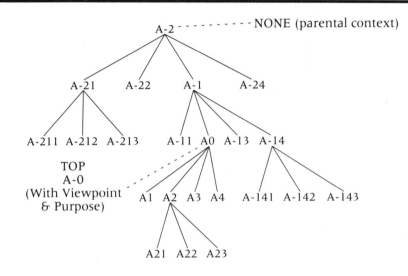

map development it is important that each new element of information be associated with the node that brought it into consideration.

For each form (FEOs, text, and glossary), the node-numbering extension notation consists of a single letter appended to the associated node number. For example, node numbers for FEOs shall contain an "F" for FEO (e.g., A312F).

Some IDEF users record glossary definitions on IDEF diagram forms, even though the use of this form for glossaries is not required. In this case, a glossary page can define the key words, phrases, and acronyms used with a particular associated IDEF node. The node numbers for such glossary pages should contain a "G" for glossary (e.g., A312G).

Likewise, some IDEF users record their textual comments on IDEF diagram forms, though the use of this form for text is not required. In this case, a text page could provide the text comments for a particular associated IDEF node. The node numbers for such text pages should contain a "T" for text (e.g., A312T).

If there is more than one FEO, glossary or text page associated with a given IDEF0 node, the pages should be designated with an additional number to uniquely identify each (e.g., A312Fl, A312F2, . . . A312Gl, A312G2, . . . A312Tl, A312T2, . . .).

Name Your Process Map

Each process map should have a unique, descriptive name that distinguishes it from other process maps with which it may be associated. This process map name is normally abbreviated (uniquely) for use in node references. For example, a process map named "Manufacturing Operations" may be abbreviated MFG.

IDEF Process Map Presentation Rules

1. When there is text, it should be accompanied by the associated graphic process map diagram.

2. In nonpublication process map, the glossary associated with a specific graphic process map diagram should accompany the diagram and should also define only the key words, phrases, and acronyms used with the particular node.

3. In publication models, a glossary section should define the key words, phrases, and acronyms in alphabetical order for the entire process map.

4. When a table of contents is provided for a process map, it should be presented as a node tree or node index, and should contain node numbers, diagram titles, and box names.

HOW TO READ A PROCESS MAP

A process map is made up of a collection of process diagrams and associated materials arranged in a hierarchical manner. A node index (or table of contents) is created. Placing the diagrams in hierarchical order gives an overall view of the process and allows access to any portion of the process map.

Reading is done top-down, considering each process diagram as a center of process activity, bounded by its parent box. After the top-level diagrams are read, first-level diagrams are read, then second-level diagrams are read, and so on. If specific details about a process map are needed, the node index is used to descend through the levels to the required process diagram.

When published, a process map is bound in "page-pair" format and "node index" order. "Page-pair" format means that each diagram and the entire text associated with it appear on a pair of facing pages as shown in Figure 6.4.

"Node index" order means that all child diagrams relating to one box on a process map diagram are presented before the children of the next box. This places related process map diagrams together in the same order used in an ordinary table of contents as shown in Figure 6.5.

Exploring the Process Map

Process maps provide an overview of the whole process or details of a particular process. To read a process map to obtain an overview, use the index to find all high-level diagrams as shown in Figure 6.6.

Figure 6.4   Page-Pair Format

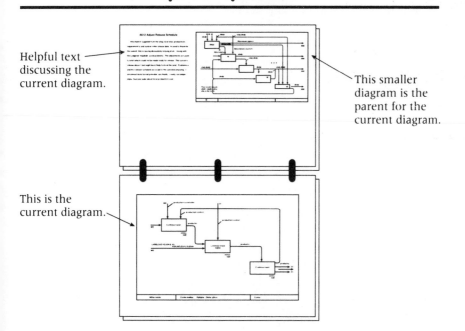

Helpful text discussing the current diagram.

This smaller diagram is the parent for the current diagram.

This is the current diagram.

Figure 6.5   Node Index Showing Diagram Order

Order of diagrams
in a document

A0   Plan for manufacture

    A1   Assume a structure and method of manufacturing

    A2   Estimate requirements, cost, time to produce

        A21   Estimate resource needs

        A22   Estimate costs to purchase or make

        A23   Estimate timing for startup and production

    A3   Develop production plans

    A4   Develop support activities plan

Figure 6.6   Node Index Showing Overview Diagrams

A0 Manufacture product
  A1 Plan for manufacture
    A11 Assume a structure and method of manufacture
    A12 Estimate requirements, time, cost to produce
    A13 Develop production plans
    A14 Develop support activities plan
  A2 Make and administer schedules and budgets
    A21 Develop master schedule
    A22 Develop coordinating schedule
    A23 Estimate costs and make budget
    A24 Monitor performance to schedule and budget
  A3 Plan production

To read a process map for detail, use the index as shown in Figure 6.7 to find all process map diagrams detailing the process of interest.

Further detailing in a process map may be traced by referring to the detail reference expression (DRE) reference (see Figure 6.8) just below the box number. This indicates the node number, Child (C-number) number, or page number of the child diagram that details the process box. In the example following, details for box 3 on diagram A24 may be found on a diagram with node number A243. If no DRE appears, the box has not yet been detailed.

Details may be shared within a process map or between different maps. In both cases, a call arrow (downward pointing), as shown in Figure 6.9, indicates where the shared detailing appears via a reference expression that may include a unique, abbreviated process name. As shown in Figure 6.9, box 4 is detailed by diagram A4 in process map MQ. In this example, the reference expression is a diagram node reference.

Process Diagram Reading Steps

The specific information about a process is in the diagrams themselves. The following "read me" sequence is recommended:

1. Scan the boxes of the process diagram to gain an impression of what is being described.

Figure 6.7   Node Index Showing Specific Detailed Diagram

A0 Manufacture product
  A1 Plan for manufacture
    A11 Assume a structure and method of manufacture
    A12 Estimate requirements, time, cost to produce
    A13 Develop production plans
    A14 Develop support activities plan
  A2 Make and administer schedules and budgets
    A21 Develop master schedule
    A22 Develop coordinating schedule
    A23 Estimate costs and make budget
    A24 Monitor performance to schedule and budget
  A3 Plan production

Figure 6.8   Example of Detailed Reference Expression (DRE)

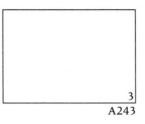

Figure 6.9   Example of Downward-Pointing Call Arrow

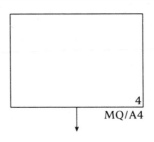

2. Refer back to the parent diagram and note the arrow connections to the parent box. Try to identify a "most important" input, control, and output.

3. Consider the arrows of the current process diagram. Try to determine if there is a main path linking the "most important" input or control and the "most important" output.

4. Mentally walk through the process diagram, from upper left to lower right, using the main path as a guide. Note how other arrows interact with each box. Determine if there are secondary paths. Check the story being told by the process map diagram by considering how familiar situations are handled.

5. Check to see if a related FEO diagram exists.

6. Finally, read the text and glossary, if provided.

This sequence ensures that the major features of each diagram receive attention. The text will call attention to anything that the process map author wishes to emphasize. The glossary will define the interpretation of the terminology used.

Each process diagram has a central theme, running from the most important incoming boundary arrow to the most important outgoing boundary arrow. This main path through the boxes and arrows outlines the primary function of the diagram as shown in Figure 6.10. Other parts of the process diagram represent qualifying or alternative conditions which are secondary to the main path.

The system's operation can be mentally envisioned by pursuing the main path. Specific kinds of data inputs, the handling of errors, and possible alternative outputs lend detail to the story. This walk-through enhances your understanding of the process map.

Figure 6.10 Example of Main Path

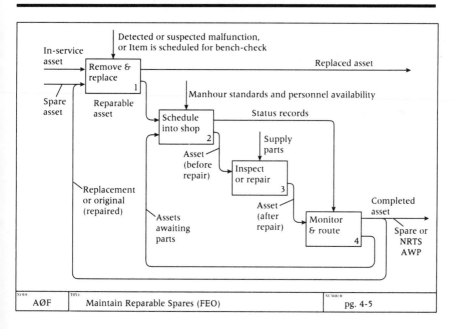

Semantics of Boxes and Arrows

The fundamental notion which must guide the interpretation of any process diagram or set of diagrams is that "only that which is explicitly stated is necessarily implied." This derives from the very nature of constraint diagrams.

Unspecified constraints must not be assumed; necessary constraints must be explicit. The corollary is: Any further detailing not explicitly prohibited is implicitly allowed.

The example shown in Figure 6.11 illustrates an assumption that can be made, that the temperature is measured "often enough" and the tolerances are changed "when appropriate" and the temperature is monitored against the tolerances "often enough" that the danger signal will be produced "soon enough." None of these intuitive understandings would conflict with subsequent process detailing which showed that:

- The temperature was measured by periodic sampling, or

- Current tolerances were requested only when the temperature increased by some fixed amount, or

- A series of temperature values produced by box 1 were stored by box 2, which examined the pattern of change to determine if the pattern was within the tolerances, and so on.

Figure 6.11   Example of Constraint

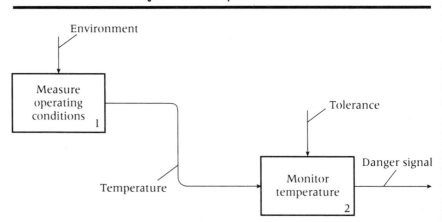

The graphic notations of a process diagram are, by themselves, abstract. However, they do make important fundamental distinctions. Their abstract nature should not detract from the intended breadth of possible interpretations that are permitted.

Constraints Omit How and When

Either of the two "how"- and "when"-dependent representations, shown in Figure 6-12, indicates that activity a2 is dependent on "d," which is created or modified by the activity a1.

Each representation defines a constraint relationship between the two boxes. All that is explicitly stated by the intermediate arrow

Figure 6.12   Illustration of Dependent Relationships

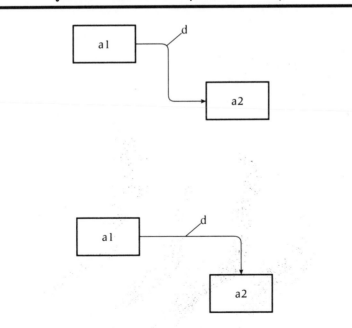

for either representation is expressed as follows: Some activation of box 2 requires something called "d" that is produced by some activation of box 1.

Frequently, process diagrams imply strongly that two or more boxes may need the contents of an arrow. The meaning of the boxes and arrows shown in Figure 6.13 is that something produced by box 1 is needed by box 2 and by box 3. It may be that an activation of the arrow's "source" (box 1) must precede every activation of its "destination" (box 2 or box 3). It may be that one activation of the source is sufficient for every activation of any destination. Without additional information, the boxes and arrows alone permit either interpretation.

Multiple Inputs, Controls, and Ouputs

The basic interpretation of the box shown in Figure 6.14 is that in order to produce any subset of the outputs (01, 02, 03), any subset of the entries (Il, I2, I3, Cl, C2, C3, C4, Ml, M2, and M3) may be required. In the absence of further process detailing it cannot be assumed that:

- Any output can be produced without all entries present, or
- Any output requires all entries for its production

Figure 6.13   Two Boxes Using the Contents of the Same Arrow

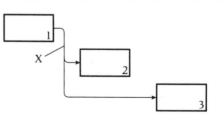

Figure 6.14   Illustration of ICOM Coding

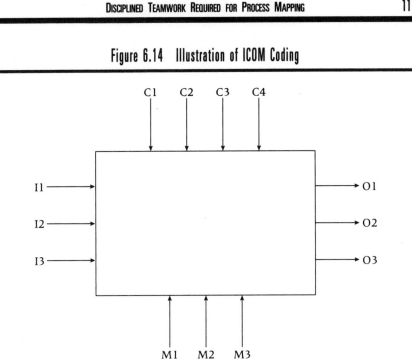

The partial detailing of the box (shown in Figure 6.15 as it might appear in a FEO diagram) indicates that I3, C2, C3, and C4 are not required for producing O1. Figure 6.15 illustrates the point that:

- Some form of further detailing will specify the exact relationship of inputs and controls to outputs
- Until the detailing is provided, limiting assumptions about relationships "inside" each box should not be made, and
- Reading of a diagram should concentrate on the arrows, which are explicit, rather than on box names, which are only implicit

DISCIPLINED TEAMWORK REQUIRED FOR PROCESS MAPPING

The IDEF process mapping approach includes procedures, as described in Chapter 10, for developing and critiquing process maps

Figure 6.15 FEO Representing Detailing of Multiple ICOMs

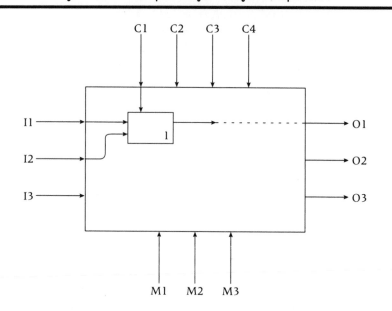

by a large group or team of people, as well as integrating support subsystems. Additional supporting procedures, such as librarian rules, and review cycle procedures are included as part of the IDEF0 process mapping methodology.

These rules of the road should help you understand the nature of IDEF process mapping and how to interpret the diagrams.

CHAPTER 7

Create a Process Mapping Team

As your work becomes increasingly sophisticated and as the demands for your business to improve performance and adapt to ever-faster changing conditions accelerate, there is an ever-greater need for you to map your processes by creating teams to examine how every process can be improved, simplified, or eliminated.

Process mapping teams are one of the most common and effective near-term strategies that business leaders can use to improve their bottom-line performance. This chapter describes process team building, describes when process team building is an appropriate activity, presents clearly the overall process mapping team building approach, and discusses the impact of process teams on your business.

However, before addressing creation of your process mapping team, it is important to understand what makes an effective team.

WHAT IS A PROCESS MAPPING TEAM?

Almost everyone has experience either being on a team or watching one in action. Sports teams, such as those in football and soccer, are obvious examples, but they also exist in business organizations, churches, community groups—even in families. And while there may be tremendous differences in their task, structure, and makeup, teams share several key characteristics:

- The team members share a common vision of what they are committed to achieve, based on a clear perception of the value that the team can provide for its customers.

- The team has a well-developed strategy for realizing its vision.

- Team members collectively possess the necessary skills and knowledge, and they share responsibility for fulfillment of your survival strategy.

- The procedures, systems, and methods are appropriate, clear, efficient, and adaptable as needed.

- Relations among team members are open, challenging, and supportive.

- There is active participation and communications between the team and other individuals and organizations to ensure that the team remains vital, adaptable, and relevant to the task at hand.

Virtually every team possesses these characteristics to some degree; it should be your objective to help your organization fully implement these winning team characteristics. Process team building is a structured effort that is based on organizational development concepts. As most commonly practiced, team building is often based around one or more key improvement activities such as process mapping and process improvement.

During the process team building phase, team members learn how to work together and resolve operational problems. The team identifies specific process areas that are either inhibiting their performance or could be strengthened and comes to agreement on ways to reach a higher level of performance. In the General Electric model, process mapping team members come together to describe and recommend immediate action for their managers to resolve. General Electric calls their process "work-out" and it was designed to improve their team communication and performance; it is a proven process for near-term breakdown of organizational stovepipe boundaries in their business. You can use these concepts today in your own business.

During the team building process, teams focus on a variety of business process improvement issues. In addition, the team also periodically steps back to reflect on its own processes of communication, problem solving, and decision making during the team building effort. In this way, team building is both a planning and problem-solving effort that is used to better understand your team's own strengths and weaknesses.

CREATING YOUR PROCESS MAPPING TEAM

Business survival goes beyond management leadership and decision making—it includes defining the problem, generating alternative process solutions, evaluating alternatives, selecting alternatives, and implementing the solution. The problems may be multileveled, multidimensional, and multidisciplinary—all of the information required to make sound decisions to solve your near-term problems may not be available, and the available information may be based on "seat of the pants" judgment and your own experience. Your business survival depends on complex human interaction among your co-workers with diverse backgrounds and from various disciplines.

The success of each process improvement effort depends on the ability of your team members to work together; thus, team satisfaction with the change process and the resulting process definition is important. Achieving consensus among members of your team means arriving at a process definition that your co-workers can agree upon. Each member may not think the new approach is the absolute best attainable, but in agreeing to a particular process, each member must believe that it is a "good" process and that all essential elements have been included. Having all members satisfied with the change process ensures ownership and responsibility among your team members. Once consensus is achieved among the team members, it is essential that buy-in is achieved from management. The preferred method is by maintaining open communication during the process to prevent management objections during the process implementation phase.

The multifunctional nature of the process mapping teams complicates the group dynamics because of technical language barriers, perceptions of unequal status, and general cultural barriers to teamwork. Some of the disconnects include:

- Rigid, functionally dominated organizational structures exist that resist any change.

- Everyone's functional organization base becomes the center of their universe.

- Process analysts and software and hardware engineers see themselves as creative individuals who do not want that creativity restricted by having to accommodate functional or process concerns.

- Manufacturing is concerned with satisfying customers' current orders and maintaining their production flow stability.

Management must overcome these obstacles if your process mapping team is to work effectively.

Some of the various organizational and management strategies business is practicing to fully utilize process mapping teams[1] are summarized here:

Teams of Teams

A general rule for effective group interaction is that the process team's size should not exceed 8 to 12 members. However, the development of a complex product or service can require hundreds of people from various functional groups in an organization. The total team performs, therefore, as a team of teams. The use of the team here has more to do with a way of thinking about process problem solution than the size of the group. The typical process improvement team consists of co-workers who operate from a shared agenda and a common view of their assignment.

A multifunctional team or a team of teams is usually a hierarchy of teams that follows the decomposition of the process down to the smallest element of action. The term "hierarchy" here does not apply to the status of the teams or team members but rather to the relationships among the teams and how these relationships correspond to process elimination, simplification, or other process changes. Communication can be maintained among teams by placing a member (usually the team leader) from a lower-level team on a team at the next highest level. The high-level team defines the strategic or system integration of the results of the other teams.

There is usually at least one team for each node of your process development. If the process definition for the next level requires more than a dozen people, the teams are further divided by discipline or technology. The decomposition occurs until the subsystems can be defined by a manageable group (8 to 12 people). The theory behind organizing the teams along discipline or technology lines within a process element is that grouping people by functional or technical discipline is a way to break the language barrier so often encountered when people who have traditionally performed different functions try to communicate. Most members of the same discipline speak the same language, regardless of their function. For example, mechanical engineers, whether from the engineering, manufacturing, or a support group, will understand most of one another's technical terms because of common education. Financial officers, human resource specialists, and different technical and information specialists have similar common vocabularies and viewpoints and they must be able to talk with one another. The problem is to get your process mapping groups to communicate with each other to help solve your problems.

Team Management

Successful management of a team relies on the same types of effective policies and actions to make management of any business organization successful. A team is, after all, like a small business organization. Following are some of the activities that characterize effective team management:

- Effective structuring of the team's organizational design (roles, responsibilities, authority, and accountability)

- Preparation of a clear, concise process team mission statement

- Identification of the goals or milestones that the process mapping team is expected to accomplish in working toward its mission or purpose

- Delineation of the strategy of the process mapping team to include major policies, programs, procedures, plans, and budgets

Regardless of the type of organizational structure selected for process mapping team formation, each team needs to have a sponsor. The team sponsor can be either a person or a team of people at the management or supervisor level, such as a designated vice president or the process improvement or reengineering champion. For projects that involve more than one company, the multicorporation team should involve individuals from all the companies involved. This oversight management team is the sponsor of all teams involved in improving your processes.

The team sponsor supports the team's activities, secures resources, and opens communication lines between the team and the rest of the department, the division, and the organization. Sponsors should possess a personal stake in the success of your effort, control over the resources needed to launch and sustain the effort, and the authority to empower the team and remove any roadblocks to its success. The sponsor can do a lot to help the team overcome inefficient processes embedded in the culture of the organization. For example, a reason might once have existed for extensive paperwork between people on a process mapping team. Many decisions can be reached through the face-to-face interaction of the team members. The extensive paperwork may no longer be needed, but not only is it required by the organization's business practices, it is instilled in the cultural practices of the team members. The sponsor should help remove these inefficiencies in existing "cultural" processes.

Team Membership

Much of the success of a team is determined by the choice of your process mapping team members. Teams may involve blue-collar, white-collar, and professional staff members and union and non-union workers. Achieving the required level of team-work requires a structured process and competent people with specific expertise and understanding of the customer needs, product or process requirements, technology base, information, materials, production capabilities, and administrative support capabilities.

The formation of your team carries with it no guarantee that team members will talk to one another. The team must include the right leader as well as the right team members. Peter Scholtes has defined team leaders as the members responsible for managing the team. His or her duties include:

- Calling and directing all team meetings

- Orchestrating all team activities

- Overseeing the preparation of reports, presentations, meeting agendas, and minutes

- Handling or assigning administrative detail

- Ensuring timely analysis and resolution of technical decisions

Team leaders can be responsible for specific processes under examination. The team leader is a full-fledged team member who shares the responsibilities of attending meetings, carrying out assignments between meetings, and generally sharing in the team's work. In addition, the team leader is the point of communication between the team and the rest of the organization—specifically, the team sponsor.

One organizational element that has proven successful for many process mapping teams is co-location of the team members. The benefits of collocation include:

- Fostering of informal communication among strategic and operational team members

- Reduction in functional allegiance and adversarial relationships

- Cultivation of flexible relationships, an appreciation of each other's concerns

- Creation of a participative atmosphere

Often the collocated members change over the duration of the project. As its work progresses, the process mapping team may recruit new people to solve specific problems. Originally all the team members may be collocated, but as the size of the team grows, collocation of all the new members may not be possible. At some point teams may become so large that many of the benefits of collocation are no longer realized—a person is limited in how many other people he or she can informally communicate with within any given time period.

How to Run Better Team Meetings

Effective team meetings are one of the best opportunities to enhance the team building process and make progress toward accomplishing your goals. To enhance the effectiveness of your process mapping team meetings, the following procedures are often recommended:

- Limit the duration of team meetings.
- Use agendas and record minutes.
- Do not end a meeting without specifying and assigning the action items.
- Do not let more than two weeks elapse between meetings.

Discipline is an important element contributing to the success of your process mapping team meetings and, thus, to the team itself. You should emphasize that each meeting must be held for a specific purpose and not merely just to have a meeting. Meeting activities should be strictly limited to the agenda items, and all of these activities have a deliverable focus. In addition, what is said is recorded. This level of meeting documentation should be created for all of the meetings as well as the management reviews.

HOW TO START A PROCESS MAPPING TEAM

Creating a process mapping team is an appropriate management tool under any one of four different scenarios:

1. A new product or process improvement has been authorized, a new team has been formed to address the specific problem, and the team needs to create a clear working arrangement for itself.

2. The improvement activities undertaken by your business are causing difficulty or distress, either in performance or communication of your process change needs.

3. The process improvement activities have been narrowly focused, and a more diverse set of corporate functional process areas need to be brought together in process mapping teams to resolve "bigger" problems, to obtain higher productivity, or to reach significant new levels of change in order to assure your survival.

4. You need to periodically reassess your performance, resolve any complex issues before they become serious or chronic, and identify new opportunities for change, growth, and development.

As the pace of change increases and as work demands become more complex, there is an ever-greater need for your business to operate effectively in the form of teams. And as managers look for new ways to start their teams off in an effective way, they often consider developing process mapping teams.

If you are such a manager, the following points have been prepared to help you understand the overall objectives of starting a process mapping team, when it might be appropriate, what conditions must be met in order for your effort to succeed, how the process works, and what its likely impact would be. Guidance is also provided regarding how you can proceed, should you decide that a process mapping team approach makes sense for your business.

Effective process mapping teams, regardless of where they exist, share certain characteristics:

- Team members have a clear commitment to the team's goals and find that their individual goals are highly compatible with the team's.

- Team members' roles and responsibilities are clear, including their relationships with one another.

- The established procedures for functioning are clear, appropriate, efficient, and open to modification as needs arise.

- Relationships within the team are characterized by open communications, direct messages, high conflict over substance and low conflict over interpersonal issues, and mutual trust and dependability.

While it may be idealistic to expect a team to fully possess each of these characteristics, it is the goal of the team leader to start groups in that direction.

In the past 10 to 15 years, a great deal has been learned about how to develop teams so they focus on near-term achievement of your business goals. Teams are usually newly formed work groups, be they process improvement teams, product development groups, task forces, ongoing work teams, or any of these which have substantially new members or new mission focus.

Your new team start-up orientation should occur as quickly after the team has been created as possible and before any major efforts are made to organize or move toward mission accomplishment. The team orientation can be done in a retreat format, away from the work site, to provide uninterrupted time for team members to get acquainted and to focus on the team building and empowerment process.

The creation of a team may be appropriate under several scenarios, including:

1. The team is relatively new and wants to establish beneficial patterns of performance from the outset.

2. The team members are coming together from different organizations and want to clarify their values, perceptions, and team mission.

3. The team has been established to operate effectively together but believes that an even greater level of performance or satisfaction is possible.

In general, new teams will only work when there is a perceived need from within the team, as opposed to being seen as a "good thing to do," the latest fad, or the result of someone else thinking it should be done. In particular, it is critical that the team leader be fully committed to the process.

There are basically five conditions that need to be met to assure a successful team effort. There must be:

1. Perceived need on the part of the team leader and, hopefully, the team for such an effort

2. Involvement of a qualified facilitator, preferably a member of your internal staff (or external), who understands your business

3. Commitment of time: for the team leader and the facilitator to plan the overall startup process, structure the session, and for all members to participant.

4. A commitment on the team leader's part to the philosophy and practices of teamwork, especially around open communications, and the participation of process mapping team members in decision making.

5. Commitment of the process mapping team to actively engage in the change process, including implementing decisions made at the sessions and additional change activities that are needed.

THE TEAM DEVELOPMENT PROCESS

There is a basic sequence of tasks that comprise most new process mapping team start-up efforts, as shown in Figure 7.1, consisting of tasks that occur prior to the team session, during the session, and after the session.

Presession

1. The process mapping team leader defines objectives and develops the plan for the overall process mapping effort.

2. The process mapping leader meets with the entire team to discuss objectives, explain the overall process, and identify

Figure 7.1 Process Mapping Team Start-up Process

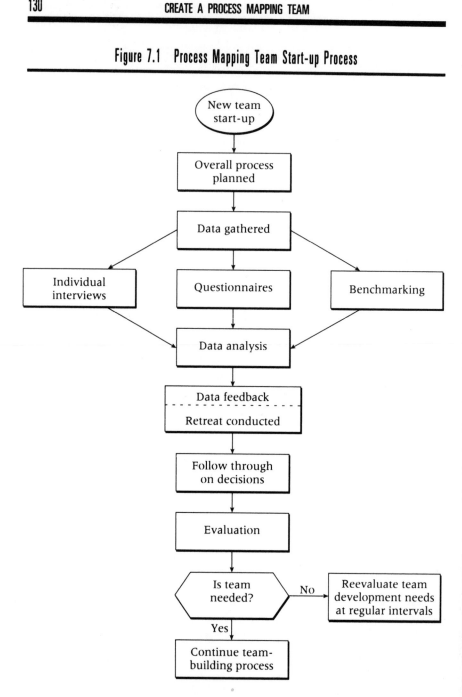

any particular areas that team members would like the leader to focus on during the team session.

During Session

There are seven basic questions that the process mapping team needs to address during the start-up session:

1. What vision and goals should the process mapping team's mission have?

2. What are the specific individual roles and responsibilities?

3. How will the process mapping team coordinate plans and strategies for mission accomplishment?

4. How will the process mapping team interact with other teams and your clients?

5. What criteria will be used to assess team effectiveness?

6. How can the team interact to meet individuals' needs regarding work style and preferences?

7. What kinds of norms will the group adopt regarding giving of feedback, support, and resolution of conflicts (personal and role)?

Usually the agenda is planned in advance by the team leader and facilitator, with input from the team members.

Postsession

1. The process mapping team follows through on decisions that are made.

2. At a predetermined time, the process mapping team reassembles to review its progress, to identify additional issues needing to be addressed, and to work on achieving problem resolution.

These are the basic steps, but they may be modified or enhanced depending on the needs of the process mapping team or the particular style of the team leader.

TEAM DEVELOPMENT RESULTS

New process mapping team start-up sessions usually result in the team's addressing issues that can provide a firm foundation for future working relationships of team members. In many cases, the press of business simply prevents the kind of thorough and open communication that is possible in this kind of setting. There is often a palpable "sigh of relief" as a result of new team start-up because feelings and thoughts are aired, usually without the negative consequences which may have been anticipated.

In addition, new team start-up usually results in:

- Norms of behavior being set or reinforced

- Plans to improve communication and performance

- Increased commitment to the team's goals and the process mapping team approach

- Enhanced appreciation of the contributions each member makes to the process mapping team's mission

The decisions that are made and the tone that is set in the process mapping team start-up sessions need continuing attention on the part of the entire team, especially the team leader. In addition, a follow-up session is usually important in order to assess the team's development and continue the team building process.

What has been provided here is a variety of factors to consider when weighing the potential value of process mapping teams. This is likely to be a valuable option if there is a strong desire to enhance your business effectiveness and where the necessary conditions exist, including the willingness to commit the financial and staff resources to make this process work.

Process mapping team building usually results in significant improvements in communication and performance. This comes about as a result of learning more about what it means to operate as a team, addressing issues that are getting in the way of your team's effectiveness and learning new techniques and principles that foster cooperative and synergistic teamwork.

Some process mapping teams have been involved in team building as a single and isolated event in the life of their organization. When this occurs, the value of the session often drops off quickly, as the initial glow of a successful process improvement effort wears off. There may be various reasons for this, but often it has to do with how realistic expectations are concerning the team development process.

On one level, team building can be seen as the beginning of functioning differently, by focusing on the collective responsibility of the team's accomplishments in changing your business processes. As with any change, it is critical to allow a period of time following your team start-up for full implementation of the agreements and principles developed during the process improvement sessions. This period of implementation should then be followed with another session (often briefer than the first) to review progress and make corrections, adjustments, or enhancements.

Therefore, process mapping team building is best seen not as a one-time event but rather as an ongoing process of team growth and renewal.

CHAPTER 8

Process Mapping Software Tool Selection

This chapter provides a brief overview of state-of-the-practice process mapping software tools and information regarding the characteristics and source of these products. It describes the available process mapping tools from graphic sketch pad workflow diagrams to computer-aided process mapping products, to sophisticated computer "What-If" simulation products.

The author thanks the Society for Enterprise Engineering (formerly the IDEF Users Group), the Society for Computer Simulation, and various vendors that allowed time for personal interviews or demonstrations, provision of test software, and use of vendor catalog specification data.

The validity and currency of the product data, specifications, or performance attributes are subject to almost continuous change. Therefore you are advised to contact the vendors for their latest product or performance data. Neither the author or the publisher guarantees the accuracy of the product information.

This chapter concludes with a comparative assessment and "Best Buy" suggestions regarding these process mapping tools.

GROWTH IN PROCESS MAPPING TOOLS

The need for process mapping tools for reengineering use in both the private and public sector is growing rapidly. According to the International Data Corporation, the business process reengineering market is expected to be $2.2 billion in 1996. In addition, they estimate that the market for process mapping and simulation software tools that can be applied to reengineering initiatives will be $150 million in 1996. Tremendous growth in reengineering is expected in both the United States and with our global competitors.

There are both old-line military-type IDEF process modeling and simulation products and the new generation of reengineering process mapping and simulation tools being created to support this growth market. In this regard it is important to highlight some of the trends in process mapping and simulation product development and delivery:

- If reengineering-focused process mapping is to be widely adopted, the software products will require user-friendly access. But far more important—the process mapping *and* simulation software will require that vendor training be constrained to the "help" instructions contained in the software. For process mapping to be effectively made available to every reengineering "process analyst" in your business, you can't afford to send your staff off to weeks of training on the software product. Vendors are just beginning to realize that the "mass market" potential for process mapping and simulation products requires a paradigm shift in their training and support concepts.

- The cost of many process mapping and in particular simulation products sold to Uncle Sam is excessive, and even the government should not be spending money on "gold-plated" simulation systems. Neither should the commercial market pay for excessive product features and unneeded complexity. This situation is similar to when computer-aided design (CAD) systems required special computers and cost a fortune. Today these computer-aided design products sell for less than a thousand dollars and run on desktop personal computers. That is the direction that process simulation and mapping products are going.

- The shift to distributed personal computers is driving software vendors to provide Windows-type delivery on desktop computer platforms. Those companies that don't shift away from expensive and or unique hardware systems will not succeed in this new market, particularly in the case of simulation products.

- The functions of process mapping products are moving toward "integrated" suites of software products. Many vendors have renamed or made minor modifications to existing process mapping products to play in the reengineering growth market. As process analysts increasingly adopt reengineering concepts, they are pressuring software vendors to develop a suite of products that have seamless integrated interfaces designed for process mapping, simulation, and Activity-Based Costing that can be effectively applied to your business process reengineering needs. These integrated products may be created totally in-house—or, even better, they could be based on partnerships with other vendors who have the "Best Product" in their niche.

AN INTRODUCTION TO PROCESS MAPPING SOFTWARE TOOLS

A brief description of the basic process mapping software tools is broken into five categories: (1) simple flow-chart graphic software, (2) process mapping products, (3) IDEF process mapping products, (4) process simulation products, and (5) process-mapping-related Activity-Based Costing (ABC) products. Each of these type tools is briefly described below:

Simple Flow-Chart Graphic Tools and Software

Probably the simplest process mapping tool is the pencil and paper. In many cases, in particular when you are trying to begin your process mapping effort, you can start with pencil sketches that describe the key boxes or elements of your processes. This can be expanded to writing your process block-diagram information on 3M Post-It-type notes and pasting them on oversize sheets of paper, or they can be applied to a blackboard sort of wall surface. This will enable you to begin to see the magnitude of your process mapping effort. The use of this simple approach is often sufficient to begin process improvement; you can begin to communicate to your process mapping team the priority areas of interest and potential improvement.

Several inexpensive and very-easy-to-use software products are described in this chapter that can be used to document your processes. With their aid you can begin to develop a computer process map that can be shared across your business organization.

One basic software tool in this category is Micrografx's *ABC Snap-Graphics 2.0,* which costs approximately $50.00, is very easy to use, and can be used to describe and document your basic process map. *ABC Snapgraphics 2.0* provides a flow-chart template gallery so you can map out a process or procedure so simply that anyone can understand how it works. This product is user-friendly, runs on Windows, and supports OLE 2.0 to facilitate software integration.

VISIO 2.0 for Windows is the next-higher level of flow-chart graphic software product. As noted by the Motorola software evaluation team, VISIO 2.0, "due to its low cost and its ability to provide double-digit productivity improvement, should be a standard utility in all Windows-based PCs." VISIO's "software intelligence and techniques allow . . . the intended mission [to be performed] faster and easier than any other known product." Motorola was searching for the ideal flow-charting tool (that is, a tool that can reduce the necessary time to produce the most sophisticated flow-chart diagrams by 75 percent) and found that VISIO met their ideal requirements for a flow-charting tool. In Motorola's evaluation VISIO had perfect evaluation scores for flow charting and advanced flow charting ease of use, ease of comprehension, reliability, compatibility with other software products, and customer service.

VISIO is the state-of-the-practice "Best Buy" product for this type of process mapping software tool.

Process Mapping Software Products

With the explosion of interest regarding business process reengineering, a whole new set of process mapping software products are beginning to emerge that are specifically created to focus on the needs of reengineering process improvement users.

In some quarters of the business community this interest in non-IDEF-type process mapping tools is gaining strength. This is in part due to the concern about being tied to a bureaucratic set of standards that may be more complex than necessary. Or it may be due to the business community's misunderstanding regarding the ease of use or validity of government-defined software products. Vendors are developing very effective new process mapping software products to meet the needs of the commercial product and service reengineering business community that are not necessarily IDEF driven. One excellent example is Logic Works Inc., which has brought to market their powerful Windows-based product *BPWin*. BPWin is an excellent example of an integrated software approach that provides process mapping and simulation, and also provides an easy link to ABC software products. Expect to see more of these sorts of integrated process mapping products hit the market.

IDEF Process Mapping Software Products

The fundamental concepts of IDEF (Integrated computer-aided DEFinition) process mapping are based on the ideas of structured analysis that have produced significant payoffs in diverse business applications. Such benefits include reductions in development costs, fewer system integration failures, and uniformly better communication.

For new business systems, new products, or new functional processes, IDEF software tools may be used to help specify the process requirements and functions and then be used to improve the process in order for you to meet your customer's requirements.

For existing processes, IDEF software tools can be used to analyze the purpose that your processes serve and the functions performed. In addition, these IDEF software tools can be used to record the mechanisms by which your processes are accomplished. In all cases, the result of applying IDEF software tools is the refinement and documentation of your own unique process(es). An IDEF software-created process map consists of diagrams, text, and glossary that are cross-referenced to each other. Either paper or computer graphic process map diagrams are the major output of the IDEF process mapping software products.

IDEF software tools provide a disciplined way of graphically describing the detailed structure of your processes and how they relate to one another. Since understanding process hierarchy is important in understanding large complex systems, IDEF software products are particularly useful, since IDEF includes hierarchy as a basic element of its process mapping capability. IDEF process mapping software provides a tool that can be effectively used linked to your process simulation, process analysis, and process improvement efforts.

Process Simulation Software Products

Generally, process simulation software tools are used to address the dynamic properties such as "What-If" and "To-Be" process mapping analysis steps that often provide the greatest benefit to your process improvement initiatives. Process mapping simulation software tools provide an effective means to examine potential process improvements before substantial funds are invested in a new product or process improvement effort; they also provide an early warning if disconnects or implementation conflicts can be identified without actually making the planned change in your process.

The use of simulation software products to analyze your processes is important for four specific reasons:

- Process simulation provides a means of measuring overall changes in the value (output) of your system, product, service, or functional process that can be attributed to actual or planned changes in your processes.

- Process simulation software graphic capabilities are a very valuable tool in helping decision makers understand complex operations through a relatively simple graphic representation. You can actually see the workflow process in the midst of operation or as it might be when the process is changed.

- Process mapping simulation software can be used to identify utilization rates of (money, time, people) activities, revealing bottlenecks or underutilized process activities. Bottlenecks or "white space" tells you where to apply resources or to suggest a redesign of your processes. Underutilized activities tell you where waste exists and help identify resources for reallocation and activities that can be discontinued for a cost savings without degrading overall productivity.

- Simulation also supports functional process economic analysis in that it increases the possible dimensions of your cost/benefit analysis.

In the context of other process mapping methodologies, there are two general areas to which process simulation software may contribute uniquely. These are in (1) dynamically measuring process utilization and (2) system workload.

Process Utilization. In a steady-state environment, process activity utilization can be measured using static techniques. Activity-Based Costing is an accounting technique that involves measuring both the cost and value of process activities. It may be possible to identify the resources supporting each process activity and their sunk costs in dynamic processes but difficult to measure the proportion of these resources actually devoted to one activity. Process simulation software can provide these metrics. Simulation software is very effective in demonstrating bottlenecks and underutilization of process activities or equipment, enabling management to redistribute resources or restructure processes to enhance overall efficiency.

System Workload. Another capability simulation software provides is in linking local changes to global performance improvements. One aspect of process mapping is the development of a "To-Be" map. The options for projecting a "To-Be" map can be almost unlimited. Many different collections of relationships can be redefined between process activities, and the application of resources used by process activities can be varied in many different ways. When two or more "To-Be" map configurations are under consideration, how do you choose the best alternative? Simulation software provides a means of measuring anticipated global performance improvements when changes are made locally.

Process mapping simulation tools are of two general types that include (1) discrete event and (2) continuous event. The benefits of each are described below:

1. Discrete event simulations show processes as a sequence of events in which each event has a beginning and an ending

point usually measured by time. Consequently, discrete event simulations are often called time-step simulations. Associated with these discrete points in time are state variables that measure the state of the process being simulated. Therefore, as a simulation proceeds through a series of events, the process under simulation will be viewed as a series of state changes. Analysis can focus either globally or locally as defined in your process mapping approach for your specific simulation.

2. Continuous event simulations show processes with mathematical expressions that do not delineate discrete events. The process analyst can designate a sequence of points in time to provide a sequence of snapshots of the simulated process.

There are advantages and disadvantages to either type of simulation. Discrete event simulations generally provide a better format for analysis in that it may be easier to structure a process simulation through the building block approach provided by them. Discrete events facilitate postsimulation analysis, keyed to the initiation and completion of events. The downside of discrete event simulation includes the increased labor required to construct a simulation at a discrete event level and the demands on computational capability required. Some discrete event simulations may not be feasible because of the number of events that would be evaluated.

Continuous event simulations are easier to use after a choice has been made of the mathematical expressions used to construct them. They generally require less time and labor in setup and in postsimulation analysis. They can also demand less computer power. For these reasons, they support more computer runs, allowing wider alternative options to determine the breadth and depth of your analysis. Their weak point is in how well the mathematical expressions fit the processes being simulated. Although some expressions provide excellent representations of simulated processes, others may include unacceptable errors or unknown side effects.

Several current simulation techniques are worthy of comment. Several software techniques selected for comment here include petri nets, *ITHINK*-type system dynamics, *SIMSCRIPT* military-type simulation software, custom software packages, and less complex inexpensive simulation products.

- Petri nets are particularly useful in discrete simulation. IDEF process maps can be used with petri net structures and are easy to construct and analyze. They can be used to replicate phenomena difficult to map using other simulation techniques. An excellent petri net process simulation tool is called *Design/CPN*, which was developed and is widely marketed by Meta Software.

- ITHINK is a Macintosh-based system-dynamics continuous-type tool for the evaluation of resource allocation. ITHINK is a commercially developed software program that does not require a lot of expertise to apply. A weakness is that it would be difficult to integrate with IDEF-type process activity maps.

- SIMSCRIPT is a programming language that facilitates the development of simulation software featuring robust user interface capabilities. *SIMPROCESS* is a CACI Products Company product written in SIMSCRIPT that is designed to represent sequential activities graphically, as if viewed from above a factory floor.

- Custom simulation software is not generally recommended for business process reengineering use because of the high cost required to develop the software, to provide user friendliness, and to provide training support required for a valid product. Custom or special-purpose simulation software may be a viable solution for replicating process dynamics if cost is not a factor. Data modeling performed in conjunction with process mapping can define data structures, which supports the use of standard relational database management structures.

- There are inexpensive simulation software products that are oriented toward using *Microsoft Windows* flow-chart graphic techniques. One of these products is called *OPTIMA*, and it is developed by AdvanEdge Technologies Inc. in Tualatin, Oregon. OPTIMA is a business process mapping package that provides "What-If" simulations, and provides a report writer. This type of software product is particularly good for applications that are characterized by relatively small processes being evaluated and where a large number of individual concurrent process mapping and simulation efforts are underway.

The trend in simulation software is to use IBM-compatible personal computers, off-the-shelf rather than custom software products, less expensive software products, and products that are very easy to learn and apply to the majority of your process mapping needs.

Activity-Based-Costing Software Products

ABC segregates and manages product and process costs differently and better than the traditional cost accounting approach. ABC is a proven methodology that measures the cost and performance of activities, resources, and cost objects. Resources are assigned to activities; then activities are assigned to cost objects based on their use. ABC recognizes the causal relationship of cost drivers to process activities. ABC can be described as a relatively simple concept that says you should break up your overhead into small batches of cost drivers that are the specific factors that determine the final cost of a process operation. Although the business community has been looking at ABC for more than a decade, recent paradigm shifts brought on by business process reengineering, concurrence by the accounting profession on the methodology for ABC, and the development of application-oriented software products have all accelerated the use of ABC.

In General Electric's early analysis they recognized that over half of their manufacturing expense was indirect cost. The General Electric team focused on "capturing the upstream drivers and reflect[ing] the actual work that is going on down on the factory floor in terms of the drivers that cause them."

Business process reengineering has refocused our attention on the management of process activities as the route to improving the value received by our customers and the profit we achieve by providing better value. Business process reengineering is not just about understanding our process; it also includes cost driver analysis, process activity analysis and simplification, and performance measurement linked to specific products or services.

A very good example of ABC software for business process reengineering is *Easy ABC Plus* by ABC Technologies Inc. It is a state-of-the-practice tool and is one of our "Best Buy" software products.

DESCRIPTION OF PROCESS MAPPING TOOLS

The leading process mapping tools (including vendor address and brief product descriptions) are divided into five categories: (1) Simple Flow-Chart Graphic Software, (2) Process Mapping Products, (3) IDEF Process Mapping Products, (4) Process Simulation Products, and (5) Process-Mapping-Related ABC Products:

Simple Flow-Chart Graphic Software

Micrografx Corporation
1303 Arapaho Street
Richardson, Texas 75081
(214) 234-1769
(800) 733-3729

Micrografx, a pioneer in the development of flow diagram software products, has revised their earlier SnapGrafx product. Their new product, now called *ABC SnapGraphics 2.0,* provides a good basic software product that is intuitive, easy to use, and inexpensive (costs approximately $50.00). It is a process mapping flow chart tool. ABC Snapgraphics 2.0 provides a flow-chart template gallery so you can map out a process or procedure so simply that anyone can understand how it works. ABC SnapGraphics 2.0's handling of flow-chart connecting lines is very good, and it is easy to change connect points. Choosing art from the shape template palettes is a simple matter of dragging and dropping the process block to the diagram page.

The ABC Snapgraphics capability is also available bundled as part of *ABC Flowcharter 4.0,* a more expensive (approximately $495) workflow software product by Micrografx. ABC Flowcharter 4.0 integrates ABC SnapGraphics 2.0 and *ABC DataAnalyzer* to create a dynamic flow-charting package. New features in this integrated package include full object linking and embedding 2.0 support, a user interface compatible with Microsoft Office from Microsoft Corporation, and automatic line-routing features.

The Micrografx products are very user friendly, run on Windows, and support OLE 2.0 to facilitate software integration.

Shapeware Corporation
Maryann Kluster
520 Pike Street, Suite 1800
Seattle, Washington 98101-4001
(206) 521-4500
FAX (206) 521-4501/4561

You may not be an artist, but you probably communicate through process-map-type drawings every day. Many people draw ideas,

sketches, processes, and directions instead of writing them down—
pictures are often faster to create and easier to understand than
words for the same information.

The *VISIO 3.0* process map-drawing tool allows you to communicate ideas quickly through the powerful medium of an inexpensive
and very-easy-to-use computer-aided drawing tool. VISIO 3.0 is
the current version of Shapeware's best-selling Windows drag-and-
drop software program. It is designed for business and technical
individuals or team members who need to create high-quality
computer-aided process maps quickly and easily.

Some of the user-friendly features of VISIO 3.0 are drag-and-
drop drawing, smart process block connectors, predrawn process
stencils and templates, click-and-type text, click-and-drag editing,
and OLE 2.0 support. VISIO 3.0 includes a new "Universal Connec-
tor Tool" that automatically connects process shapes together, making it easier and faster for users to create process maps. VISIO's
implementation of OLE enables users to edit process maps "In
Place" without leaving the application they are working in.

In an independent assessment Motorola evaluated VISIO 3.0
and awarded it their "Gold Excellence Award for Most Productive
Graphic Object Drawing Tools."

In the "Best Buy" portion of this chapter we recommend VISIO
3.0 as the number 1 product in this category.

Scitor Corporation

Julie Clarke
333 Middlefield Road
Menlo Park, California 94025
(800) 549-9876
(415) 462-4200
FAX (415) 462-4201

Scitor Corporation recently introduced *Process Charter 1.0* for Windows. It has been designed to provide the essential tools you may
need to create process map flow charts. It lets you go further with
its internal process analysis and simulation capabilities, which are
integrated into one product. Process Charter may be used to perform
ABC, resource analysis, value-added analysis, and total throughput
analysis to facilitate process improvement. Process Charter includes
customizable flow-chart shapes and arrowheads, style palette management, activity calendars, key variable values, process analysis,

color animation tracing, "What-If" scenario analysis, and master page templates. Process Charter also provides the ability to customize the specific attributes of a flow-chart graphic element. Process Charter can also easily accommodate parallel tasks with several branches since in reality process flows do not always occur in series sequence.

With Process Charter, process analysis is a four-step process. First, the process map structure is defined using the versatile flow-charting tools. Second, the necessary resources for the process are identified in the resource spreadsheet. After the resources have been defined, the third step is to assign the resources to the different steps of the process. Finally, the process simulation is executed and the results are presented in the form of graphics and statistics. All four steps are accomplished within Process Charter.

Scitor has taken its experience in project management software *(Project Scheduler 6 for Windows)* and built Process Charter based on their very strong customer experience base.

Process Charter version 1.0 was released at the time this book was being created. However, early user reviews indicate that it could be one of the "breakthrough" software products of the 1990s because it recognizes the potential of easy-to-use Windows programs that provide an affordable integration of process map flow charting, process analysis, resource analysis, simulation, and "What-If" analysis. Time will tell how Process Charter is accepted by the user community. But we suggest that you keep an eye on this product and include it in the list of tools you may be evaluating.

Process Mapping Products

The Jonathan Corporation—Systems Group
Jose A. Villalobos
5898 Thurston Ave.
Virginia Beach, Virginia 23455
(804) 363-0880
FAX (804) 363-8841
E-mail: josev@neptune,wyvern.tom

The Jonathan Corporation—Systems Group developed and markets *Plexus,* a client/server system designed to support business reengineering and system integration projects. Plexus can be used to illustrate process maps of business processes, to analyze their cost and performance, and to integrate enabling software products, proprietary and third party, into a seamless operating environment.

Logic Works, Inc.
Jeffrey Mershon
1060 Route 206
Princeton, NJ 98540
(609) 243-0088
(800) 783-7946
FAX (609) 243-9192

BPwin is a powerful Windows-based business process mapping tool that helps define and optimize your business process. Featuring an intuitive point-and-click interface that helps create process maps quickly, BPwin uses a graphical toolkit of boxed (activities) and arrows (data flows) to quickly build a process map that clearly shows results of activities, the resources needed to perform them, and their relationships. BPwin's modeling intelligence maintains diagram referential integrity—preventing incorrect arrow connections and ensuring arrow consistency throughout the model. BPwin can generate activity reports directly into Microsoft Excel for simulations and *BPwin/ABC*—a special version of BPwin— includes a link to ABC Technologies' *Easy ABC Plus*, offering a complete ABC management solution from activity definition through detailed accounting. Through point-and-click menus, BPwin can import process data map information from *ERwin*, Logic Works' Entity-Relationship (ER) database design tool to improve model quality and consistency while reducing development time.

Scitor Corporation
Julie Clarke
333 Middlefield Road
Menlo Park, California 94025
(800) 549-9876
(415) 462-4200
(415) 462-4201 (FAX)

Scitor Corporation recently introduced *Process Charter 1.0* for Windows. It has been designed to provide the essential tools you may need to create process map flow charts. It lets you go further with its internal process analysis and simulation capabilities, which are integrated into one product. Process Charter may be used to perform ABC, resource analysis, value-added analysis, and total throughput analysis to facilitate process improvement. Process Charter includes customizable flow-chart shapes and arrowheads, style palette management, activity calendars, key variable values, process analysis, color animation tracing, "What-If" scenario analysis, and master page templates. Process Charter also provides the ability to customize the specific attributes of a flow-chart graphic element. Process Charter can also easily accommodate parallel tasks with several branches, since in reality process flows do not always occur in series sequence.

With Process Charter, process analysis is a four-step process. First, the process map structure is defined using the versatile flow-charting tools. Second, the necessary resources for the process are identified in the resource spreadsheet. After the resources have been defined, the third step is to assign the resources to the different steps of the process. Finally, the process simulation is executed and the results are presented in the form of graphics and statistics. All four steps are accomplished within Process Charter.

Scitor has taken its experience in project management software *(Project Scheduler 6 for Windows)* and built Process Charter based on their very strong customer experience base.

Process Charter version 1.0 was released at the time this book was being created. However, early user reviews indicates that it could be one of the "breakthrough" software products of the 1990s because it recognizes the potential of easy-to-use Windows programs that provide an affordable integration of process map flow charting, process analysis, resource analysis, simulation, and "What-If" analysis. Time will tell how Process Charter is accepted by the user community. But we suggest that you keep an eye on this product, and include it in the list of "Best Buy" tools you may be evaluating.

IDEF Process Mapping Products

Coe-Truman Technologies, Inc.
Joann Van Nuys

1321 Duke Street
Suite 301
Alexandria, VA 22314-3563
(703) 836-2671
FAX 703/836-2563

Coe-Truman Technologies, Inc. (CTT) provides the Cosmo software suite, which is designed for easy use and claims to be an integrated Windows-based toolset compliant with the IDEF Standards:

- *COSMO-0:* An integrated IDEF0 process modeling tool
- *COSMO-PRO:* An IDEF-based prototyping tool

D. Appleton Company, Inc.
Neil Snodgrass
222 Las Colinas Blvd.
Suite 1141
Irving, TX 75039
(214) 869-1066

D. Appleton Company's approach focuses on business rule development and integrates ABC and Functional Economic Analysis (FEA) for federal government business case development. Their *BUSINESS ENGINEERING TOOLKIT* integrates multiple vendors' tools and provides a process mapping management environment. D. Appleton Company is one of the pioneers in the development of IDEF.

KBSI (Knowledge Based Systems, Inc.)
Contact: Elena M. Cigainero or Umesh Hari
One KBSI Place
1408 University Drive East
College Station, TX 77840-2335
(409) 260-5274
FAX (409) 260-1965

Knowledge Based Systems Inc. (KBSI) is a provider of "intelligent" IDEF tools. KBSI offers an integrated set of IDEF tools including *AIO Win* for Windows, which provides IDEF0 Function Modeling support; *ProCap,* a process mapping tool; and *ProSim,* a pushbutton AT&T WITNESS simulation model generation created from IDEF process maps.

ProCap is a process mapping tool that offers OSTN (Object State Transition Network) support. ProCap has three window formats in which process maps may be developed, edited, and analyzed. The Matrix Window is a spreadsheetlike interface that allows the user to quickly define the interaction between processes and their associated objects. The Indented Nodelist is an expandable outline format that displays the hierarchical arrangement of the processes. The Diagram Window is a graphical representation of processes, their sequence, and their associated decision points.

Each KBSI tool comes equipped with *SmartDraw* for point-and-click ease of use; one-time, one-place data entry; background quality checking and advisory support; hands-off model drawing and layout; and model revision support.

Meta Software Corporation
Andrew Levin
125 Cambridge Park Drive
Cambridge, MA 02140
(617) 576-6920
FAX (617) 661-2008
E-mail avl@metasoft.com
or
Kevin Coombe
12020 Sunrise Valley Drive, Suite 100
Reston, VA 22091
(703) 476-2235
FAX (703) 476-2234

Meta Software's *Design/IDEF* fully supports both IDEF0 Functional/Process mapping and IDEF1X Data/Information Modeling. In addition, the "Meta WorkFlow Analyzer" enables the automatic simulation of IDEF0 workflow models ("Dynamic Analysis") and does not require programming skills. Design/IDEF and the "WorkFlow Analyzer" simulation product make it easy to identify the bottlenecks and idle resources that hinder system performance. Design/IDEF also supports integrated ABC for the dynamic analysis of system costs.

Design/IDEF also supports IDL, AML, and SML for export and import of IDEF0 and IDEF1X data and provides a direct link to KnowledgeWare's ADW CASE toolset and the Easy ABC Plus Activity-Based-Cost Management tool from ABC Technologies.

Design/IDEF is available for MS-Windows, Macintosh OS, Sun SPARC, and HP9000. Models are transferrable across hardware platforms. Design/IDEF is available throughout Europe and Asia from, among others, MicroMatch (U.K.), C.I.T. GmbH (Germany), Sumitomo Metals (Japan).

Meta Software's Design/IDEF process mapping tool is considered a "Best Buy" product.

Texas Instruments
Mike Amundsen
6620 Chase Oaks Blvd.
MS 8507
Plano, TX 75086
(214) 575-4942
FAX (214) 575-4144

Texas Instruments (TI) provides business reengineering solutions, which include a methodology called Business Process Engineering (BPE) and a tool called *Business Design Facility* (BDF) to support business reengineering projects. The Business Design Facility can be used to map your business processes as well as other business objects in multiple formats including IDEF0.

Triune Software, Inc.
Keith Comstock
2900 Presidential Drive
Suite 240
Fairborn, OH 45324
(513) 427-9900
FAX (513) 427-9964

Triune's *"ABLE PM"* version 2.0 is the first Automated Business Logic Engineering (ABLE) product line and is based on the IDEF0 methodology. ABLE PM is available for both the Windows and Macintosh operating environments. ABLE PM's intelligent ability to "ripple" changes throughout the process mapping model at the user's discretion is simplied by its intuitive graphical user interface.

Through its ease of use, ABLE PM guides the user to process decomposition all the while maintaining parent/child integrity and IDEF0 compliancy.

ABLE PM for Windows offers activity-based costing data collection and provides a seamless, round-trip interchange of data between ABLE PM and Easy ABC Plus, one of the industry's leading ABC products. They have added an icon-based tool bar for quick access to highly used functions, increasing ABLE PM's "userability." And ABLE PM for Macintosh provides a full upgrade path from its predecessor, AutoSADT. ABLE PM is available in an author/reader version, facilitating an electronic author/reader review cycle.

Triune is presently developing round-trip interfaces with other software tools such as CASE/IDEF1X tools, project management tools, workflow managers, simulation tools, and financial analysis tools.

ABLE PM 2.0E, The Executive Version, provides the power of ABLE PM at a more affordable price. Most features and limited process map development are supported.

UES, Inc.
Vijay Shende
Knowledge Integration Center
5162 Blazer Parkway
Dublin, OH 43017
(614) 793-2559
FAX (614) 792-0998

The UES Knowledge Integration Center (UES-KIC) is the developer of *KI Shell*, a workflow process management system, UES-KIC provides the Kl Shell tools for creating and deploying IDEF-consistent process and information process maps.

The early development of KI Shell was under USAF Wright Laboratory programs (successors to ICAM and IISS), and thus KI Shell maintains a clear relationship to the IDEF process mapping methodology.

KI Shell products and services go beyond modeling to generate deployed information systems consistent with the IDEF models.

Wizdom Systems, Inc.
Rita Feeney
1300 Iroquois Avenue

Naperville, IL 60563
(708) 357-3000
FAX (708) 357-3059

The Wizdom Systems, Inc.'s *IDEFine* tools and methodologies automate the IDEF modeling process and provide proper syntax and consistency. It is possible to transform IDEF activity process maps developed from Wizdom Systems Inc.'s IDEFine software tool into CACI Products Company's *SIMPROCESS* simulation product.

The IDEFine products are IBM-AT compatible and are available in both DOS and Windows versions.

- IDEFine-0 creates and maintains IDEF0 models within and across projects within integrated diagrams and text.

- IDEF glossary provides definitions of all terms in the process map model.

- IDEFast is a time-line approach to identify bottlenecks.

- IDEFsim exports files into simulation applications to perform dynamic "What-If" analysis.

- IDEFbpi allows the user to capture process improvement information and impacts, prioritize projects, and identify activities to be changes.

- MINERVA is a business process reengineering toolkit supported by computer-aided process reengineering.

Wizdom Systems Inc. also integrates Micrografx ABC Flowcharter in their process mapping applications and distributes process diagrams using the ABC Viewer component of ABC Flowcharter.

Process Simulation Products
AdvanEdge Technologies, Inc.
Kenneth A. Carraher
10170 S.W. Hedges Court
Tualatin, Oregon 97062
(503) 692-8162
FAX (503) 691-2451

OPTIMA is AdvanEdge Technologies' relatively inexpensive simulation software product that is oriented toward using Microsoft Windows flow-chart graphic process mapping and simple simulation techniques. OPTIMA is a business process mapping package that provides "What-If" simulations and is also a report writer. OPTIMA is not tied to IDEF process mapping standards. However, the price for this simulation product is approximately a thousand dollars and is a bargain. It provides a simple-to-use process mapping and simulation product to start your process mapping and simulation analysis. This type of software product is particularly good for applications that are characterized by relatively small-scale processes being evaluated, and where a large number of individual concurrent process mapping and simulation efforts are underway. Because it is not expensive, nor hard to learn and apply, you can buy and distribute this product around different divisions of your company or request that your suppliers acquire and use the product to improve your total process value stream and interteam communication process.

Application Development Consultants, Inc.
3802 Gunn Highway
Suite B
Tampa, FL 33624-4720
(800) 910-4ADC
(813) 265-3708
FAX (813) 265-3028

ADC Inc. has developed the *ADC ProcessSimulator,* which visually simulates the passage of work through a business process on-screen and produces reports and graphs to aid process improvement. On-screen simulation gives the ability to "run the model," providing powerful visual communication of the performance of one business process design compared to another. It enables better evaluation of solutions through "What if" analysis of alternatives, from simple fine tuning of process operations or staffing options to radical changes, on a quantitative basis. ProcessSimulator fully supports ADC's event-driven Process Dynamics Modeling extensions, which have evolved through the process redesign work of their customer base, in addition to the formal IDEF0 notation. ProcessSimulator runs on MS-Windows and is designed with an open-architecture shared repository to integrate with most popular ICASE and repository environments, including Rochade, Excel, CASEwise Modeler, KnowledgeWare ADW, Bachman Analysts, Excelerator, ORACLE*-CASE, and so on. Integration is through CASE Data Interchange Format (CDIF) and custom import/export bridges, ILE, and Windows and Windows cut-and-paste.

AT&T ISTEL
Visual Interactive Systems Inc.
Margaret Coyte
25800 Science Park Drive
Beachwood, OH 44122
(216) 292-2668
FAX (216) 292-2861

The AT&T ISTEL *WITNESS Simulation Software* product was designed to provide a simulation tool that can help you support business process reengineering sorts of business decisions, formulate new process solution options, and reduce the risk of change. WITNESS Simulation Software provides the user with a broad range of information with which to make decisions, predict outcomes, improve processes, analyze problems, and formulate solutions. It can handle the simulation of complex large process systems.

The AT&T ISTEL WITNESS Simulation Software may be used to create graphical process maps of manufacturing plants or other complex business environments using simple pull-down menus. The WITNESS Simulation Software can represent real-world operations by creating an animated color view of the flow of objects through a facility or process. The WITNESS Simulation Software approach utilizes a template of objects from which you can build a process model and simple forms to describe those objects.

The WITNESS Simulation Software product can be used to test capacity planning options and generate performance statistics, return on investment scenarios, or "What-If" analytical scenarios.

It operates on a variety of systems, including IBM-compatible PCs, Hewlett-Packard, SUN, and IBM Unix workstations, and DEC VAX/VMS workstations.

Refer to the comparative assessment section for more information on the AT&T ISTEL WITNESS Simulation Software product.

CACI Products Company
Hal Duncan

Winston Haight or
Scott Swegles
333 N. Torrey Pines Court
La Jolla, CA 92037
(619) 457-9681

CACI's *SIMPROCESS* and *SIMPROCESS II* provide a sophisticated simulated view of complex business processes. It can be used to dynamically assess functional process maps for low output, to help in identifying bottlenecks and inefficient use of resources, to break out "product" resource and activity costs, and to help substantiate your business case for resource allocation and process improvement. SIMPROCESS is a CACI Products Company product written in SIMSCRIPT that is designed to represent sequential activities graphically, as if viewed from above a factory floor.

SIMPROCESS can be used to predict the performance of a proposed workflow and provides measurements for convenient analysis of alternatives. SIMPROCESS can be used to display your current situation and predict the impact of changes before you commit to a new course of action. The SIMPROCESS tool can be used to evaluate fluctuating workloads, processing rules, equipment capacities, varying work times, resource assignments, and scheduled and unscheduled breaks.

SIMPROCESS accepts your workflow description through a mouse-driven graphical interface and can give you statistics regarding the number of items processed, total processing time, waiting time and other process delays, resource usage, number of items departing without service, percent value-added activities, and processing costs.

SIMPROCESS extends the IDEF methodology by capturing attributes in a process map of your organization's "As-Is" situation, providing formulation of "What If" alternatives and allowing the user to address technology insertion issues. SIMPROCESS provides a "fly before you buy" evaluation of a selected reengineered process and organization.

Some of the unique features of SIMPROCESS are flexibility, interactive graphical interface, animated results, and curve fitting.

It is possible to transform IDEF activity process maps developed from the Wizdom Systems, Inc., software tool IDEFine into SIMPROCESS.

SIMPROCESS does not accommodate process activity hierarchy and seems to be weak in its facilitation of some simulation dynamics. It still requires extensive training to apply this software product. SIMPROCESS obtained some of its initial success as a more expensive tool applied to complex simulation needs and defense-oriented factory-floor-type manufacturing applications.

Refer to comparative assessment near the end of this chapter for more information on SIMPROCESS.

Imagine That, Inc.
Kathi Hunt
6830 Via Del oro, Suite 230
San Jose, CA 95119
(408) 365-0305
FAX (408) 629-1251

Imagine That Inc. markets *Extend + BPR* (a Macintosh-based product) for business process reengineering applications. It is based on their *Extend* software tool, which provides an integrated product for discrete event and continuous simulation applications. In Extend + BPR they have added an additional library of blocks to support total quality management and process improvement efforts.

KBSI (Knowledge Based Systems, Inc.)
David Rice or Elena M. Cigainero
One KBSI Place
1408 University Drive East
College Station, TX 77840-2335
(409) 260-5274
FAX (409) 260-1965

KBSI (Knowledge Based Systems, Inc.) offers *ProSim*, a process mapping tool that automatically generates simulation models and offers OSTN (Object State Transition Network) support. ProSim has three window formats in which models may be developed, edited, and analyzed. The Matrix Window is a spreadsheetlike interface that allows the user to quickly define the interaction between processes and their associated objects. The Indented Nodelist is an expandable outline format that displays the hierarchical arrangement of higher-level and lower-level processes. The Diagram Window is a graphical representation of processes, their sequence, and their associated decision points.

ProSim automatically generates simulation models, including user-selected reports and graphs. Information on simulation goals, process time, what objects are being processed, resource utilization, costing, labor requirements, and setup time can be captured in the simulation model. Errors are reported by the system, which allows time to edit processes, reallocate resources, and update decision logic before the simulation is run.

Each KBSI tool comes equipped with *SmartDraw* for point-and-click ease of use; one-time, one-place data entry; background quality checking and advisory support; hands-off model drawing and layout; and fast model revision support.

Meta Software Corporation
Andrew Levin
125 Cambridge Park Drive
Cambridge, MA 02140
(617) 576-6920
FAX (617) 661-2008
E-mail avl@metasoft.com
or
Kevin Coombe
12020 Sunrise Valley Drive
Suite 100
Reston, VA 22091
(703) 476-2235
FAX (703) 476-2234

Meta Software Corporation was founded in 1985 to develop graphical software tools that enable organizations to map, simulate, and analyze complex business systems. Meta Software offers a suite of IDEF and process simulation products. Their *WorkFlow Analyzer* provides a proven integrated approach to solving business process improvement and reengineering problems. Meta Software had a vision of providing business tools that would allow people to quickly and easily create powerful behavioral process maps of business systems. They found that traditional IDEF-type static maps (in more than 50 percent of their clients' applications) were not enough to support or justify complex system process changes. They believe that static models, while useful as a starting point for process analysis, do not provide a complete understanding of a system's behavior. They believe that the process maps must become more dynamic so business leaders/managers can be provided with new business insights into the processes you are building or trying to improve.

Meta Software has also recognized that simulation software products must be easier to use and be transitioned to desktop computer platforms. It was Meta Software's belief that desktop computing technology could provide the power and the platform needed to use simulation and process mapping tools as a regular part of the business decision-making process, not just as a tool for a few computer whiz kids. This recognition of the need for user-friendly, personal-computer-oriented simulation products is in tune with current market demand.

Today their tools not only describe the physical elements of a system, they report on the dynamic relationships between elements, like time duration, costing, and resource allocation.

Meta Software's tools allow users to build and study "As-Is" process maps of their operational workflows and then simulate the effects of proposed "To-Be" changes so that critical business process reengineering decisions are made with confidence, based on actual hard evidence, not guesswork.

The process maps created with Meta Software's tools empower organizations to test common assumptions. Frequently, what is perceived as a problem in a system is not the real issue at all. But without a tool to test the workflow, it is impossible to validate your assumptions or identify the real bottlenecks. Meta Software's WorkFlow Analyzer delivers this capability, and it does so by providing measurable results. The ability to generate solid evidence of the value of proposed changes or the inherent problem(s) enables organizations to approach business process reengineering with greater confidence, which inevitably improves process improvement implementation and ultimately increases your chance for success. As Dr. Hammer has noted, more than 70 percent of reengineering projects fail. Use of tools that provide a sound basis for change can protect your organization and your job!

Meta Software process mapping and simulation tools are among the most used products of their type. They are used throughout the global marketplace in businesses such as banking, insurance, manufacturing, and government.

Some of their simulation applications have been included in the success stories noted in Chapter 5.

Meta Software's WorkFlow Analyzer enables the automatic simulation of IDEF0 workflow models ("Dynamic Analysis") and requires no programming skills. The Meta Software WorkFlow Analyzer is designed to help reengineer your business processes. The WorkFlow Analyzer software product permits business analysts to develop graphical process maps of "As-Is" workflows and then identify bottlenecks, and it can help you assess your resource usage and related process costs to improve your performance.

Meta Software also developed *Design/CPN*, which is a very sophisticated, graphically based simulation software product. Design/CPN has been designed for integration with process activity maps using an automatic programming feature and is very flexible in the range of simulations to which it can be applied. Meta Software's Design/CPN can be an effective tool not only to map your processes; it can also be used as a graphical report-writing product that can help better document your processes.

The integration feature of Design/CPN is so strong that it could accurately be described as a CASE tool that semiautomatically converts information requirements into computer code. It uses colored petri-net techniques for performance evaluation and validation testing of very large and complex processes. It is very useful for applications that involve concurrent improvement issues. Design/CPN provides a variety of analytical reports that can be used to assess and optimize your business processes.

Meta Software is uniquely recommended for process mapping and simulation efforts where a larger number (more than 250) of process nodes need to be examined. Some comparable products cannot process the number or range of process nodes that Meta Software can.

Meta Software tools are "Best Buy"-type products.

Micro Analysis & Simulation Software, Inc.
Catherine Drury
4900 Pearl East Circle, Suite 201E
Boulder, Colorado 80301
(303) 442-6947
FAX (303) 442-8274

Micro Analysis & Simulation has developed *Micro Saint*, a discrete-event network simulation system. Once you have created your process map you can build a simulation of your process with Micro Saint. Its Action View capability provides a library of icons that can be animated to create a realistic image of your process as it is being simulated.

Micro Saint has been created so that "no programming" is required. It features menus and tools in a structure that lets you build simple or complex simulation models with the same basic techniques. Micro Saint is available for the popular operating systems, including DOS, Macintosh, Microsoft Windows 3.0, and UNIX. The optional Action View animation capability is available for the Windows and Macintosh operating systems.

Additional features of Micro Saint include diagram tools that let you build your process map model graphically, by "drawing" it. It also provides on-line user guidance, powerful windowing capability, and the ability to model a wide range of applications.

Performance Systems, Inc.
Natalie Lasky
45 Lyme Road, Suite 300
Hanover, New Hampshire 03755
(603) 643-9636
FAX (603) 643-9502

Performance Systems Inc.'s simulation product is called *ITHINK*. ITHINK is a powerful Macintosh-based system-dynamics continuous-type tool for the evaluation of resource allocation. ITHINK is a commercially developed software program that does not require a lot of expertise to apply. Weak properties are that it would be difficult to integrate with IDEF-type process activity maps. You can create your simulation by visually manipulating graphic objects. Some of the features include automatic sensitivity analysis and both discrete and continuous process analysis.

PROMODEL Corporation
Bruce Gladwin or Ken Tumay
1875 South State
Suite 3400
Orem, UT 84058
(801) 226-6036 or (801) 223-4612
FAX (801) 226-6046

PROMODEL Corporation provides *ServiceModel* and *PROMODEL* simulation process mapping software for business and manufacturing process reengineering. Their animated simulation process mapping tools are very easy to use and can help put your process improvement efforts into motion more quickly. Their simulations allow you to ask "What If" questions taking into account the dynamics, variability, and unique nature of your service or manufacturing processes. PROMODEL has designed its software products to create scenarios that can be modified by adjusting variables using a run-time interface.

Their products are point-and-click menu driven, easy to learn, easy to apply, and provide interactive process analysis coupled with colorful animation. A key feature of their products is their ability to provide automatic data editing and error checking.

ServiceModel is a powerful simulation tool for analyzing "service" business processes of all types and sizes. By defining resource characteristics and process requirements you can experiment with different operating strategies and staffing levels to achieve the best possible system performance for your service functions. Typical applications for ServiceModel include: process design, business process reengineering, workflow analysis, staffing and resource allocation, and logistics management.

One of the significant advantage of the PROMODEL products is that they have been designed so that you can apply these sophisticated products with only a brief orientation, and they do not require simulation software programming experience. PROMODEL design philosophy was used to create products that are created for the typical potential user, rather than a computer programmer.

With ServiceModel's convenient constructs and graphical user interface, process map simulation is quicker and easier than the early military-type complex simulation software products. All you need to do is define how your particular system operates and then run a simulation of your process. Automatic error and consistency checking is provided. During simulation, ServiceModel displays an animated representation of the system and gathers statistics on performance measures. Statistics are then automatically tabulated and graphed.

PROMODEL (PROduction MODELer) *version 2.0* is a very powerful, Windows-based simulation tool for structuring and analyzing manufacturing production systems. PROMODEL is also designed for easy use and it is menu driven. It can accurately simulate the range of characteristics that are both common and peculiar to manufacturing systems. PROMODEL provides engineers and managers the opportunity to test new ideas for system design or improvement before committing the time and resources necessary to build or alter the actual system. PROMODEL focuses on issues such as resource utilization, production capacity, productivity, and inventory levels. By modeling the important elements of a production system such as resource utilization, system capacity, and production schedules, you can experiment with different operating strategies and designs to achieve the best results.

As a discrete event simulator, PROMODEL is intended primarily for simulation and mapping discrete part manufacturing systems. Process industries can be simulated by converting bulk material into discrete units such as gallons or barrels. PROMODEL is designed to map systems where events occur at definite points in time, and the time resolution is controllable.

Typical applications for PROMODEL include assembly lines, job shops, transfer lines, JIT, and KANBAN systems, and flexible manufacturing systems.

To use PROMODEL, you define how your particuliar system operates, mostly through process maps showing part-flow and operation logic.

For existing customers, The 32-bit upgrade provided in PROMODEL Version 2.0 adds a facility for tracking manufacturing speeds, a graphics editor for representing factory layouts, a resource tracker, and a debugger.

Thomas Jones, manager of performance improvement for Ernst and Young, said that by using PROMODEL, "We now can simulate what we think will happen before we build a capital-intensive project."

Bruce Kaiser, of GE Nuclear Energy in Bloomington, North Carolina, noted that they, "tried a flowcharter program, but we wanted to go deeper"; so they evaluated PROMODEL by creating an extensive map of their process and checked to see how closely PROMODEL represented their current process. They checked to see how correctly the product reflected their known bottlenecks. Then "they did What-If analysis and demonstrated different scenarios." Kaiser noted that PROMODEL's "active display and visual look is an improvement over other similar products that just emphasize huge data outputs on a number of printer pages."

ServiceModel and PROMODEL are true Windows products that take full advantage of Microsoft's Graphical User Interface (GUI) operating environment.

These products offer all the advantages associated with other applications designed to run on the Windows platform. These features include a standard user interface, cooperative multitasking, built-in printer drivers, and point-and-click operation. Windows provides a seamless interface with other product applications that may provide input data. For example, schedule data may be created in a spreadsheet and read directly into ServiceModel or PROMODEL. Other data can be read from or written to general text files.

Refer to comparative assessment review near the end of this chapter for more information.

PROMODEL simulation products are "Best Buy"-type products.

Software Consultants International, Ltd.
Contact: Lawrence Peters
13812 SE 240th Street
Kent, Washington 98042-3321
(206) 631-4212
FAX (206) 631-2328

Software Consultants International (SCI) Limited has produced a business process reengineering product called *TemPRO version 2.5*. The key to successful improvement of your business processes is to really understand your processes. This can be accomplished by (1) mapping your processes, (2) simulating your processes, (3) process analysis, and (4) changing your existing or planned process solution using products such as TemPRO. The TemPRO technology has been designed to address the problems of business process reengineering implementation by using graphical process mapping and simulation techniques.

With the technology embodied in the TemPRO tool, business process reengineering process mapping teams and analysts can easily use this approach, without having to write simulation equations or pseudocode. One powerful and unique aspect of TemPRO is that its graphical interface and accompanying dialogues result in the actual execution of the process map rather than its simple documentation. The graphical user interface of the Microsoft Windows environment was chosen as the target environment because it is widely used and very simple to apply. TemPRO provides both static and dynamic process mapping capabilities.

TemPRO version 2.5 incorporates a feature called "Personality." Personality enables users to model business processes that have different behaviors. Each behavior is dependent upon how the process is initiated. This feature addresses situations where a process activity initiates in several different ways with each enabling condition having its own set of outputs and processing times. For example, an activity like "Review Loan" may be enabled by a mailed-in loan application, a Client-delivered application, or a request from the VP for Corporate Affairs. Although the basic Loan Approval process may be the same in each of these three examples, the priority, the duration, and the results may be different. The "Personality" feature in TemPRO enables users to relate these different outcomes with each of the corresponding inputs or enabling conditions and their processing times.

The design of TemPRO insulates the user from the complexities usually required to perform process simulation. This has been accomplished through the use of graphical interfaces, on-line help, and a great deal of "bulletproofing" to prevent misuse and incorrect results.

Through the use of TemPRO users are able to perform detailed analysis and simulations of current and future business processes within the relatively inexpensive Microsoft Windows environment release of 3.1 or above. Timing, interactions, priorities, concurrencies, and random events can all be mapped using TemPRO. TemPRO's combination of object-oriented and business process reengineering concepts provides a tool that lets users focus on their business problem without being distracted from the theoretical and complex world of the computer simulation software specialist. TemPRO greatly simplifies process simulation while reducing the time it takes to get results.

TemPRO provides a complete set of process mapping capabilities, including cyclic-time-based activities, probabilistic behavior, multiple priority levels, interrupts, variable flow times, "What-If" analysis, personalities, and real-time monitoring during process simulation. TemPRO is compatible with IDEF methods.

Systems Modeling Corporation
Adrian Wood or David M. Profozich
504 Beaver Street
Sewickley, PA 15143
(412) 741-5635

Systems Modeling Corporation has developed the *ARENA* simulation software product. One of the unique aspects of ARENA is the Application Solution Template, which consists of specific modules that can be used to tailor ARENA to your particular needs.

Activity-Based-Costing Products

ABC Technologies
Ernest Halperin or Chris Pieper
5075 S.W. Griffith Drive, Suite 200
Beaverton, OR 97005
(503) 626-4895
FAX (503) 626-4003

Easy ABC Plus is the premier activity-based-costing product available today. Easy ABC Plus provides an easy to use Activity-Based-Costing and report generation software tool. It facilitates process mapping analysis by allowing process analysts and managers to identify process activities, their true costs, and significantly improve metrics. With its graphical approach, the Easy ABC Plus software suite allows users to identify a set of process activities, establish linkages to general ledger data, assign performance metrics, and prepare appropriate reports. Some of the features of Easy ABC Plus include attribute costing, unit costing, performance measures, incremental cost allocator, multistage assignment, multiple periods, file security, and display of actual and budgeted costs. Easy ABC Plus uses standard graphical user interfaces and supports OS/2, Windows, or Apple Computer's System 6/7.

ABC Technologies Inc. and Meta Software Corporation have developed an interface from Meta Software's *Design/IDEF* version 3.0 process mapping product to Easy ABC Plus. This link allows Design/IDEF process analysts to export IDEF0 process and cost information directly to the Easy ABC Plus "Decomposition by Level" format for detailed ABC analysis. The process analyst can then apply the full range of Easy ABC Plus analytical capabilities to the business process reengineering effort. The ability to assess this level of detail information gives Design/IDEF users the ability to determine the true cost of a process and learn whether it is a candidate for reengineering redesign. For the user of Easy ABC

Plus it is an important interface because one can now build Design/IDEF process maps which provide a starting point for business process reengineering, workflow analysis, activity-based costing and management, and process simulation.

KBSI (Knowledge Based Systems, Inc.)
Elena M. Cigainero
1408 University Drive East
College Station, TX 77840-2335
(409) 260-5274
FAX (409) 260-1965

AIO WIN's Function Modeling tool also offers Activity-Based-Costing support. AIO WIN can be used to capture process time and resource costs for process activities, resources, and products. AIO WIN automatically calculates total activity costs and collates and reports the results for each activity in a "Cost Roll-up" dialog. The dialog's "Build Report" option generates formatted text output of the results, which can be exported to a ASCII-compatible spread-sheet. AIO WIN can share information with other tools such as ABC Technologies' Easy ABC Plus through the IDEF0 IDL inter-face.

Logic Works, Inc.
Jeffrey Mershon
1060 Route 206
Princeton, NJ 98540
(609) 243-0088
(800) 783-7946
FAX (609) 243-9192

BPwin is a powerful Windows-based business process modeling tool that helps define and optimize your business process. BPwin can generate activity reports directly into Microsoft Excel for simu-lations and *BPwin/ABC*—a special version of BPwin—includes a link to ABC Technologies' Easy ABC, offering a complete activity-based management solution from activity definition through de-tailed accounting.

Triune Software, Inc.
Keith Comstock

2900 Presidential Drive
Suite 240
Fairborn, OH 45324
(513) 427-9900
FAX (513) 427-9964

ABLE PM 2.0 for Windows offers activity-based costing data collection and provides a seamless, round-trip interchange of data between ABLE PM and Easy ABC Plus, one of the industry's leading ABC products. It includes an icon-based tool bar for quick access to highly used functions, increasing ABLE PM's "userability."

ABLE PM 2.0E, The Executive Version, provides the power of ABLE PM at an affordable price. Most features and limited model development are supported.

COMPARATIVE ASSESSMENT OF PROCESS MAPPING SIMULATION TOOLS

Business process reengineering is being used to eliminate, simplify, or improve current or planned work processes and reduce your resource requirements. According to Kevin Coombe of Meta Software, of those organizations that examine their processes via IDEF method, at least 50 percent of those organizations extend their analysis by applying process simulation techniques.

Many organizations have now mapped their "As-Is" process and need to answer the "What-If" questions, which can be better examined by business process reengineering simulation software products.

Major customer-driven changes are rapidly affecting simulation software product development and delivery for business process reengineering. The trend is away from very expensive, total system simulation products, which require special computer hardware and simulation software products. The status of the development of simulation products today is similar to the situation in the late 1980s and early 1990s when vendors were trying to sell complex "Cadillac"-type computer-aided-design and artificial intelligence software and hardware systems.

The simulation software product users are still not satisfied with complex military-type process mapping or computer simulation tools that may offer more complex features that are not required for business process reengineering assessment. They want easy to use, integrated, nonthreatening, lower-cost simulation systems matched to the scope of their problem analysis needs. They do not have time or money to send everyone that should simulate their processes away for weeks of training. Those simulation systems that will survive the growing business process reengineering market competition will be geared to the business process reengineering simulation user versus the computer programmer/analyst.

Pressure is being placed on vendors whose old products need weeks of off-site training to understand their product or whose products are grossly overpriced (software purchase price plus total training cost) to meet the needs of their new potential customers. The choice for these vendors is to sell a few very burdensome products or sell simulation tools to each of the business process reengineering simulation analysts in the service and manufacturing market.

At the time this book was being written we could find only one public domain independent assessment of simulation products designed to support business process reengineering. It is a report entitled *An Assessment of Simulation Systems Applicable to Business Process Reengineering at the Army Directorate of Public Works*, U.S. Army Corps of Engineers, USACERL Technical Report FF-94/31, September 1994, by Edgar "Skip" Neely, James H. Johnson, and Mark J. Orth. After examination of this independent assessment and discussion with various users we feel comfortable in sharing the results of their assessment with our readers. The system comparison provided in their report is described below. For full background regarding their methodology, please refer to the original source.

The evaluation criteria used in this study consisted of determining the simplicity and ease of use of several leading simulation products that could be used for business process reengineering.

Preliminary screening assessments were made of candidate simulation packages. The documentation provided a means of determining the release/revision history, the number/level of simulation features, any parallel processing limitations, ability to process graphics, automated statistical aids, and summary activities or total process reporting capabilities. Demonstration or test simulation models also provided indications of user friendliness and whether needless complexities were included.

A review of the demonstration packages and documentation resulted in three systems being selected for more detailed analysis. They included SIMPROCESS, WITNESS, and PROMODEL. Each of the evaluations for these products is summarized below:

SIMPROCESS Evaluation

The logic of SIMPROCESS is entity based. The complete path of individual units through a process must be specified.

One advantage of SIMPROCESS is the animation, which shows the number of work orders that has begun and completed a certain activity during a simulation run. This is helpful in verifying and demonstrating the simulation of the model.

In terms of disadvantages, the SIMPROCESS use of attributes and expressions is confusing and often leads to errors in the simulation process. For instance, setting the cost of a certain work order is difficult. In most simulation languages, a line of code such as "cost = 1" or "cost = high" would be sufficient. In SIMPROCESS, the equivalent line of code is "atr(cost(self)) = 1."

Editing in SIMPROCESS is cumbersome. Several windows must be opened before reaching the editing mode. It is quicker to edit manually from a file or to copy lines of code.

The complete path of an item through a process must be specified. This can be laborious. Considering the number of activities and the number of different work orders involved, the entity-based logic of SIMPROCESS is not efficient.

A review of the SIMPROCESS functional characteristics shows that there was no convenient way to use global variables (e.g., a record of the current calendar year). In most simulation packages, a variable can be created and assigned a value. In SIMPROCESS, a separate entity must be created and given an attribute; then values are assigned to that attribute.

Another difficulty is that a work order cannot be simply changed from "new" to "subject to availability of funds." SIMPROCESS requires you to remove one work order ("new") and then create another ("subject to availability of funds") in its place.

A valid model needs to include the ability to simulate shifts easily, but SIMPROCESS cannot. IN SIMPROCESS, a separate entity must be created, which interrupts the activities or workers, to simulate these breaks.

An important aspect of a simulation package is the ease and clarity with which it displays results for observation and analysis. Problems were encountered with the output reports of SIM-PROCESS. After a simulation run, no reports were able to be viewed. Instead, a message was given, such as, "No data to display."

Another problem was that the SIMPROCESS documentation was unclear and did little to lessen the difficulties encountered in learning the software system.

WITNESS Evaluation

The WITNESS Simulation Software product is an activity-based simulation tool. When a work order arrives at a certain activity or location, all work delays and variable assignments are performed. The work order is then sent to its next location.

An advantage of WITNESS is that when a work order changes, for example, from "new" to "carry over," it can be done by using a simple "CHANGE" statement. When editing, appropriate changes are made throughout WITNESS automatically.

One of the disadvantages of WITNESS is that editing is difficult because the placement of the cursor does not correspond to the text that is being edited. The screen font is very small and difficult to read. No means were found to increase the font size.

In reviewing the WITNESS functional characteristics, problems were encountered in limiting the run length. WITNESS would run until it was manually stopped. Use of global variables, attributes, and shifts is much easier in WITNESS than in SIMPROCESS. The animation in WITNESS is adequate and fairly easy to incorporate. Output reports in WITNESS are simple to view but are not very detailed.

The documentation in WITNESS is good.

PROMODEL Evaluation

PROMODEL is an activity-based simulation product. A simulation in PROMODEL is run as a network consisting of locations, and resources within the locations, which are connected via paths. A typical operation list in PROMODEL has the logic for routing, and assigning values to attributes is fairly straightforward. In the simula-

Table 8.1 "Best Buy" Process Mapping Software Tools

Simple flow-chart graphic software

Number 1.	Shapeware *VISIO 3.0 for Windows*
Number 2.	Scitor Corporation *Process Charter 1.0 for Windows*
Number 3.	Micrografx Inc. *ABC SnapGraphics 2.0* and *ABC Flowcharter 4.0*

Process mapping products

Number 1.	LogicWorks *BPwin*
Number 2.	Scitor Corporation *Process Charter 1.0 for Windows*
Number 3.	Shapeware *VISIO 3.0 for Windows*

IDEF process mapping products

Number 1.	Meta Software's *Design/IDEF*
Number 2.	Wizdom System's *IDEFine*

Process simulation products

Number 1.	PROMODEL Corporation PROMODEL and *ServiceModel*
Number 2.	Meta Software's *WorkFlow Analyzer*
Number 3.	AT&T ISTEL *WITNESS Simulation Software*

Activity-based-costing product

Number 1.	ABC Technologies *Easy ABC Plus*

tion, a work order can be changed from "new" to "carry over" by simply modifying the output of the routing.

One of the advantages of PROMODEL is that editing is easy. Similar lines of code can be copied and pasted, which eliminates repetitive keyboard input. Creating the model was at least twice as fast using PROMODEL compared to the two other systems evaluated. When changes are made, PROMODEL queries the user if corresponding changes should be made throughout the model. The animation capabilities of PROMODEL are superior to the two other products evaluated.

In reviewing the functional characteristics, the use of global variables, attributes, and shifts is similar to WITNESS. The reporting capabilities of PROMODEL are slightly more enhanced than those of WITNESS.

PROMODEL has an extremely good documentation and tutorial package, which aids in the learning process.

As noted in the original study, of the three simulation systems assessed, PROMODEL was recommended for business process reengineering applications. It was recommended because it is easy to learn, it requires the least amount of labor hours to create a simulation, and its capabilities allow the user to create more valid simulations.

Simulation products are continuing to change and improve to meet the needs of the business process reengineering analyst. Review the above study results as part of your own assessment of simulation products. All of these products are basically acceptable, but some are better than others.

"BEST BUY" SUGGESTIONS

Based on the author's experience, research involved in developing this book, industry leaders' and users' comments, and independent and personal evaluation of various products—including their user-friendly operation, performance, documentation, training approach, and overall value—"Best Buy" process mapping tools are suggested. The "Best Buy" process mapping products that are suggested in Table 8.1 should be on your own list of products that you should evaluate in terms of your own specific process mapping needs.

CHAPTER 9

How to Collect Data for Process Mapping

This chapter provides a detailed methodology that you can use to gather data and related information. It provides a proven step-by-step interview approach that can help improve the effectiveness of your data collection and process mapping efforts.[1]

THE ROLE OF THE DATA GATHERER

So far, this book has discussed concepts and guidelines that precede the collection of "hard" information and the actual drawing of a process map. Before discussing the details for process map data gathering and interviewing activities, it may helpful to show the overall context in which data gathering via interview techniques plays a part.

In process mapping, many aspects of the technique need to be considered, but in an orderly manner. If you can train yourself to be consciously aware of the different stages of process authorship that currently occupy your mind, you can significantly improve your ability to free the power of your creative analytical process.

Through discipline, extraneous factors can be held aside, leaving a crisp and clear set of work processes at each stage, and you can be astonishingly inventive, creative, and productive.

To create your process map several phases of author/interviewer activities need to be completed, including:

1. Data gathering phase

2. Process map structuring phase

3. Map documentation phase

4. Feedback interaction phase

Each of these phases is briefly described here:

Data Gathering Phase

Read Background Information The process map author gains familiarity with information about the subject matter area by collecting and reading source information prior to interacting with the process experts to be interviewed.

Parallel Interviews The author would normally be interviewing other "process experts" concurrently who may provide information with respect to the process that will be focused on in the new interview effort. Maintaining separate data-gathering files will help eliminate the comingling of apparently similar process information.

Outside-the-Box Thinking The process author should allow sufficient analysis time to see the big picture—to "ruminate." Every once in a while you must merely stand back and let all of the process bits and pieces sink into place. This type of "outside-the-box" thinking time is the unstructured time that precedes actual process mapping.

Priority Setting In this stage, the process map author examines the need for the preparation of key process maps to be created or analyzed and establishes priorities as to the sequence of interviews that should be conducted.

Process Map Structuring Phase

Draw Your Map The interviewing effort begins the actual creative process of generating a process map diagram. It is not limited to sketching process boxes and arrows; it also includes the identification and listing of random data elements, making preliminary sketches, and so on, which precede drawing formal process map boxes and arrows. This step can begin with sketch-type maps or computer-generated process flow diagrams.

Redraw Redraw includes the analysis and reexamination stage of process mapping, corresponding to editing and rework of the verbal text. The mapping activity here is concerned not with creating but with graphical editing, clarifying, simplifying, and rearranging the process map information gathered during the data-gathering interviews.

Map Documentation Phase

Write Text This is the writing of properly structured text, based on your interview and data-gathering research, for your process map. On occasion, beginning analysts write lengthy descriptions of what they mean by high-level process map boxes before they have progressed to actually diagramming those boxes at the next level.

Edit This is, similarly, the editing of proper structured process map text. It corresponds to "Redraw" of the graphic notation.

Make Process Mapping Kit Collect and make copies of collected data, diagrams, drawing node diagrams, and assembling reader process mapping kits for review are then completed.

Proofing This phase concentrates on proofreading and correction of publication versions of process maps. It consists primarily of reviewing the mechanical steps of publication performed by other analysts, reviewers, or team members.

Feedback Interaction Phase

Read It This normally applies to process mapping kits prepared by other process analysts, but on occasion, especially when a process author has been interrupted for some length of time, it may also include reading of a process map that which you have authored.

Reaction This refers to your reaction to reader comments that are returned to you. It is a combination of reading and annotating, to add your reactions to the reader comments.

Talk This represents time spent when an author, the process expert, and reviewer/reader(s) could actually get together and talk about the reactions to the process map and other reviewers' comments. It should be used only for this type of talking. "Interviewing" and "Group Meetings" cover the other "talking" activities of a process map interviewer/author.

Group Meetings This is all the time spent in group or team meetings reviewing progress or brainstorming next steps in developing your process map. The minutes of the group meeting should identify the subject matter under discussion. All such activities are lumped in this single category. Group meetings are generally much less efficient than one, two, or at most three people carrying out a properly structured "Interview," "Draw," or "Talk" activity when an author cannot make progress alone. Hopefully, interviewers/ authors will use such meetings only to indicate progress and review the results of individual efforts in these other categories.

THE PURPOSE OF INTERVIEWS

The purpose of an interview is to gather information from an individual who possesses expertise considered important to the process mapping analytical effort. A key part of the interviewing process is to record the information obtained. This can be done as informal notes, as activity and data/object lists, as a formal matrix of functions, or as process diagram or sketches.

When analyzing or designing a process map, it may be necessary to obtain or verify facts about the process or subject matter at hand. For the process map creator/author, there are many sources of factual information including:

- Reading of existing specification, drawing and process documents, using the Table of Contents and Index to locate needed information.

- Observe the process in operation, if it already exists

- Survey a larger group of process owners or users, through questionnaires or other such means

- Talk to one or more "process experts" who possess the desired knowledge.

- Use the inherent expertise and experience of the process map author

- Create or invent a hypothetical description and ask readers to help bring it closer to reality

Of all these methods, the most important is face-to-face interviews with the process expert. Seldom will all existing information be written. Preconceived notions that are reflected in questionnaires are often faulty.

There are four types of interviews that might be conducted during the course of performing the process mapping analysis phase of your process improvement effort.

1. "Fact Finding" for understanding current process operations. This type of interview is used to establish the scope and basic elements of a process or to help better understand the existing process environment.

2. "Problem Identification" to assist in the identification and discussion of current "As-Is" process problems or to help communicate the need for process changes. This type of interview is used to validate the current process and to provide the foundation for your process mapping work.

3. "Solution Discussion" regarding "What-If" and "To-Be" process options. This type of interview shares discussion and

analysis of process alternatives. This type of feedback-oriented interview can be very effective if supported by analytical process mapping tools, process simulations, and activity-based costing techniques. This type of interview is used to help establish the basis for recommending process change.

4. "Process Resolution Talk Session" in which the interview is used to resolve process problems or "bottlenecks" that have surfaced during the construction of your process map.

The reason for identifying types of interviews is that during the course of performing an actual interview, ingredients of each type of interview may appear. The respondent might tell the interviewer facts about a given system in terms of problems. Also, the respondent might identify problems in terms of solutions to the problems. By constantly classifying the respondents' remarks, the interviewer can better appreciate the process expert's point of view.

THE DATA-GATHERING INTERVIEW TOOLKIT

A "standard" data-gathering interview toolkit can be created and used to capture and organize your process mapping interviews. It should be stored in a process mapping "interview file" from which it can be distributed to appropriate process mapping analysts or process improvement team members. By creating a basic interview toolkit the fundamental data-gathering elements can be applied to each process mapping effort in order to provide a degree of consistent data collection for your efforts. You can make this "standard data-gathering toolkit" available to other members on the process mapping analysis team or even the interview respondent for corrections, additions, and deletions. The interview kit could contain:

I. Process under review cover page

II. Interviewer and record follow-up

    A. Interviewer name (author name)

    B. Interview date (process map diagram date)

    C. Interview duration (start time, end time)

    D. Respondent name

    E. Respondent title and organizational responsibility

    F. Respondent telephone number and extension

    G. Additional sources of information identified

        1. Process document—title and location

        2. Other suggested interviewees—name, title, organizational responsibility, address, telephone number

        3. Collection of all paper data.

    H. Essential elements of information—a summary of the key points covered in the interview including:

        1. Follow-up questions and/or areas of concern either not covered during the interview or postponed

        2. New terms for unique glossary of process-related terms

  III. Activity and process data lists

  IV. Agenda for interview (developed as part of preparation for interview)

   V. All interview notes and rough process maps

HOW TO CONDUCT DATA-GATHERING INTERVIEWS

The purpose of an interview is to gather information from an individual who possesses an expertise considered important to your process mapping assessment. There are four basic types of data-gathering interviews that are conducted during a process mapping project:

- *Fact Finding:* To understand current process operations or foreseen conditions

- *Problem Identification:* To assist in defining problem levels or requirements

- *Solution Discussion:* Regarding future process options or capabilities

- *Author/Reader Talk:* Sessions to resolve process problems that have surfaced during the Author/Reader interview cycle

During an actual interview, ingredients of each type may appear. The process expert tends to tell the interviewer "facts" about a given system in terms of problems. The process expert also tends to identify "problems" in terms of solutions to the problems. The interviewer should establish an atmosphere conducive to the purpose of the interview and prevent side issues from clouding the discussion. On the other hand, any and every relevant topic should be discussed in each interview. In the real world, the interviewer may have only one "shot" at the expert and must try to obtain facts, identify problems, and discuss solutions entirely during that one interview. Remembering the types of interviews will help the interviewer conduct the actual discussion with your process expert(s).

There are five stages to a successful data-gathering interview. Each must be conducted so as to assure that the most useful information is obtained and recorded in the least amount of time. The basic data-gathering interview steps are:

Step 1: Preparing for the interview

Step 2: Opening the interview

Step 3: Conducting the interview

Step 4: Terminating the interview

Step 5: Completion of the interview

In each stage of an interview there are certain basic activities which will help the interviewer establish an atmosphere of professionalism and trust with the process expert.

Step 1: Preparing for the Interview

This stage of the interview is directed at preventing a "pregnant pause" from occurring during an interview. Making an expert struggle to recall information may be a valid interview technique.

But it is undesirable for you as the interviewer to be stumped—and at a loss for how to proceed. By thinking through certain key interview needs before the interview, a more organized and efficient dialogue can occur. Preparation for your process expert interview should include the following basic activities:

I. Select interviewee (process expert)

   A. From areas of organizational or process responsibility

   B. From recommendations of others

   C. From multifunctional teams

   D. From different levels of the organizational hierarchy— upper levels useful for "big picture strategy," lower levels for detail process information, and middle levels for bridging the gap

II. Make appointment

   A. Short-duration interview—half to one hour

   B. Identify purpose of interview

   C. Explain the role of the interviewer

   D. Confirm process expert's name, title, address, telephone number

III. Establish tentative agenda

   A. Topical operational or process areas—used as a foundation for interview (this helps prepare "broad general questions")

   B. Develop specific questions

IV. Review available background information

V. Review appropriate terminology

VI. Ensure coordination with other interviewers

   A. Avoid duplication by checking to ascertain that the respondent has or has not been previously interviewed. If the interview is a follow-up, then examine the results of the previous interviews

   B. Assure information transfer to other team members

Step 2: Opening the Interview

This stage of the interview is directed at establishing a rapport between the interviewer and the process expert. The initial courtesy introduction and peer recognition provided at the start of an interview are usually of short duration. This time is extremely important in motivating the process expert to help the interviewer. This stage of the interview should include the following topics:

I. Provide the process expert with a tangible means of introduction, including your business card to establish your authority in the process.

II. Describe in some detail the purpose of the interview.

    A. Expand on information provided in initial contact

    B. Establish point of view for the interview, e.g., interview type

    C. Always establish purpose, even if the interview is a follow-up interview

III. Confirm that note-taking is acceptable. If the expert requires confidentiality and accuracy, document the results of the interview immediately after the interview has been completed. Be sure to use the standard process mapping toolkit forms for note-taking. Write down the date, place, time, and participants' names.

IV. Establish quickly the process expert/author relationship. Alleviate the fear that the interview will be used to tell the process expert how to do his or her job, or that the expert's job is in jeopardy.

V. Start with broad, general questions that will get the expert talking. These should be based upon the topical areas identified in the agenda

VI. Assess the expert's ability to provide pertinent information. If the information is too general or too detailed for the stage of the process map being prepared, redirect your interview strategy or terminate the interview, if necessary.

VII. Begin to formulate specific questions that complement the agenda.

STEP 3 : Conducting the Interview

While it is impossible to define every possible question that should be asked during an interview, it is possible to identify specific question guidelines which can be used during the interview. You may learn more from the process expert about process or related operational problems from your own evaluation of their process description. The first set of guidelines deals with qualifying the information being obtained. The second set of guidelines relate to stimulating the information flow.

Information Qualification The human mind can comprehend at more than twice the rate at which most people speak. The danger in interviewing is that this rate difference is typically used by the listener to not think about what is being said, but rather about what should be said in response to what is being said. The problem is one shared by both the processes expert and the interviewer.

In any event, to assist the interviewer in thinking about what is being said, there are basic questions that may help the interviewer qualify the information being provided:

- What supporting facts are being provided for the main points being discussed?
- How recent is the information?
- How complete is the information?
- Do I really understand what is being said?
- Is the level of detail appropriate for my purpose?
- Are there areas being omitted?
- Has this information been discussed with someone else?
- How does this information compare with what was obtained previously?
- How important is this information?
- Are side topics being discussed?
- Has the process expert's viewpoint changed?
- Is the information fact or opinion?

These questions are certainly not complete, but rather should be used by the interviewer to think about what is being said. Constantly qualify the information being obtained.

Information-Flow Stimulation The following guidelines should be used to stimulate the process expert into providing reliable information.

- Make certain that extraneous comments and conversations are kept to a minimum. The interview is used to obtain information, not to make friends or sell ideas.

- Do not use "yes"- or "no"-type questions; such questions elicit snap judgments from the expert.

- Provide the expert time to think. Do not suggest answers or ask another question. This type of pause in the interview is useful to allow the expert to recall vital pieces of information. Your silence may force the process expert to think and talk beyond what he or she was willing to share with you.

- Try to avoid outside distractions, which tend to uncouple the train of thought. If at all possible, conduct interviews outside of the expert's normal habitat.

- Be aware of internal distractions—signs that the expert is not comfortable or at ease with the interview.

- Encourage elaboration by asking for a rephrasing or a summary of the information presented.

- An interview is no place for sarcasm.

- Ascertain the expert's background and association with the subject matter being discussed. Valuable insight can be obtained by knowing the expert's relationship with the organization and systems.

- Record all questions asked by the expert.

- The interviewer should answer all questions except those dealing with user organization management, plans, or personalities.

- Above all, show interest in what the process expert is saying.

- Concentrate on the unfamiliar and difficult aspects of the subject being discussed. Avoid the obvious.

- Be alert for the inconsistent or incorrect use of process-defining words. Ask for definitions of any unfamiliar or questionable terms. Record the definition for the project glossary.

- Do not contradict the expert even if facts do not support what is being said. Use the process mapping review cycle approach to resolve such conflicts.

- Be humble. The respondent, not the interviewer, is the process expert.

- Postpone subjects that cannot be fully covered within the agreed-upon time frame. Do not extend the interview time, but rather make another appointment.

STEP 4: Terminating the Interview

The interview should be terminated for any of the following reasons:

- The information being obtained in the interview is not appropriate.
- The time limit has been reached.
- The interviewer has been saturated with information.
- There is a clash of personalities between the interviewer and the process expert.

Depending on the cause of termination, the following topics should be considered during the termination of the interview:

- The interview should not be closed abruptly. Rather, end it with a few minutes of informal conversation.
- The main points of the interview should be summarized.
- Identify areas of concern or further analysis that have not been covered or are being postponed.
- A follow-up interview, if necessary, should be arranged.
- Ask the process expert to suggest other persons who should be interviewed.

- If the interview results are to be reviewed by the process expert prior to distribution, this fact should be mentioned during the closing of the interview.
- Thank the process expert for his or her time and effort.

STEP 5: Completion of the Interview

This stage of the interview is directed at assuring that the information obtained during the interview is properly recorded and disseminated to the process team. If note-taking was not permitted by the expert, the interviewer should, upon termination of the interview, immediately write down the salient points discussed. Completion of the interview includes the following:

- Identify additional sources of information.
- Summarize the essential elements of information.
- Identify new terms for the project glossary.
- List follow-up questions and areas of concern either postponed or not covered during the interview.
- Complete activity and data lists.
- Expand notes with any information recalled from the interview.
- Prepare rough process map sketches and diagrams that reflect the information obtained.
- Identify any assumptions being made or any items that are not clear.
- Publish and distribute a reader kit for your team members and reviewers.

TIPS FOR CONDUCTING DATA COLLECTION
AND INTERVIEWS

Several tips are provided below to help gather relevant data and facilitate your interview process.

TIP—Catch Glossary Terms While Fresh in Your Mind

Glossary definitions should be captured when fresh in your mind. You can perfect these terms later. Stale glossary definitions are awful to write and that makes them awful to read and understand. Remember that one of the key purposes of process mapping is to do a complete job of communicating your understanding of the process under evaluation. If special terms with special meanings arise, make them clear. Keep an eye out for new terms and sketch their meanings as you go along—usually as a design note or comment on a process map sketch. Don't get hung up with writing a dictionary definition—that will come later.

TIP—Find the Right Experts

No one person understands everything about a particular subject or process, and frequently, no one at all will know the answers to some very pertinent questions. Process mapping is never merely a mechanical transcription of all the know-how that resides in one person's head. The whole point of the process mapping analysis is to help enable your multifunctional team to improve your performance by correcting "unrecognized" problems by determining what is really going on in your process.

TIP—Stay the Course

Just because the process understanding job is difficult does not mean that the strictures of the process mapping discipline that you have chosen should be set aside or distorted by reverting to text writing and group-think methods. You can make it work, and the real problem is for each individual process map author/ interviewer to find his or her own way of making it work. The bounded context, stick-to-the-subject discipline is intended to give you some controlled amount of information to work with.

TIP—Call for Assistance When Needed

The steps will work if you are not too concerned, to begin with, whether things come out right the first time. Get it on paper, critique it, and then correct it, using the process mapping box and arrow-type notations. Don't make the mistake of trying to write your muddled thoughts in English text or excessively long and "complete" lists. When you are really stuck, find the expert who knows about the topic that's holding you up. Don't let reworking the same information lead you to overlook the hard facts.

TIP—Guidelines for Note-taking

The interviewer should always receive permission from the expert to take notes. Note-taking tends to keep the interviewer's mind on the subject matter. Note-taking may be the only way of retaining specific facts. Your notes, even if short and incomplete, assist in recalling details. Note-taking should not become stenographic or the interviewer will tend to lose control of the interview. Be aware that note-taking can inhibit the expert from talking freely; adapt to the situation. Note-taking may also cause excessive attention to fact with little regard to ideas, opinions, and questions.

TIP—Be a Doubter

Qualify the information you have obtained by data collection or interviews. Do not assume just because it is written down that it is correct. Be skeptical and determine accuracy by cross-checking data sources and interviews. Be aware that you need to distinguish between information based upon facts and information based upon emotion or opinion. At the same time you can discover reality by appreciating different opinions on the same subject. Use separate process maps to show these opinions and to resolve conflicts.

TIP—Experience Counts

With experience, a process map creator/author becomes accustomed to changing mental gears between several different concurrent process mapping activities. In keeping track of the time spent in various process mapping activities, you will find that the data-gathering process becomes both smoother and more effective. Being aware of what you are doing at a given moment and where it is leading, is the discipline that gives form to thought and understanding. The only way to become proficient at process mapping is through practice. Keeping track of the time spent on each of the possible process authoring activities provides the measurable feedback that you need to improve your own performance.

SUMMARY OF APPROACH TO DATA GATHERING

When analyzing or designing your process mapping approach, it is necessary to obtain or verify facts about the process to be mapped. To create your process mapping database you should begin by collecting and entering in your process mapping files the following information.

- Create a baseline information file that collects all process documentation, process drawings, performance specifications, process metrics, and customer and quality data.

- Read all the existing product or service performance and process specification data. Identify and collect all key information. Identify possible information "disconnects." Knowing what has already been done to document the process should be used to help you better understand the real process.

- Determine the business strategic goals and core process requirements that provide value so you can meet your customers' needs in your process improvement effort.

- Discuss the process with product and process owners, lead managers, and the individuals who are involved with the process under examination. Include your notes of these first-impression interviews in your process mapping data file.

- Create an initial high-level process map that shows the input-through-output stages in your process. This process map can be a simple "brown bag" sketch or, if the process is more complex, you can use process mapping flow-chart-type graphic software.

- Observe the process in operation. Talk with every "process expert" (the person actually doing the work) to discover how the process is really performed. You should expect that the actual process will often be performed entirely differently than as defined in the documentation or as management thought or assumed it would be. Identify these disconnects and add them to your process database.

- Create a detailed "As-Is" process map using the software tools and techniques suggested in Chapter 8.

- Have your process improvement team return to your process experts to solicit their ideas and suggestions regarding how they think the process could be simplified, improved, or eliminated. Add these ideas to your process improvement database and process map.

- Conduct exploratory "benchmarking" assessments of how similar processes are currently executed within your organization and, if appropriate, within your competitors' business. Add this process intelligence to your database.

- Begin to develop your "To-Be" process improvement process mapping toolkit. Select the appropriate process mapping and simulation software to meet your analytical needs. Enter your collected process data and assumptions in the software products so you can begin your "What-If" process improvement analysis.

- Now use these data and process mapping tools to explore the options for process improvement.

Of all the above steps, the most important is face-to-face interview interaction with the actual work process expert. Seldom will all the relevant information be written. Preconceived notions regarding how people believe the process proceeds are usually wrong.

These simple process mapping data collection and interview procedures and tips, which are based on years of experience, will help you complete your process mapping efforts with less pain and more gain.

CHAPTER 10

Process Map Implementation

In Chapter 6, the IDEF process mapping methodology was described in terms of the background, concepts, and basic language needed to help explain the approach. The information presented in Chapters 4 and 8 through 11 serve as the awareness or pre-implementation process steps that you should review before implementing process mapping in your organization. In this chapter the key elements of the IDEF implementation process[1] are described.

BASIC PROCESS MAP GOALS

One of the primary goals of creating your process map is to describe the functions of your business processes in order to simplify, elimi-nate, or improve your processes to provide your products and ser-vices cheaper, better, and faster. The person responsible for creating the process map is called the "author." This chapter provides a description of the basic steps for authoring process map activity diagrams and shows how the logical, hierarchical, step-by-step dis-cipline of authoring makes it possible to create process map dia-grams that form useful and coherent graphic representations of your real processes. For any process map effort the creative concerns of authoring break naturally into a series of six different phases that are described here:

1. First try to *bound the process activity* more precisely than the title of the process activity box that our assigned task suggests. This is done with a list of data (objects or information) impacted by the process activity.

2. Then try to let your mind respond to that bounded set of process activities so you can *start forming some possible subactivities* of which the total process activity may be composed.

3. Then look for natural *patterns of interconnection* of those process subactivities, while raising various questions about the completeness of your original understanding of the bounded process activity.

4. During this effort you may find better process subactivities, so you can *split and combine* different process elements to make new process activity boxes.

5. The preceding steps will lead to a *complete set of interconnections* among the process activities, and you would then feel that you have succeeded in creating your baseline process map. At this point, you have a process structure that is well understood but not well expressed graphically.

6. Now draw an integrated version of the *process map diagram* with careful attention to layout and clarity so that we have a well-structured expression of your process. The process map diagram is now complete. What remains is to have our understanding of the process peer reviewed and confirmed by your team members.

Repeating this process helps to continuously refine and improve your understanding and expression of the process being improved and the related processes that are involved in your business.

GETTING STARTED

The basic generic steps involved in creating your own process map are described here:

Selecting a Context, Viewpoint, and Purpose

Before beginning any process mapping effort, it is important to determine the focus of your process map. This includes its context, its viewpoint, and its purpose.

The context establishes the subject of the process map as part of a potentially larger process map. It creates a boundary with the process environment by describing external interfaces. These limits help pin down what the process under analysis is and is not.

The viewpoint determines what can be "seen" within the context, and from what "slant" or perspective the map is being developed. It helps position the author's viewpoint as an observer of or participant in the process. Depending on the audience (management, technical, customer, etc.), different viewpoints may be adopted that emphasize different aspects of the process or omit some aspects altogether.

The purpose establishes the intent of the process map or the goal of communication that it serves. Purpose embodies the reason why the process map is created (cost reduction, faster cycle time, "white space" reduction, functional specification definition, implementation of "best practice" design, customer service improvement, etc.).

These concepts guide and constrain the creation of your process map. While they may be refined as authoring proceeds, these guidelines should be used to be consistent throughout your process map if its purpose is to remain clear and undistorted.

Creating the Context Diagram

To start your process map, create the A-0 diagram. Draw a single process activity box containing the name of the process activity that encompasses the entire scope of the process or system being described. Use arrows entering and leaving the box to represent the data interfaces of the process to its environment. This single-box process diagram defines the boundaries and the context for the entire process map and forms the basis for further process decomposition.

Creating the Topmost Process Activity Diagram

All process activities should lie within the single box shown on the A-0 diagram. The diagram is, therefore, said to bound the context of the process. The A0 diagram decomposes into the A-0 diagram, which contains from three to six major process activities. These are represented as boxes (and their interface arrows) which cover exactly the same scope of information covered by the A-0 parent.

The real "top" of the process map is the A0 diagram. It is the first, and most important, expression of the process map's viewpoint. Its structure clearly shows what the A-0 process box name describes. The terms and structure of A0 also bound every subsequent process level because it is a complete description of the chosen process. Lower levels make clearer what each of the A0 box names are intended to say. If the purpose of the process map is to be achieved, this chain of detail must be carefully followed at each subsequent step. This is the challenge of effective process map authoring.

To begin your first draft of the A-0 process map diagram based on the initial requirements and constraints, some authors find it easier to sketch the A0 level and then draw the single process box and interface arrows that capture all of the details shown at level 0. You may find it necessary to switch process diagramming techniques back and forth between A-0 and A0 several times to obtain a good start for the process decomposition.

In many instances, you may discover that the A-0 diagram has begun at too low a level of process detail. In this case, make the A-0 box the basis of a new level 0 diagram and move up one level to a new A-0 starting level. Repeat this process until an A-0 is reached that has sufficient scope to cover all aspects of the process.

Creating Subsequent Diagrams

To form the structure of your process map diagrams, decompose each box on the A0 diagram into its major parts. Treat each box on the A0 diagram like the A-0 box; that is, decompose it into its major parts to form a new diagram that covers the same topic as its parent process activity box but (again) in more detail.

To decompose each box obtain the needed additional facts from your work experience, from system specification and related documents, or through interviews (as described in Chapter 9). Create a first-draft process map diagram by listing all data items and activities that fall under the process box being decomposed. Take care that these lists cover the entire topic of the parent box, so that no portion is lost in the decomposition. To create the draft process activity diagram, draw boxes that are based on these lists and draw interface arrows between these process activity boxes.

To derive the clearest possible process activity diagram, modify or redraw the diagram several times until you are satisfied. Split (break up a process activity box into two or more parts) and cluster (combine two or more parts into a single process activity box) until you are satisfied with the clarity and simplicity of this step.

While creating a draft process activity diagram, you may wish to generate portions of additional process diagrams at a more detailed level to explore points that need additional clarification or come to mind at this step in your analysis process. Therefore you may create three or four process diagrams as a set at the same time, rather than just one process activity diagram at a time.

Writing Text

Eventually, each process activity diagram will be accompanied by a page or less of carefully written narrative text. The text associated with the A-0 diagram should complete the process map's orientation by being written when the A-0 diagram is created. The text complements the context (expressed in A-0 itself) by stating the viewpoint and purpose of the process map.

Text for every other process map diagram, however (including A0), is quite different. It tells a brief, concise story and does not duplicate what the graphic process diagram already says better. At every level, this captures the viewpoint in a way that furthers the purpose of your process map analysis.

Selecting a Box to Decompose

The following tips are provided to help you create process activity boxes.

Keep an Even Level of Description Given a complete parent process map diagram to work from, you should try to "firm up" the higher levels of your process map before overcommitting to sublevel process details. That is, given A0, try to emphasize work on A1, A2, A3, and so on, rather than on A1, A11, A111, and so on. If changes are made to higher-level diagrams, this can help avoid potential rework. Also, errors and oversights are more likely to be caught earlier if this approach is used.

However, detailing a process map "horizontally" (keeping an even depth or level of detail) is not a strict rule. The amount of depth at any time depends on whether more depth would capture meaning better than one process activity diagram. And sometimes it does. In other words, you may well sketch ahead several levels (to A11 and A111, for example). The important thing is to treat all such forays as sketches until the "horizontal" even level is confirmed. Be ready to rework the A111 material if it conflicts with A2, A3, and so on. But don't put off doing a good A111 sketch while the ideas are fresh and while you know what you would like to do.

Selection Based on Degree of Difficulty Given an even depth of coverage in your process map, and the availability of information on each process area, there will still remain a choice as to which process activity box should be decomposed next. Two guidelines are helpful in deciding which process activity box to decompose:

1. Start with the "hard part"—the part that is least familiar or is least clear.

2. Select the process activity box whose decomposition will give the most information about the other boxes.

Use either of these two criteria in deciding which process box to decompose. In short: Leave the simpler or better-understood process boxes for later decomposition. The simpler topics can be more easily decomposed later, with less risk of error or oversight, and can be easily manipulated to fit the decomposition of the more complex process issues.

Stick to Your Purpose Without conscious effort, in the process of creating detail, you can stray from the original purpose of your process map analysis effort.

Remember that the starting point for every process map analysis is to bound the context of your process map. You should decide what to focus on before even the topmost process activity box is created. If you do not continue to concentrate on your primary purpose, you may drift away from your starting point.

Every process activity step should be checked against the original starting purpose. Things that don't fit may be noted as subjects for further analysis.

By doing a thorough job as you go along you will be able to create more precise texts to be written for the high-level process activity diagrams of your process map. The reader should clearly understand your purpose from the start.

In the authoring process you will arrive at clarity from the rigors of detailing your process activities. Knowing how far to go, when to stop, when to change gears, and how the pieces fit together will always depend on the purpose for which the process map is created. Pick your context, viewpoint, and purpose. Know what you are and are not trying to address in your process activity effort.

Concentrate on Only One Viewpoint Don't confuse yourself or your reader by mixing apples and oranges. One process map should be used to describe only one purpose and should present only one viewpoint.

Multiple process activity diagrams of relatively shallow depth are better than a giant map that tries to be all things to all people. Once you've picked a viewpoint, be careful that you stick to it.

It is very natural during your analytical process to have a wide range of interests, even as you work within a bounded context. The deeper you go into learning about how things really work, the more you understand, and the more you want to tell about the process. Other process viewpoints and impacts can come from above, beside, or below your current process activity.

But be careful! Keep an eye out for opportunities to make a cross-reference to a companion process map. Don't distort the one you're working on. Remember that even the most astute and virtuous reader may not really match your own grasp of the entire process.

To convey your insights fully and correctly, you must always impose order and structure. A well-placed reference cuts off misplaced elaboration here, while motivating well-structured presentation in another process map.

Make a cross-reference now and also make a note for the other process map so it isn't overlooked. And then proceed with the business at hand! Don't let this flurry of activity prematurely stop your treatment of this viewpoint. Stick to the process you are analyzing and more good process understanding and improvement ideas will come to you.

THE PROCESS MAP ACTIVITY PHASES

So far, in this chapter we have discussed process mapping guidelines that precede the actual drawing of a process activity diagram. Before discussing "drawing" activities, it may be helpful to briefly describe some of the typical process map author activity phases that you will want to better understand and utilize, including (1) data gathering, (2) structuring, (3) presentation, and (4) interaction. With experience, an author becomes accustomed to changing mental gears between these activity phases. By keeping track of the time spent in each of these activities, you may find that the process becomes both smoother and more effective as you gain experience. Being aware of what you are doing at a given moment, and where it is leading, is the process mapping discipline that gives form to thought and understanding. At any time, an author may be engaged in any of the activity phases that are described in more detail on the following pages.

The only way to become proficient at process mapping analysis is through practice. Experience has shown that process mapping is a discipline of thought, which is simply assisted by the graphic conventions and tools. The practice of process mapping is, and must be, a very personal and individual thing. As in good technical writing, process mapping analysis requires understanding and skill on the part of an author to be effective.

In process mapping, many aspects of the discipline must be considered, but in an orderly manner. If as the author you can school yourself to be consciously aware of which of the many stages of authorship concurrently occupies your attention, you can significantly improve your ability to create efficient and effective process maps.

Data-Gathering Phase

As noted above, we described the various phases that authors need to consider in creating their process map. The first phase—Data

Gathering—is described in substantial detail in Chapter 9. A brief description of the basic elements of data gathering include the following:

- The author gathers information about the process by reading source information without interacting with other people.

- The author actively interviews the process "experts" about the process under analysis. This "interview" data-gathering step is not used for multiperson planning or review meetings.

- The process map author needs time to think about the overall process and the system interactions. This step is neither fact gathering, nor creating process activity diagrams, nor writing text. This "think" time is the unstructured examination, analysis, and thinking that precedes actual process map creation.

- In this step the process author selects the process activity box starting point by roaming over the full set of system and process activity diagrams, but this time with the specific objective of figuring out which box is the appropriate one to detail next.

Structuring Phase

A brief description of the basic elements for your creation of the process map structure includes the following:

- The first element of structuring is drawing the process activity diagram. This encompasses the actual creative process of drawing the process map diagram. It is not limited only to drawing boxes and arrows, however, for it also includes the listing of random data elements, making sketches, and so on, which precede drawing boxes and arrows.

- The redraw step covers the digestion stage of process map diagramming, corresponding to editing and rework of verbal text. The activity here is concerned not with creating but with graphical editing and rearranging your description of the process activity for clarity.

- At this point you can begin to fix the master diagram. This applies to the correction of master drawings to incorporate improvements and rework modifications. It is primarily a mechanical operation—a type of overhead—which results from the fact that masters are set aside while tinkering is done on the work in process copies.

Presentation Phase

The basic elements of the presentation phase are described here:

- Next is the writing of properly structured text. On occasion, beginning process map analysts write lengthy descriptions of what they mean by high-level boxes before they have progressed to actually diagramming those boxes at the next level. Such activity is not "Write Text" but instead is a nongraphic form of "Draw." "Write Text" means the writing of precise, structured text intended for ultimate publication.

- The edit step is, similarly, the editing of proper structured text. It corresponds to "Redraw" in the graphic notation.

- The editing step is followed by making the actual process kit, which consists of creating this set of kit forms (as described in more detail latter in this chapter), making copies of process diagrams, drawing node diagrams, and assembling reader kits.

- Time must now be devoted to proofreading and correction of publication versions of your process map. Here the mechanical steps of publication performed by others are reviewed.

Interaction Phase

The interaction communication steps are delineated here:

- Interaction starts with reading the process kit. This normally applies to reader kits prepared by other process map authors, but on occasion, especially when an author has been interrupted for some length of time, it may also include reading of a process map that you have previously authored.

- The next step is reacting to reader comments that are returned for your review and action. This step is a combination of reading and annotating, to add your reactions to the reader comments.

- At this point an author and reader actually get together and talk about the author's reactions to the reader comments. It should be used only for this variety of talking. "Interviewing" and "Group Meetings" cover the other "talking" activities of an author.

- Group meetings are designed to review progress or brainstorm the next step(s) in your process mapping effort. The minutes of the group meeting will identify the process subject matter under discussion. All such communication activities are lumped in this single category because it is the one place where the author by him- or herself is unable to furthur contribute to improving the process maps without input from his or her associates and team members. Group meetings are generally much less efficient than one, two, or at most three people carrying out a properly structured "Interview," "Draw," or "Talk" activity when an author cannot make progress alone. Hopefully, process authors will use such meetings only to accelerate progress and then review the results of individual efforts in these other categories.

HOW TO CREATE YOUR PROCESS MAP

Process activity diagram creation is the most subjective and creative activity of the process mapping process. It is open to variations between individual authors. No one set of steps will work equally well for all authors. It is useful, however, to present here a proven sequence for process map authoring. New process map authors should carefully study and follow this sequence until they have developed their own "style." The following recommended steps of authoring use data concepts to derive process activity boxes. The newly created process activity diagram is compared to the parent process activity box to ensure that the complete scope (defined by the data) is covered. The process map's purpose and viewpoint must also be consistent, as described earlier in this chapter. The recommended process activity drawing steps are:

1. Create a relevant, but not yet structured, list of data. List items that first come to mind (using a fresh process activity diagram form) within the context of the parent process diagram. Group items, if possible, to show similarities.

2. Name activities that act on the listed data, and draw boxes around the names (so that they can be connected, even if by messy arrows).

3. Sketch appropriate arrows. As each box is drawn, leave arrow "stubs" to make the box more meaningful. Make complete connections as what the process activity diagram is describing becomes obvious.

4. Draft a process layout that presents the clearest box and arrow arrangement. Bundle arrows together if the structure is too detailed. Simplify, simplify, simplify—leaving only the essential process elements. Continue to modify the process activity diagram as necessary.

5. Create text or FEO (For Exposition Only) process diagrams, if necessary, to highlight aspects that are important. Examine the process activity diagram's purpose, viewpoint, balance, and accuracy. Propose changes in the parent diagram where needed.

By following these steps and remembering certain key issues during the process map creation you will be able to create effective process map activity diagrams. As with any other "learn by doing" skill, ability improves with experience. The key issues to remember for creating your process map are summarized below.

Creating Process Activity Boxes

Once the list of data is completed, sketch your process activity boxes. Generate the process activity boxes by writing names of slightly more detailed subprocess activities that occur under the process of interest. As you create the process activity names, draw boxes around them to form the start of the actual process map diagram. Make no arrow connections between boxes at this early stage. However, you may draw individual arrows entering or leaving the isolated process activity boxes. This is helpful in making the process activity box more meaningful. It will serve as a reminder when later connecting the processs boxes to each other.

In writing the process activity names, use the major subactivities of the parent, not all of the many detailed activities that may come to mind. However, more than six activities are acceptable in this initial set, since the steps to follow will reduce the number to its proper level. Review the resulting set of process activity boxes to see if the initial process activity box names can be made more precise.

Try to avoid using special terms and abbreviations (jargon). Use them only when needed to promote communication with a specialized audience, and only at the detailed process activity diagram levels. Do not use them at the highest (A-0 and A0) levels, since these diagrams must be understood by nontechnical readers who are not familiar with the technical nature of every process. Carefully define special terms in the glossary.

In all cases, make the activity box names verb phrases. Whenever the phrase can be interpreted as either a verb or a noun, use the notation "(v)" to signify the intended verb usage.

To create process activity boxes, begin with the following steps:

1. Sketch or create in your process mapping software tool the process activity boxes by drawing them diagonally from upper left to lower right. While any layout that makes clear the author's intent is acceptable, vertical or horizontal formats tend to crowd arrows.

2. Recognize that process activity boxes placed in the upper left corner "dominate" those boxes placed lower and to the right—through the control arrows that link them. This standard style makes it easier for readers to understand your meaning. However, any layout that clearly presents your process map may be used.

3. Number each process activity box in its lower right corner. Assign the box numbers on a process activity diagram from left to right and from top to bottom. This defines the node number for each process activity box. The leading digits of the process activity box's complete node number are the same

as this process activity diagram's node number. The last digit of the node number is the process activity box number.

4. On working or draft copies, write the author C-number below the lower right corner of any process activity box that is diagrammed.

5. No process activity diagram should contain more than six boxes.

6. A process activity diagram with only two boxes is rarely decomposed enough to be useful. Try to rethink it.

TIP—A Fast Start Is OK, If It Passes Muster

If you already have experience in creating process maps you may bypass the step-by-step cold-start-up steps. You may skip ahead in the process, but be sure to follow up with a self-critique to assure that you have followed the methodology to obtain your results. These time-tested and rational process mapping start-up steps are really designed to get you started in virgin territory. Don't slavishly follow them just to be "disciplined." They are designed to help you, not to slow you down.

TIP—Avoid Concrete!

Create as many more formal process activity box sketches as you like, if you think that's best. But don't go overboard! Remember that even sketches can become cast in concrete and become hard to change because they have been put on paper or the computer screen. It's very easy to be too easily satisfied with material that is drawn.

TIP—Beware of Runaway Enthusiasm

If you go too fast you can build trouble for yourself in the future. So seek a proper balance and apply all the steps of the process map discipline even if you sometimes do them in a backwards order. There's no substitute for solid, top-down, thoughtful progress.

TIP—Don't Make Trivial Boxes

With fewer than six boxes per process activity diagram, each one must carry its own weight. Make each process activity diagram say enough to be really meaningful.

Sometimes past computer programming and flow-charting experience is carried over into process map analysis. The result shows up in the form of trivial boxes that ask a yes-no question or provoke a low-level selection from alternatives.

The corresponding effect is to make other factors of the process diagram carry too much, so that the parent diagram's function is not really factored in at all! It's like making small wood chips, one at a time, instead of splitting a large log by a well-placed blow.

Don't be surprised if it is difficult to get rid of a trivial box. It's not easy, but it is worthwhile to simplify your process activity boxes.

Creating Interface Arrows

After creating data interface arrows for each individual process activity box, connect the ends of the arrows (which have not already been connected) to show which outputs supply which inputs and controls. At this early process map diagramming stage, do not worry about the layout on the page. It is best to connect the boxes first to see the basic arrow patterns before attempting to make a clean process map drawing.

A basic rule for layout of the arrow structure is "constraint"; don't sequence. That is, make the process activity diagram structure show relationships that must be true no matter which sequence is followed.

Recall that input data are transformed by the process activity to produce the output. If an arrow contains both input and control, show it as a control. If you are uncertain whether an arrow is a control or an input, make it a control. If it is unclear whether a particular piece of data is needed at all, leave it out!

Output arrows show the results of possible occurrences of the process activity. The syntax for output arrows does not indicate which patterns of output arrows may occur under which circumstances. If the sequence is of particular interest, draw an FEO illustrating the pattern. But do not worry too much about sequence.

Just make sure that all important cases are allowed by the process activity diagram.

Bundle groups of related arrows whenever possible, resulting in fewer, more general arrows. Perhaps the most common mistake when creating arrows is to make the arrow structure or the arrow labels too detailed. Recall that the level of detail of arrows must match the level of detail of your process activity boxes. At high levels, both process activity box names and arrow labels will be abstract.

As a final check, compare all arrows to the data list to ensure that each correct element appears and that each incorrect element was indeed incorrect and not just overlooked when creating the arrows.

TIP—Think Control and Constraint, Not Flow

Don't let sequential flow, "how to do it" thinking influence you too early; it will automatically rule out potentially better alternatives.

Even though something must progress from stage to stage to reach some desired end result, do your best to express the constraints that must be satisfied or the properties that must be true rather than one specific sequence of steps that will yield that result. The reason is that any time you give a sequence, it's just that—a single sequence. There may be many possible sequences, some better than the one you may think of first.

If you build in a sequence, no other sequence is possible. If you build a proper constraint structure, any sequence—even one you haven't yet thought of—is allowed. It is always more powerful to constrain than to sequence.

Often, it is easiest at first to think of submodule actions in a particular sequence to get unstuck and get something on paper. This may be a good way to get going, but always rework your first attempt into a constraint structure.

TIP—Label Arrows for Clarity

Readers are not supposed to have to study any one process activity diagram too deeply. Subordination of unneeded details makes what's left that much more meaningful.

Don't clutter your diagrams with too much information and too many arrows.

Remember that each process activity diagram will eventually be accompanied by text describing what it is trying to say. Many times an arrow has an obvious meaning from the way you talk about it. Putting excessive labels on the diagram itself is not necessary.

TIP—Leave Out Questionable Arrows

It is often hard to determine whether to show an arrow or not. (Showing it seems rigid, not showing it seems imprecise.)

The easiest way to handle the arrow question is, "When in doubt, leave it out." If the arrow isn't really essential to the main backbone of what you have to say, if you have questions about it, you probably don't know enough to put it in correctly. If you just throw it in, it will confuse things and have to be changed later.

Remember that the process mapping discipline won't let you quit until the full job is done, so leaving the questionable arrow out now won't last forever. It will be added when it is required by the workings of some later subactivity detailing. At that time, you will have no questions about it.

Good Is Better Than Best

You should not worry about whether the expression in your initial process activity diagram is "the very best" you can do. The initial goal should simply be to complete a process activity diagram that represents a good effort and does not violate any process map syntax rules. Then, when the process activity diagram is drafted, the critical guidelines of reading and review by others can be used to improve the first try. Any process activity diagram can be modified to make a second version that is, in some sense, better than the first. The first process activity diagram will never be the very best.

The process mapping methods and procedures, implemented via disciplined teamwork, will allow you to detect flaws, make improvements, and increase the quality of your efforts. But these methods only get a chance to work when there is a first draft (however brief or unkempt) to be read, pondered, and modified. Until those first process map activity diagrams begin to appear, nothing can be done.

As skill levels develop, first diagrams get better and authors feel more comfortable with their use of the graphic language. But always, reworking of diagrams is a necessary part of the process. The key idea is to use a review cycle to make progress on paper.

Process mapping is a thought-forming aid, not just a diagram-making exercise. Even when thoughts are ill-formed, putting them on paper and letting the notation and discipline work are what keep authors and readers alike moving toward development of your process map. Rely on your ability to ask good questions, rather than on the expectation of providing "perfect" answers.

TIP—It Is More Important to Be Clear Than Correct

It's easy to restructure something that you really understand, but it's very hard to overcome the confusion of nonstructured complexity.

Let the orderliness of the process mapping discipline help you to make clear even the wrong viewpoint as long as it's on paper in process activity diagram form. Then step back and figure out what's wrong. Use the same discipline to adjust it as necessary to make it more correct.

The excessive use of text to describe process activity boxes before they've been detailed is a very bad practice, even though it appears to be natural for beginning efforts in difficult problems. It has a disastrous impact on productivity.

REDRAWING YOUR PROCESS MAP

As part of drawing your process map several key elements are described below, including the techniques for modifying your process activity diagrams.

Modifying Process Activity Boxes

When first creating your process activity diagram, recall that you must cluster activities into three to six boxes of approximately the same level of detail. If necessary, split the set of process activity boxes and cluster them again until you are satisfied with the clarity and similar level of detail among the process activity boxes. Two or more boxes may be split or clustered to provide a boundary that is more familiar, more easily understood, or that provides fewer arrows and therefore makes a simpler interaction between the process activity boxes.

Clustering represents groups of two or more process activity boxes to form a single box. Its goal is to cluster related process activities into a single, more general activity. It helps to eliminate "premature detail" that will appear at a more detailed level but that would obscure the message to be conveyed at this level. Indicate a cluster by circling the two or more process activity boxes that are to be clustered and writing the new combined box title near the perimeter of the circled boxes.

Splitting breaks a single process activity box into two or more parts. It is the inverse of clustering. Its goal is to provide more detail. One reason for splitting may be that the process activity diagram does not present sufficient new information to make it essential to an understanding of the process being decomposed. Another reason may be that a subactivity is incorrectly included inside a process activity box and should be split out to form two boxes. Indicate a split by crossing out the old process activity box and writing the new box titles adjacent to it.

Most often, splitting and clustering work together. Process activity boxes are split and the resulting pieces are clustered in different groupings to form new boxes that more closely convey the intended message. The same process matter is thus covered, but its pieces are grouped in a more understandable way.

TIP—How to Split and Rephrase

It is important that all of the boxes of a process activity diagram have a consistent "flavor." Split and rephrase boxes where required to restore the balance.

Sometimes a process activity box is found to obscure, or somehow not to fit very well with the other boxes of the current process map. Frequently the trouble is that, because other aspects of the process map have undergone change and clarification, the earlier version of the process activity that may have been a good idea initially now has the wrong slant or flavor.

Correct this problem by further dividing the offending process activity box by neatly splitting off the bad part, leaving two or more pieces, one of which still contains the essence of the original relevant process activity idea. Expect to change the wording of the box (or boxes) because with the separation of the split, you probably can make your new ideas clearer and make them mesh more closely with related process activity boxes.

TIP—How to Cluster and Replace

A solid abstraction is both clearer and more powerful than premature detail. Cluster related boxes and replace them by a single encompassing process activity box.

Frequently what you thought was a good level of process description can be made even better by clustering several process activity boxes into a more general view and moving the details to the next level down. Draw a line around the cluster and replace them all by that one boundary, suitably worded.

Clustering arises often in conjunction with splitting and is, in fact, one of the most powerful methods to use to get things to come out right. Obscure process subactivities are split off from several process activity boxes and then clustered to make better big boxes. The combined effects can give much deeper insight into your processes.

Suggesting Modifications to the Context

The detailed understanding of your processes revealed by creating new process activity diagrams will uncover errors or oversights in the original parent diagram. You may wish to create an alternate parent diagram (or rough sketch of one) just to explore some detail which needs clarification.

Parent diagram changes may represent various degrees of difficulty. If the change can be accommodated by a revision to the immediate parent only, this is simpler than a revision that involves more remote higher-level or related process activity diagrams. When proposing a change to the parent diagram do not try to make the change simple when it may in fact need to be more complex. By attempting to avoid major changes, harm can be done to the quality of the process decomposition. When the correction is completed, check all boundary connections carefully to ensure consistency. If other authors are simultaneously decomposing other portions of the same process activity diagram, inform them of the changes that you are pursuing.

Connecting Process Activity Diagrams. An important aspect of understanding process activity diagrams is the ability to scan up and down the levels of detail to help you understand the process better. To be able to perceive this connection between process activity diagrams, node numbers should reflect the structure of the process activity box decomposition, and the arrow network should provide rigorous interface connections.

To tie all arrows shown entering or leaving the sides of a process activity diagram together, write ICOM codes on all arrows having one end unconnected on the process activity diagram (called boundary arrows because they connect the arrow network across the boundary). As you draw each boundary arrow, label it with its ICOM code to specify the connection of the arrow to the parent diagram. Write the ICOM code near the end of the arrow that connects across the boundary, not near the process activity box or boxes to which it connects on the diagram being created.

When creating a process activity diagram, the only firm requirements that should be satisfied are noted here:

1. The purpose and viewpoint in your process map must match those of its context.

2. Its boundary arrows must correspond to those of its parent diagram.

3. Its content must include everything delineated in its parent box.

Good judgment ensures the first and the last; ICOM codes trace the arrows. Splitting and clustering are to be expected in your current process activity diagram and its details. But if problems appear at the boundary, use the ICOM codes to ensure that changes are properly handled in other parts of the process map.

TIP—Bound the Context, and Stick to It

It is often hard to determine what does and does not belong in a process activity diagram.

Always have in mind—and in view in front of you—the parent diagram for the process activity box you are detailing.

Don't allow things to get unclear or confusing. If your work on process activity detailing doesn't fit the context as you have sketched it, either your current work or the context is wrong. Either change the context or change your work. They must match.

PROCESS MAP GRAPHIC LAYOUT

By the time the data list and process activity boxes are drawn and the basic arrow structure is laid out, the original process activity diagram may appear quite jumbled or confused. Anticipate that several redraw steps may occur to get a careful process map diagram layout for distribution and comment. As noted earlier, lay out the process activity boxes diagonally according to the constraint structure, from upper left to lower right. That is, the usual flow of activities should be from left to right and from top to bottom, with feedback arrows going up and left. At this point, number the boxes in order, from left to right.

It is best to start this graphic layout with the most heavily used constraint arrows only, leaving out less used paths for the time being. This subset of the arrows will permit the process activity box position to be determined. Next, draw all boundary arrows shown on the parent diagram; then draw the remaining arrows.

The following tips and suggestions about using the box and arrow graphics is provided to help you create your process map. These points are most useful when cleaning up a process activity diagram to get a clear layout, after the initial rough diagramming has resolved questions about what the process activity diagram should contain.

TIP—Too Many Arrows Obscure the Message

Although no specific number of arrows is recommended as a limit, there should not be "too many" arrows between the six-or-fewer boxes of the process activity diagram.

Both arrows and boxes should be at a corresponding level of abstraction in the process activity diagram. Any time that you find lots of arrows on a diagram, this stricture somehow is being violated.

There are two basic ways to simplify your graphical use of arrows:

1. Bundle arrows with the same process activity source and destination under a single more general label, and make one arrow.

2. Rename some process activity boxes (using "Split" and "Cluster") to better distribute the process subactivities. To do this, try to create a single box that describes all the transactions a bunch of arrows are trying to carry out. Then rename the process activity box, bundle the arrows, and relabel the resulting arrow(s).

It is not necessarily true that "too many arrows" is wrong. It may be the case that you are just both accurate and precise. But it may be true that "too many arrows" is bad in that you obscure things. The ability of readers to understand what you have said is also an issue. It is better to be approximate and clear than precise and obscure.

TIPS—On How to Create Better Process Map Graphics Faster

The following tips on how to better create your process map graphics can save you valuable time.

—When an entry arrow serves both control and input functions, show it as control. When in doubt, make it control. An arrow appearing on a parent diagram as control can appear on the next level as control or input or both, padepending on its function at that level.

—Process activity boxes must always have control arrows, though they may not always have inputs.

—Boxes with neither output nor two-way input or control would have to be interpreted as "write only." They should never occur.

—In general, do not split an arrow into both a control and an input to the same process activity box. This detail is best shown on a lower-level process activity diagram where the destination of each branch and the reason for the split will appear. When you must do it, however, choose labels for the two branches that will convey your important decision.

—Draw arrows along horizontal and vertical lines, not diagonally or as curves (except at corners).

—Place arrow corners and intersections (and labels) a reasonable distance away from process activity boxes. Crowding obscures.

—Don't use the words "data," "activity," "input," "output," "control," or "mechanism" in names or labels unless absolutely necessary.

—If an arrow is long, label it twice.

—Place ICOM codes near the unconnected ends of arrows.

—Connect open-ended boundary arrows to show all the places affected. Readers may miss connections otherwise.

—Don't draw arrows all the way to the margins of the process activity diagram sheet.

—Space parallel arrows adequately. They are hard to follow visually if they are lengthy and close together.

—Place extra arrowheads along arrows where needed for clarity.

—Bundle arrows with the same source and the same destination unless the arrow is of such importance that making it part of a pipeline would decrease clarity.

—On any one side of a process activity box, there should never be more than four arrows. If there are more, bundle some, label with a suitable abstract label, and fan out branches to their destinations.

—Control feedbacks are clearer when shown as "up and over" arrows.

—More dominant constraints may be described more clearly when shown as "down and under"arrows.

—If an arrow branches and feeds into several boxes, draw it at the same relative ICOM position on each box, if possible.

—Lay out arrows so as to minimize unconnected crossings.

—Minimize curves and corners whenever possible.

—Use the expressive potential of branching arrows when it is appropriate.

—To avoid clutter when showing an external arrow that applies identically to or is obtained identically from each and every process activity box on a diagram, use a "to all" convention.

WRITING PROCESS MAP TEXT

To support the process activity diagrams, clear and easily understood text is required. The following guidance is provided to help you create useful text.

Create Process Activity Diagram Text

The text that accompanies each process activity diagram presents a brief overview of the diagram and should be less than a page in length. It highlights features that the author feels are of special interest or significance. It does not duplicate every detail shown on the diagram itself. It does "walk" the reader through the main ideas of the process map diagram. Where the process activity diagram conveys the intended message clearly the text may be omitted.

It is preferable to write the text only after the process activity diagram has received a fairly high level of review and approval—usually as a final stage in preparing the process map for publication. By not relying on textual descriptions earlier, you are assured that the process activity diagram itself is properly communicating the intended message. Tying each brief narrative to a process activity diagram results in text that is structured and as well organized as the process activity diagram itself.

Writing the A-0 Text

Since all process activity decomposition proceeds from the A-0 diagram, place any noteworthy facts that apply to the entire process map in the text associated with the process activity diagram. In particular, the A-0 text must contain a concise statement of the viewpoint and purpose of the process map. Unlike other process activity diagram text, write the A-0 level text when A-0 is first drawn, and include it whenever A-0 is presented.

TIP—Texts Tell Stories, They Don't Describe

Process map texts should lead the reader's mind. They should not duplicate, in weaker form, the information already provided in the process activity diagrams.

Remember that the text is not a specification. Its role is to bring life to its companion process activity diagram. The combination of diagram and text must make complete sense to the reader.

Don't necessarily follow the box numbering. The last box may come first in the story line.

Refer to other process activity diagrams only briefly; just tie them in. Remember, they have their own texts to cover details. Never describe each box in turn, saying in text what the next level of diagrams will say better and more clearly in graphic form. Also, don't just describe a diagram, talking about it and saying what it is.

Sometimes when writing text you may find the need for a FEO. If the need is real, add the FEO and talk to it to make your point. But don't overdo—try first to get good text without an added FEO.

TIP—Most Importantly—Tell a Story

Make it easy for the reader to dash through your text and come out at the end feeling good—that that's what he or she had already thought the process activity diagram had told him.

Text should not have to be studied to be understood. Make it easy, informative, comfortable, encouraging, and exciting reading. Make the reader eager to get on to your next process activity diagram so they can really understand your processes.

THE PROCESS MAP REVIEW CYCLE

The established process mapping review cycle consists of six subelements, including: team dynamics for the process map review cycle, the IDEF process map cycle, the process mapping kit, standard forms, file management, process map review presentation process, and meeting management guidance. Each of the critical elements is described below:

TEAM DYNAMICS FOR THE PROCESS MAP
REVIEW CYCLE

The development of any process map is a dynamic process that requires the participation of more than one person. Throughout a project, the draft iterations of the process map are created by process analysis author(s) and distributed among other team members (process improvement team members, experts in the subject matter, management, etc.) for review and comment. These draft portions of a process map are called "kits" and may contain process diagrams, text, glossary, or any other information the process analysis author feels is pertinent to the development of the process map.

It requires some training and experience to correctly read and understand process maps. Such experience is essential if the quality of the team-supplied process map is to be assured. Those process analysis team members who are skilled in reading process maps are called "readers."

The process mapping teamwork methodology identifies all the appropriate persons interested in the review of your process mapping efforts as reviewers. Reviewers that are requested to make specific written critiques of a kit are called commenters. Reviewers who receive a kit for information only are not expected to make written comments and are called readers. The process map author and the commenters share responsibility for the quality of the process map. Through their acceptance of the agreed result, the other reviewers share accountability for the utility of the process mapping results.

This discipline requires that each person expected to make comments about a kit make them in writing using reader notes and submit them to the author of the kit. Writing on the reader's copy, the author responds to each note in writing (a simple check mark, for agreement; otherwise, a note in reply). This process mapping development cycle continues, encompassing all kits pertaining to a particular process map, until the process map is complete and recommended for publication.

At regular intervals during the evolution of your process map, the master copy of the latest version is placed in the process map "library," and a copy is disseminated in the form of a kit, which is sent to readers to assist them in maintaining current information about your process map. As the comments on each kit are reviewed by the author, he or she makes changes in the master copy of the process map to incorporate corrections and changes. Another kit, which includes the latest changes, is then distributed to the list of readers. More detail is added by the creation of more diagrams, text, and glossary. More comments are made; more changes are included. The end effect of this continuous improvement process for organized teamwork review and active participation is assurance that the final process maps are valid and well expressed, and that a consensus has been reached by the set of readers who have been included in the review cycle.

The specific roles and functions of your team in developing your process maps are delineated below:

- *Authors* (analysts): Team members who prepare the process map

- *Commenters* (experts or other authors): Team members knowledgeable of the subject being mapped from whom authors may have obtained information by means of interviews, and who have enough experience in process mapping technique to offer structured comments in writing. People assigned to make a written critique of a kit

- *Readers*: People knowledgeable of the process being mapped from whom authors may have obtained information by means of interviews, and who review documents for information, but who are not expected to make written comments. (Process experts, or anyone who believes that they can contribute to process improvement, may be on the reader list.)

- *Librarian*: A person assigned the responsibility of maintaining the file of documents, making copies, distributing kits, and keeping records

All team members should be knowledgeable process map readers so they can perform the assigned functions reliably. If you are just beginning to map your processes, take the time to train your team in the basic skills for process map preparation, which can be taught rather effectively in small team groups.

An individual team member's role in the process mapping effort has nothing to do with the individual's job title, and the same person may be asked to perform several different process mapping roles. Therefore, each individual's participation is, in fact, unique and depends upon the process mapping effort involved. More information on each of the process mapping individual's responsibilities are described in more detail below.

An author interviews experts, analyzes the information, organizes it into process map diagrams, and creates the process map.

An author may or may not be the source of the technical content of a process map document.

A commenter reads the material produced by an author and verifies its technical accuracy. They are responsible for finding errors and suggesting improvements. The role of a commenter is the key to producing high-quality results. But every reader should note whether the author has followed the process mapping technique consistently; whether the viewpoint and purpose have been adhered to; and whether errors or oversights exist that should be brought to the author's attention. If a reader is a trained author, suggesting changes in the hierarchical breakdown and variations in activity box content (as well as other observations on how to enhance the communication power and utility of the process map) should be welcomed by authors.

General guidelines for authors, readers, and commenters are summarized below.

TIP—Guidelines Preferred over Rigid Process

No set pattern of questions and rules can be adequate for commenting, since subject matter, style, and technique vary so widely. However, guidelines do exist for improving quality. The major criteria for quality are:

- Will the document communicate well to its intended audience?

- Does it accomplish its purpose?

- Is it factually correct and accurate, given the bounded context?

TIP—How to Provide Notation

Make notes brief, thorough, and specific. As long as the author understands that niceties are dropped for conciseness, this makes for easier communication and less clutter.

Use the "N" notation (reader notes) to identify comments. To write an "N" note, check the next number off the READER NOTES list, number the note, circle the number, and connect the note to the appropriate part with a squiggle line.

Make constructive criticisms. Try to suggest solutions or point out sources of problems clearly. Provide useful constructive comments in the form of your notes to the author.

TIP—Get Your Comments Organized

Take time to gather overall comments. These may be placed on the cover of your kit (description to follow this material) or on a separate sheet. Try not to gather specific points onto this sheet when they belong on the individual pages. Agenda items for author/commenter meetings may be summarized. Make agenda references specific.

TIP—Provide Your Comments Now!

The length of time spent critiquing depends on a variety of things: familiarity with what is being described, the number of times something has been reviewed, the experience of the reader and author, etc. A kit returned to an author with no comments other than the reader's signature and a check mark means that the reader is in total agreement with the author. The reader should realize that there is a shared responsibility with the author for the quality of the work. Take the time to review your team's process map material when requested. Do it right the first time.

TIP—Author/Commenter Interchanges

When a reader returns a kit, the author responds by putting a check mark or "X" by each N note (reader note). A check mark means that the author agrees with the commenter and will incorporate the comment into the next version of the process map kit. "X" means the author disagrees. The author must state why there is disagreement in writing where the comment appears. After the author has responded to all comments, the kit is returned for the reader to retain.

THE IDEF PROCESS MAP KIT CYCLE

In creating an IDEF process map, materials written or gathered by an author are distributed, in the form of a "standard kit," to commenters, reviewers, and other readers. Commenters review the material and write comments about it. The commenters return the kit to the author, who reacts to comments and may use the comments to revise or expand the material. The kit is returned to the commenter with the reactions from the author. Readers may return comments to the author as well, but this is not required. This is known as a kit cycle, as shown in Figure 10.1.

The specific steps of the IDEF-type process map kit cycle are as follows:

- The author assembles the material to be reviewed into a standard kit. A cover sheet is prepared. Copies of the kit are distributed to each of the readers, and to the author. The original is filed for reference.

- Within the response time specified, the commenter reads the kit and writes comments directly on the copy in the form of reader notes, in red if possible. The kit is returned to the author.

- The author responds in writing directly on each commenter's copy, in blue if possible. The author may agree with the comment by check-marking it, noting it on his working copy and

Figure 10.1   Process Mapping Kit Cycle

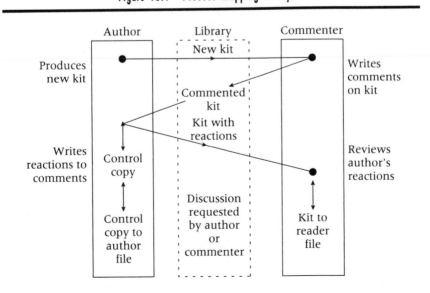

incorporating it into the next version of the model. If there is disagreement, the author writes a note of reply attached to the reader's note (no new note number). Whether or not there is disagreement, the kit is returned to the reader, completing one reader/author kit review cycle.

■ The reader reads the author's responses and, if satisfied, files the kit. (Commented kits are always retained by the reader.) If an assigned commenter does not agree with the author's responses, a meeting is arranged with the author to resolve differences. If this cannot be done, a list of issues is taken to the appropriate team leader for decision. The author is not obligated to resolve differences with every reader, but commenters are disenfranchised if their concerns are not resolved.

This cycle continues until a process map document is created that represents the careful consideration of all team project members. In addition, a complete history of the suggested process revisions has been retained.

The results of this kit cycle are a process map document to which author and commenters have contributed, and, if necessary, a list of issues that require further management action.

Throughout the cycle, a project librarian handles copying, distribution, filing, and transfer of process mapping kits between authors, commenters, reviewers, and readers.

HOW TO PREPARE A PROCESS MAPPING KIT

A process mapping kit is a technical document. It may contain diagrams, text, glossaries, decision summaries, background information, or anything packaged for review and comment.

An appropriate cover sheet distinguishes the material as a kit. The cover sheet has fields for author, date, project, document number, title, status, and notes.

There are two types of IDEF process mapping kits:

■ A *"standard kit"*: To be distributed for comment. It is considered a "working paper" to assist the author in refining his total process map.

- *An "update kit"*: Contains the latest version of your process map. It is sent for information only and is designed to aid in maintaining current information about the total process map while portions of the map are being processed through the kit cycle. The update kit may include only those pages changed since the previous updating.

Standard kits contain portions of your process map and are submitted frequently as work progresses. Standard kits are submitted through the process map kit cycle for review and are the type referred to in the rest of this chapter.

Update kits are submitted at regular intervals. These kits contain the latest version of the process map. Recipients of update kits are not expected to make comments on them although they may choose to do so. Update kits are kept by the recipients for their files.

Completing a Kit Cover Sheet

The kit cover sheet denotes the material as a process map kit. The cover sheet has fields for author, date, project, document number, title, status, and notes. Prepare one cover sheet for each kit submitted, filling in the following fields on the cover sheet as shown in Figure 10.2.

- Working information
  Name of the author or team generating the process map
  Project name and task number
  Date of original submission to library
  Dates of all published revisions
  Status of process map—working, draft, recommended for acceptance, or publication as final process map

- Reviewer information
  Filing and copying information
  List of kit reviewers
  Schedule date for various stages of kit cycle

- Content Information
  Table of contents for the kit
  Status of each kit section
  Comments or special instructions to librarian

Figure 10.2 Process Map Kit Cover Sheet

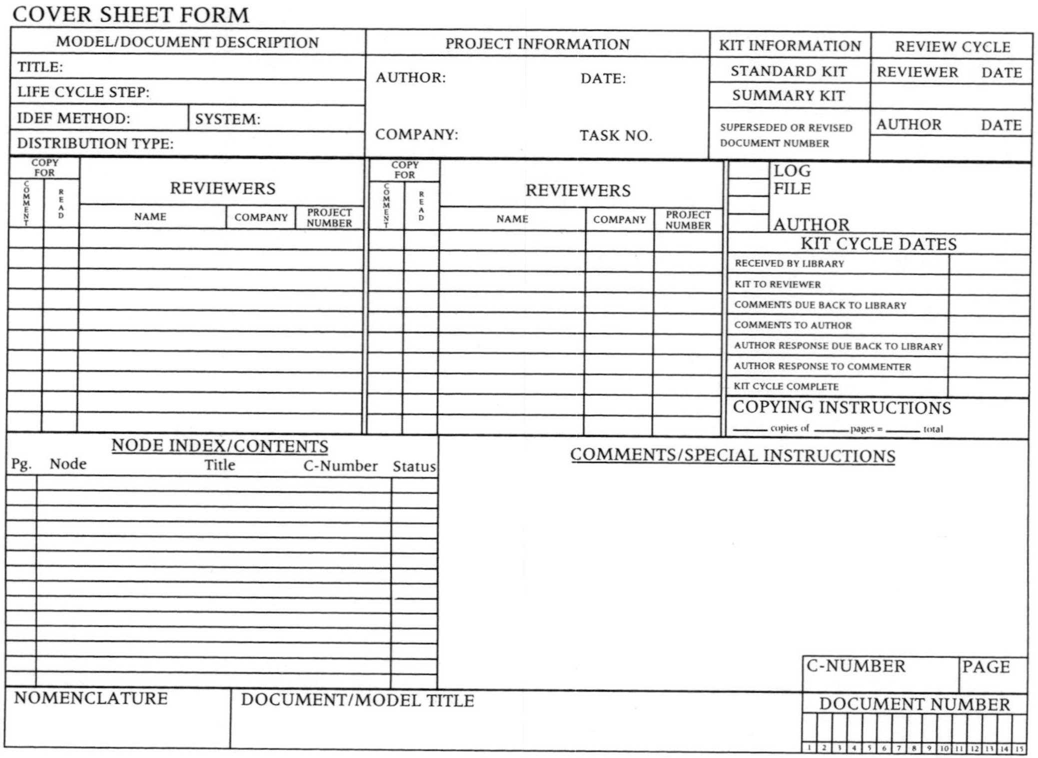

COVER SHEET FORM

MODEL/DOCUMENT DESCRIPTION	PROJECT INFORMATION	KIT INFORMATION	REVIEW CYCLE
TITLE:	AUTHOR: DATE:	STANDARD KIT / SUMMARY KIT	REVIEWER DATE
LIFE CYCLE STEP:			
IDEF METHOD: SYSTEM:	COMPANY: TASK NO.	SUPERSEDED OR REVISED DOCUMENT NUMBER	AUTHOR DATE
DISTRIBUTION TYPE:			

REVIEWERS

COPY FOR (COMMENT / READ)	NAME	COMPANY	PROJECT NUMBER

REVIEWERS

COPY FOR (COMMENT / READ)	NAME	COMPANY	PROJECT NUMBER

LOG
FILE
AUTHOR

KIT CYCLE DATES

RECEIVED BY LIBRARY
KIT TO REVIEWER
COMMENTS DUE BACK TO LIBRARY
COMMENTS TO AUTHOR
AUTHOR RESPONSE DUE BACK TO LIBRARY
AUTHOR RESPONSE TO COMMENTER
KIT CYCLE COMPLETE

COPYING INSTRUCTIONS
_____ copies of _____ pages = _____ total

COMMENTS/SPECIAL INSTRUCTIONS

NODE INDEX/CONTENTS

Pg.	Node	Title	C-Number	Status

NOMENCLATURE	DOCUMENT/MODEL TITLE	C-NUMBER	PAGE
		DOCUMENT NUMBER	1 2 3 4 5 6 7 8 9 10 11 12 13 14 15

- Identification Information
  Process map "name" (in node field)
  Title of the process map
  C-number

How to Prepare a Standard Kit

To avoid oversights, review the kit as if that were the only information available. Catch any typographical errors. Add points of clarification that come to mind as brief notes on the kit itself. Glossary definitions for terms that appear in the kit should always be appended as support material.

Gather helpful materials and append these for the reader's benefit. Never use this supplemental material to convey information which should properly be conveyed by the process map itself. Whenever possible, use the most natural means of communication—process map diagrams—to show details that are important for the reader in understanding the concepts. Combine all material with a completed cover sheet and kit contents sheet as shown in Figure 10.3, and submit to the library.

PROCESS MAP STANDARD FORMS

The process map diagram form (shown in Figure 10.4) has minimum structure and constraints. The sheet supports only the functions important to the discipline of process mapping analysis. They are:

- Establishment of context

- Cross-referencing between pieces of paper

- Notes about the content of each sheet

The process map diagram form should be a single standard size for ease of filing and copying. The form should be divided into three major sections:

- Working information (top)

Figure 10.3　Process Map Kit Contents Form

KIT CONTENTS FORM

DOCUMENT NUMBER	AUTHOR:					DATE:			STANDARD KIT	REVIEWER	DATE
						TASK NO.			SUMMARY KIT	AUTHOR	DATE
1 2 3 4 5 6 7 8 9 10 11 12 13 14 15									SUPERSEDED OR REVISED DOCUMENT NUMBER		

Pg.	Node	Title	C-Number	Status	Pg.	Node	Title	C-Number	Status

NOMENCLATURE	DOCUMENT/MODEL TITLE	C-NUMBER
		PAGE

228

Figure 10.4 Standard Process Map Diagram Form

KIT DIAGRAM FORM

Used at:	Author:		Date:	WORKING	READER	DATE	Context:
	Project:		Rev:	DRAFT			
				RECOMMENDED			
	Notes: 1 2 3 4 5 6 7 8 9 10			PUBLICATION			

| Node: | Title: | Number: | Page: |

229

- Message field (center)

- Identification fields (bottom)

The form diagram shown in Figure 10.4 should be used for everything written about your process map if you elect to use the IDEF methodology. The form is designed so the Working Information Fields at the top of the form may be cut off when a "final approved for publication" version is completed.

The identification fields at the bottom are designed to show, one under the other, when the forms (with tops intact for tracking) are spread vertically and thumbtacked, in top down order, on a corkboard, wall, or in a Window-type computer process mapping tool. The exposed identification field strips act as a thumb index arranged in node index (outline) order. If the two-sided page-pair publication format is followed, with the text-and-context page bottoms toward the binding, then their information becomes visible when the wall-mounted ancestor forms are lifted up to see the message field of each diagram.

How to Fill in the Working Information Form

The typical Working Information notation that is applicable to the Standard Process Map Diagram Form shown in Figure 10.4 is briefly described below:

1. The "Author/Date/Project" Field This field tells who originally created the process map diagram, the date that it was first drawn, and the project title under which it was created. The "date" field may contain additional dates, written below the original date. These dates represent revisions to the original sheet. If a sheet is re-released without any change, then no revision date is added.

2. The "Reader Notes" Field This provides a check-off for reader notes written on the diagram sheet. As a comment is made on a page, the corresponding note number is crossed out. This process ensures that each reader note on a diagram is assigned a unique note number and that the note numbers on each diagram are consecutive.

3. The "Status" Field The status classifications indicate stages of approval. They are:

- *Working:* The working process map diagram represents a major change and restarts the approval sequence. New process map diagrams are, of course, working copy, but it also is usual for process map diagrams to remain working for several revisions before advancing. A new author for a process map diagram usually resets the status to working as well.

- *Draft:* The diagram is a minor change from the previous process map diagram and has reached some agreed-upon level of acceptance by a set of readers. Draft process map diagrams are those proposed by a task leader (who may be the author). Draft process map diagrams may undergo further revisions if they are included in a current kit along with other diagrams or are brought back into consideration from some reader's file, even though they are not in the current kit. Draft status remains until the process map diagram is accepted by a review meeting of the technical committee or coalition.

- *Recommended:* Both this process map diagram and its supporting text have been reviewed and approved by a meeting of the technical committee or coalition, and this diagram is not expected to change.

- *Publication:* This page may be forwarded as it has been completed for final printing and publication.

4. The "Reader/Date" Field This area is where a reader should initial and date each form.

5. The "Context" Field A sketch of only the box layout of the Parent process map diagram is shown in Figure 10.5, with the Parent box highlighted. The Parent process map diagram's node number is written in the lower left of the context field.

The box number of the Parent box may be written in the highlighted box, even though it also is the last digit in the Child diagram's node field entry.

6. The "Used At" Field This is a list of process map diagrams, other than the Parent context, which use or reference this process map diagram form page in some way.

Figure 10.5   Illustration of Context Field

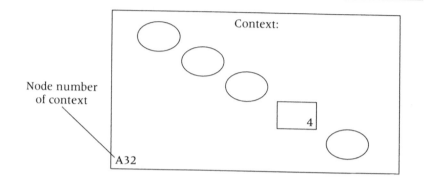

The most common use is a listing of one or more node references to submaps for which this Child diagram's Parent box supplies support for calls into this Child's. With support to a remote submap supplied by this "Used At" field, then any Child box on this Child diagram (or more generally, even the Parent box that supplies the support, or any offspring boxes) may be called upon to supply details for some reachable offspring box of the supported box (treated as the top box of a submodel) whose node reference appears in the "Used At" field. A reachable offspring box is a box that is reachable by a branching mechanism support arrow whose source is ICOM code connected to the mechanism support.

If the top of the diagram is cut off, for publication, then the contents of the "Used At" field must be copied into the Message field as an N note (map note).

7. The "Message" Field The Message field contains the primary message to be conveyed. The field is normally used for diagramming with a process map graphical language, such as IDEF. However, the field can be used for any purpose: glossary, checklists, notes, sketches, and so on. Process map team members should not use other types of process map diagram forms to assure that the reference-number-based filing system can provide a complete process map record. This can be facilitated by process mapping software tool support that includes E-mail and Bulletin

Boards, with automatic C-numbering and "preference" settings for each participant.

8. The "Node" Field This field contains the complete node reference for the sheet (including map model_name, slash, Node Number, and "F" [for FEO], "T" [for text], or "G" [for glossary]—with the page number "1" or "2", and so on, appended at the end to indicate overflow pages, if necessary), so that the sheet is uniquely located for any and all reference purposes.

9. The "Title" Field The Title field contains the name of the material presented on the process map diagram form. If the message field contains a process map diagram, then the contents of the title field must precisely match the name written in the parent box.

10. The "Number" Field The "Number" field (large area) contains the C-number. The C-number is composed of two or three letters of the author's initials (chosen to be unique among team participants) followed by a number sequentially assigned by the author. This C-number is placed in the lower left corner of the Number field and is the primary means of reference to a sheet itself, because the sheet as a process map diagram form in use can only be created once. Every process map diagram form used by an author receives a unique C-number, which habitually should be the first mark made on the form.

If the process mapping team elects to track version history, then the C-number of the process map diagram form of which this sheet is an altered version shall be written in parentheses (space optional) following the author's C-number entry in the C-number field. For example "AB34(CD123)"indicates that this sheet ("AB34") is intended to be a replacement for the already-existing "CD123."

When a process map is published, the C-number may be replaced by a standard-sequential page number.

The "Number" field ("Kit Page Number," small rectangular area) is written by the librarian at the right-hand side of the number field inside the small rectangle. This is composed of the process map document number followed by the letter identifying the sheet within the process map document.

PROCESS MAP FILE MANAGEMENT

Each officially assigned participant in a process mapping project should maintain reader/author files of the documents received. The librarian should maintain the official Master and Reference files of the project, archiving each kit submitted during the course of the process mapping project.

Variations in the filing process may occur based on individual preferences, but the following minimum files should be maintained in alphabetically sorted reference number order as the primary organizational filing structure:

- Standard kit files

  Maintained by authors, commenters and perhaps other readers. File Kit Cover Sheets chronologically, as a master log, but extract and file most C-pages in appropriate process maps, in node-reference order. When in doubt, leave sheet in filed kit, perhaps adding cross-referencing Reader Notes on already-filed process map diagram forms in selected other-filing places, as well. (Every sheet is the property of the reader, and reader-note numbering restarts fresh for each C-numbered sheet, so the added personal filing reader notes cannot do any harm.)

- Updated current model files

  Maintained by authors, commenters, and readers from update kits that are received. May be culled in favor of project master versions, as the process mapping effort progresses.

- Working files

  Maintained by authors—and any reader who initiates any ad hoc interchange between participants that has no official author assigned. The process map kit cover sheet for such a reader-started topic should be suggestively named, so that an alphabetical filing of kit contents can parallel the official working files of process maps, and so on.

- Project files

  Maintained by the librarian to standards set by the process mapping management team.

THE PROCESS MAP REVIEW PRESENTATION PROCESS

In addition to the kit cycle, a process map walk-through review presentation process should be developed as a guide for presenting the results of your process map analysis information to your group of "reviewers." It does not substitute for the reader/author kit cycle review process that is central to the quality of your process map, but it may be streamlined for periodic project use at the technical level to provide an opportunity for all participants to share or develop common interpretations that may not surface in the one-on-one kit-based interchanges.

1. Present the process map to be analyzed by using its node index. This is the process map's table of contents. It can provide a quick overview of what is to come.

2. Present selected glossary terms. Encourage each reviewer to replace personal meanings of words with those that the presenting team has chosen.

3. Present each process map diagram for review.

The process map diagram walk-through review process is an orderly, step-by-step process where questions can be asked that may identify potential weaknesses in the process map or its text. Six steps of a structured process map walk-through presentation review are delineated below. Process map corrections may be proposed at any step. These corrections may be noted for execution at a later date or adopted immediately.

Step 1: Scan the Process Map Diagram

This step allows the reader to obtain general impressions about the content of the process map. Typically, the reader will have reviewed the parent diagram that depicted the current process map diagram as one of its boxes. The reader is now examining how the author decomposed that function.

Criteria for acceptance:

- The decomposition is useful for its purpose and is complete within the context of its Parent box. All lower-level functions can clearly be categorized under each of its boxes.

- The diagram reflects, in the reviewer's opinion, a relevant point of view based on the purpose of the process map.

- In the opinion of the reviewer, there is enough new information provided to extend understanding of the Parent box. There is not so much detail that the process map diagram looks complex and is hard to understand.

Unless a problem is rather obvious, criticism may be delayed until Step 3 below. However, first impressions should not be lost. They might be put on a blackboard or flip chart pad until resolved.

Step 2: Examine the Parent Process Map

Once the reader understands the current process map diagram's decomposition, the Parent diagram should be reviewed to ensure compatibility.

Criteria for acceptance:

- The decomposition covers all of the points the reviewer anticipated when reading the Parent diagram.

- Now that the decomposition of this portion of the Parent diagram is revealed, the detail which the reviewer envisioned for this box should still seem correct. If not, note the missing detail.

It might be worthwhile at this step to return to the Parent diagram briefly and add new N notes (reader notes) or embellish existing ones based upon the added insight gained from this look at the decomposition.

Step 3: Connect the Parent Box and the Detail Process Map Diagram

This step tests the arrow interface connections from the Parent to Child diagram.

Criteria for acceptance:

- There are no missing or extra interface arrows.

- Boundary arrows are labeled with proper ICOM codes.

- Child arrow labels are the same or an elaboration of its Parent's matching arrow. Labels convey the correct and complete arrow contents.

- Examination of the connecting arrows reveal no problems in the Parent process map diagram. (An added interface may create a misunderstanding of the message conveyed by the Parent.)

A clockwise tour of the four edges of the Parent box, checking each arrow, will provide a methodical way to check matching of ICOM codes boundary arrows to the parent arrows.

Step 4: Examine Internal Arrow Pattern

The pattern of boxes and arrows constitutes the primary expression of the process map being created.

Each box will be examined in node number order and each arrow followed in ICOM order for each box. When this process is complete, the process map reviewers should be led through the diagram to explore the consequences of situations with which reviewers are familiar and to test the process map diagram's capability to simulate the relationships known to exist.

Criteria for acceptance:

- The process map diagram does not look cluttered. The number of arrow crossings and bends is minimized.

- The boxes should be balanced with regard to detail. There should be an equal amount of detail within each box. However, compromises on this criterion are acceptable for the sake of clarity.

- The process map diagram should be consistent with the reviewer's experience and knowledge of the subject matter. Feedback and error conditions should be shown as the reviewer expects.

- The level of detail of the arrows should match the level of detail of the boxes. Bundling of arrows into more general arrows should be considered.

Step 5: Read the Supportive Documentation

This step examines the points that the author highlights in the text, glossary, and For Exposition Only (FEO) documentation.
Criteria for acceptance:

- The text confirms the interpretation obtained from examining the process map diagram itself.

- Normal paths, feedback, error-handling, and other features suggested by the text are found in the process map diagram or found in an FEO diagram.

- Significant process map diagram features uncovered during Steps 1 through 4 are found in the text, glossary, or FEO.

- References to the process map diagram are detailed enough to connect text, glossary, or FEO to specific parts of a diagram.

Step 6: Set the Status of the Process Map Diagram

Set the status of the diagram (as defined earlier) to one of the following:

- Working
- Draft
- Recommended
- Publication

The process map development procedures noted above provide a clear framework for you to begin your process mapping effort.

HOW TO RUN A PROCESS MAP MEETING

Until comments and reactions are on paper, readers and authors are discouraged from conversing. When a process mapping meeting is required, the procedure is as follows:

1. Each meeting should be limited in length.

2. Each session should start with a specific agenda of process map topics that relate to one or more of the comments and author responses, and the session must stick to these topics.

3. Each session should terminate when the participants agree that the level of productivity has dropped and individual efforts would be more rewarding.

4. Each session should end with an agreed list of action items that may include the scheduling of follow-up sessions with specified agendas.

5. In each session, a "scribe" should be designated to take minutes and note actions, decisions, and topics.

6. Serious unresolved differences should be handled professionally by documenting both sides of the picture.

The result of the meeting should be a written resolution of the issues or a list of issues to be settled by appropriate managerial decision. Resolution can take the form of more study by any of the participants.

CHAPTER 11

Change It!

It is now time for you to apply the tools and techniques described in this book, and you are encouraged to begin today to implement process mapping. Process mapping has been demonstrated to provide you with effective tools and techniques to help you provide your products or services cheaper, better, and faster to satisfy your customers.

The critical factor in implementing process improvement is to focus on change. Once you understand your "As-Is" process you must not only describe the "To-Be" process, you must implement the new processes. Without changing inefficient processes, or elimination of non-value-added processes, you will have wasted a lot of time and money. The degree of significant "bottom-line" improvement changes made to improve your process is the real performance metric for process mapping.

It is time to "Just Do It!"

Notes

Chapter 1   Do You Need a Roadmap?

1. *Control Your Destiny or Someone Else Will,* Noel M. Tichy and Stratford Sherman. Currency Doubleday, 1993.
2. *Improving Performance: How To Manage the White Space on the Organization Chart,* Geary A. Rummler and Alan P. Brache. It was published by Jossey-Bass in 1994 and has been used in Chapter 1 to present a coherent view of "process" to initiate your exploration of process mapping. I thank the authors and Jossey-Bass, their publisher, for permission to use portions of this excellent book.
3. I thank Bruce Gladwin and Kermin Tumay for their input and permission to quote from their work entitled *Modeling Business Processes with SimulationTools,* courtesy of PROMODEL Corporation, Orem, UT, 1995.

Chapter 2   Reengineer Your Business Process

1. *Reengineering—Leveraging the Power of Integrated Product Development,* V. Daniel Hunt. Essex Junction, VT: Omneo-Oliver Wight, 1993.
2. *Reengineering the Corporation,* Michael Hammer and James Champy. New York: Harper Collins Publishers, 1993.
3. *Reengineering for Results,* Sharon L. Caudle, Ph.D. Washington DC: Center for Information Management, National Academy of Public Administration, 1994.

Chapter 3   Role of Process Mapping in Reengineering

1. *Reengineering for Results,* Sharon L. Caudle, Ph.D. Washington DC: Center for Information Management, National Academy of Public Administration, 1994.
2. *Reengineering—Leveraging the Power of Integrated Product Development,* V. Daniel Hunt. Essex Junction, VT: Omneo-Oliver Wight, 1993.

Chapter 4   Do You Really Understand Your Processes?

1. The continuous process improvement steps in this chapter are based on *An Introduction to the Continuous Improvement Process— Principles and Practices,* by Nicholas R. Schacht and Brian E. Mansir, April 1989, developed by LMI under DoD contract MDA903-85-C-0139. We thank the U. S. Department of Defense and LMI for permission to use the public domain material. This material has been revised to emphasize the role of process mapping.
2. *Dynamic Manufacturing—Creating the Learning Organization,* Robert H. Hayes, Steven C. Wheelwright, and Kim B. Clark. The Free Press, 1988.

Chapter 7   Create a Process Mapping Team

1. *Reengineering—Leveraging the Power of Integrated Product Development,* V. Daniel Hunt. Essex Junction, VT: Omneo-Oliver Wight, 1993.

Chapter 9   How to Collect Data for Process Mapping

1. The author thanks all of the individuals and companies that have contributed their time and talent to the development of the IDEF0 concepts, publications, and standards. This chapter reflects some of the fundamental elements of the IDEF methodology.

Chapter 10   Process Map Implementation

1. The author thanks D. T. Ross, J. W. Brackett, R. R. Bravoco, and K. E. Schman, Jr., for their groundbreaking initial structural analysis concept and application work that resulted in the *Architect's Manual, ICAM Definition Method, IDEF0*, prepared by Sof-Tech, Inc., in 1979 for the U. S. Air Force. This material has been substantially updated, edited, and abridged in this chapter.

Suggested Reading

Books

Bruce, Thomas A. *Designing Quality Databases With IDEF1X Information Models.* Dorset House Publishing, 1992.

Camp, Robert C. *Benchmarking: The Search for Industry Best Practices That Lead to Superior Performance.* Milwaukee, WI: Quality Press/ American Society for Quality Control, 1989.

Davenport, Thomas H. *Process Innovation—Reengineering Work Through Information Technology.* Boston: Harvard Business School Press, 1993.

Drucker, Peter F. *Managing for the Future—The 1990's and Beyond.* New York: Truman Talley Books/Dutton, 1992

Drucker, Peter F. *Post-Capitalist Society.* New York: Harper Business, 1993.

Galloway, Dianne. *Mapping Work Processes.* Milwaukee, WI: ASQC Quality Press, 1994

Harrington, H. James., *Business Process Improvement.* New York: McGraw-Hill, 1991.

Hammer, Michael and James Champy. *Reengineering the Corporation—A Manifesto for Business Revolution.* New York: Harper Collins Publishers, 1993.

Harrell, C. R. and Ken Tumay. *Simulation of Manufacturing and Service Systems.* New York: IE Management Press, 1995.

Hunt, V. Daniel. *Quality in America.* Burr Ridge, IL: Irwin Professional Publishing, 1995.

Hunt, V. Daniel. *Reengineering—Leveraging the Power of Integrated Product Development*. New York: John Wiley & Sons (formerly Omneo-Oliver Wight), 1993.

Imai, Masaki. *Kaizen: The Key to Japan's Competitive Success*. New York: Random House, Inc., 1986.

Ishikawa, Kaoru. *What Is Total Quality Control? The Japanese Way*. Englewood Cliffs, NJ: Prentice-Hall, 1985.

Mintzberg, Henry. *The Structuring of Organizations, A Synthesis of the Research*. Englewood Cliffs, NJ: Prentice-Hall, 1979.

Nadler, D. A., Gerstein, M. S., Shaw, R. B., Associates. *Organizational Architecture: Designs for Changing Organizations*. San Francisco: Jossey-Bass, 1992

Peterson, Donald E. *A Better Idea—Redefining the Way Americans Work*. Boston, MA: Houghton Mifflin, 1991.

Porter, Michael E. *Competitive Advantage, Creating and Sustaining Superior Performance*. New York: The Free Press, 1985.

Price Waterhouse Change Integration Team, *Better Change: Best Practices for Transforming Your Organization*. Burr Ridge, IL: Irwin Professional Publishing, 1995.

Schein, Edgar H., *Process Consultation*. Reading, MA: Addison-Wesley, 1992.

Scholtes, Peter R., et al. *The Team Handbook—How to Use Teams to Improve Quality*. Madison, WI: Joiner Associates, 1988.

Rummler, Geary A. and Alan P. Brache. *Improving Performance— How to Manage the White Space on the Organization Chart*. San Francisco, CA: Jossey-Bass, 1990.

Tichy Noel M. and Sherman Stratford. *Control Your Destiny or Someone Else Will*. New York: Currency Doubleday, 1993.

Wheelright, Steven C. and Clark, Kim B. *Revolutionizing Product Development*. New York: The Free Press, 1992.

Reports or Studies

An Assessment of Simulation Systems Applicable to Business Process Reengineering at Army Directorates of Public Works, Neely, Edgar "Skip" and Johnson, James H., and Orth, Mark J., USACERL Technical Report FF-94/31, September 1994.

Functional Process Simulation Guidebook, Director of Defense Information, Office of the Assistant Secretary of Defense, January 1, 1993.

IDEF Architects Manual—IDEF0 Definition Method, SofTech Inc., Report No. 7500-15.

Integration Definition for Function Modeling (IDEF0), U. S. Department of Commerce, Technology Administration, National Institute of Standards and Technology, Federal Information Processing Standards Publication, Report Number FIPS PUB 183, December 1993.

Reengineering for Results—Keys to Success from Government Experience, Dr. Sharon L. Caudle, Center for Information Management, National Academy of Public Administration, August 1994.

SADT—Structured Analysis & Design Technique, D. Marca, C. McGowan, Eclectic Systems, San Diego, CA.

Magazine and Journal Articles

Hall, G., J. Rosenthal, and J.B. Nicholson. *How to Make Reengineering Really Work.* Harvard Business Review, 1993, 71(6):119–131.

Moravec, Robert D. and Michael S. Yoemans. *Using ABC to Support Business Reengineering in the Department of Defense.* Journal of Cost Management, Summer 1992.

Stewart, T.A. *Reengineering: The Hot New Management Tool.* Fortune, 1993, 128(4):41–48.

Conference Proceedings

Cullinane, Thomas P. *The Human Elements of IDEF,* IDEF Users Group Conference Proceedings, May 1990, pp. 177–194.

Cullinane, Thomas P. *Teaching and Using IDEF0.* IDEF Users Group Conference Proceedings, February 1989, pp. 101–106.

Lantzy, Mark and Bob Moir. *Business Process Reengineering—Successfully Managing the Results,* IDEF Users Group Conference Proceedings, October 1992.

Patel, Kamla and Charles R. Tye. *Business Process Improvement—An Integrated Approach Using IDEF, ABC, TQM, and Benchmarking Methodologies.* IDEF Users Group Conference Proceedings, May 1993, pp. 59–73.

Seltzer, Robert. *Establishing IDEF in the Business Process Improvement Marketplace.* IDEF Users Group Conference Proceedings, October 1992.

Seltzer, Robert. *Design IDEF—Automated Support for IDEF/SADT Modeling.* IDEF Users Group Conference Proceedings, February 1989, pp. 112–122.

Snodgrass, B. Neil. *Integrating Activity Based Costing with IDEF Modeling.* IDEF Users Group Conference Proceedings, May 1992.

Acronyms

ABC	Activity-Based Costing
BIC	Best-in-Class
BOS	Business Operating System
CAD	Computer-Aided Design
CASE	Computer-Aided Software Engineering
CAM	Computer-Aided Manufacturing
CAPP	Computer-Aided Process Planning
CBAM	Cost Benefit Analysis Methodology
CE	Concurrent Engineering
CIM	Computer Integrated Manufacturing
CIM	Corporate Information Management (DoD)
CMS	Cost Management System
COQ	Cost of Quality
CPI	Continuous Process Improvement
CVI	Continuous Value Improvement
DBMS	Data Base Management System
DDSS	Design Decision Support System
DFA	Design for Assembly
DFM	Design for Manufacturability
DoD	Department of Defense
DOE	Design of Experiments
ECO	Engineering Change Order
EDI	Electronic Data Interchange
FEA	Functional Economic Analysis
FEM	Finite Element Modeling

FEO	For Exposition Only
GT	Group Technology
I-CASE	Integrated Computer-Aided Software Engineering
ICOM	Input, Control, Output, Mechanism
IDEF	Integrated DEFinition Language
IRR	Internal Rate of Return
ISO	International Standards Organization
IT	Information Technology
JIT	Just in Time
LCC	Life Cycle Cost
MDT	Multidisciplinary Team
MRP	Material Requirements Planning
MRPII	Material Resource Planning
NPV	Net Present Value
OSI	Open Systems Interconnection
PDCA	Plan-Do-Check-Act (Cycle)
PMAP	Process Mapping
QA	Quality Assurance
QFD	Quality Function Deployment
ROI	Return on Investment
SADT	Structured Analysis and Design Technique
SCM	Strategic Cost Management
SPC	Statistical Process Control
SQC	Statistical Quality Control
TCM	Total Cost Management
TDP	Technical Data Packages
TQM	Total Quality Management
VCI	Value Cost Improvement
WIP	Work in Process

Points of Contact

The following points of contact are based on brief product and/or service summaries provided by the IDEF Users Group and the Society for Computer Simulation and on additions suggested by the Technology Research Corporation. As in all rapidly changing product and service information—changes can be expected. Contact the specific organization for their latest information.

PROCESS MAPPING SOFTWARE SUPPLIERS

ABC Technologies, Inc., Ernie Halperin, 5075 S. W. Griffiths Drive, Beaverton, Oregon 97005, (503) 626-4003/4895.

Action Technologies, 1301 Marina Village Parkway, Suite 100, Alameda, California 94501, 1-800-WORKFLOW.

AdvanEdge Technologies Inc., Kenneth A. Carraher, 10170 S. W. Hedges Court, Tualatin, Oregon 97062, (503) 692-8162, FAX (503) 691-2451.

Application Development Consultants, Inc., 3802 Gunn Highway, Suite B, Tampa, Florida 33624-4720, (800) 910-4ADC, (813) 265-3708, FAX (813) 265-3028.

AT&T ISTEL, Scott Broker, 25800 Science Park Drive, Beachwood, Ohio 44122, (708) 437-2444.

CACI International, Inc., Contact: Hal Duncan, Scott Swegles, or Winston Haight, 3333 N. Torrey Pines Court, La Jolla, California 92037, (619) 457-9681, FAX (619) 457-1184.

Coe-Truman Technologies, Inc., Contact: Joann Van Nuys, 1321 Duke Street, Suite 301, Alexandria, Virginia 22314-3563, (703) 836-2671, FAX (703) 836-2563.

D. Appleton Company, Inc., Contact: Neil Snodgrass, 222 Las Colinas Blvd., Suite 1141, Irving, Texas 75039, (214) 869-1066.

Imagine That, Inc., Kathi Hunt, 6830 Via Del Oro, Suite 230, San Jose, California 95119, (408) 365-0305, FAX (408) 629-1251.

The Jonathan Corporation—Systems Group, Contact: Jose A. Villalobos, 5898 Thurston Avenue, Virginia Beach, Virginia 23455, (804) 363-0880, FAX (804) 363-8841, E-mail: josev@neptune, wyvern.tom.

KBSI (Knowledge Based Systems, Inc.), Contact: Elena M. Cigainero or Umesh Hari, One KBSI Place, 1408 University Drive East, College Station, Texas 77840-2335, (409) 260-5274, FAX (409) 260-1965.

Logic Works, Inc., Contact: Jeffrey Mershon, 1060 Route 206, Princeton, New Jersey 98540, (609) 243-0088, (800) 783-7946, FAX (609) 243-9192.

Meta Software Corporation, Contact: Andrew Levin, 125 Cambridge Park Drive, Cambridge, Massachusetts 02140, (617) 576-6920, FAX (617) 661-2008, E-mail avl@metasoft.com.

or

Meta Software Corporation—Federal Systems Office, Contact: Kevin Coombe, 12020 Sunrise Valley Drive, Suite 100, Reston, Virginia 22091, (703) 476-2235, FAX (703) 476-2234.

Micro Analysis & Design Simulation Software, Inc., Catherine Drury, 4900 Pearl East Circle, Suite 201E, Boulder, Colorado 80301, (303) 442-6947, FAX (303) 442-8274.

Micrografx Corporation, Richardson, Texas, (800) 733-3729.

Performance Systems, Inc., Natalie Lasky, 45 Lyme Road, Suite 300, Hanover, New Hampshire 03755, (603) 643-9636, FAX (603) 643-9502.

PROMODEL Corporation, Contact: Bruce Gladwin or Ken Tumay, 1875 South State Street, Suite 3400, Orem, Utah 84058, (801) 226-6036/4612, FAX (801) 226-6046.

Scitor Corporation, Julie Clarke, Business Solutions Group, 333 Middlefield Road, Menlo Park, California 94025, (415) 462-4223, FAX (415) 462-4201, Compuserve 76163.2132, E-mail: jclarke@-scitor.com.

Shapeware Corporation, Maryann Kluster, 520 Pike Street, Suite 1800, Seattle, Washington 98101-4001, (206) 521-4500, FAX (206) 521-4501/4561.

Software Consultants International, LTD., Contact: Lawrence Peters, P.O. Box 5712, Kent, Washington 98064, (206) 631-4212, FAX (206) 631-2328.

Systems Modeling Corporation, Adrian Wood or David M. Profozich, 504 Beaver Street, Sewickley, Pennsylvania 15143, (412) 741-5635.

Texas Instruments, Contact: Mike Amundsen, 6620 Chase Oaks Blvd., MS 8507, Plano, Texas 75086, (214) 575-4942, FAX (214) 575-4144.

Triune Software, Inc., Contact: Keith Comstock, 2900 Presidential Drive, Suite 240, Fairborn, Ohio 45324, (513) 427-9900, FAX (513) 427-9964.

UES, Inc., Knowledge Integration Center, Contact: Vijay Shende, 5162 Blazer Parkway, Dublin, Ohio 43017, (614) 793-2559, FAX (614) 792-0998.

Wizdom Systems, Inc., Contact: Rita Feeney, 1300 Iroquois Avenue, Naperville, Illinois 60563, (708) 357-3000, FAX (708) 357-3059.

IDEF PROCESS MAPPING TRAINING VENDORS

American Management Systems (AMS), Contact: Gordon McDonald, 17777 North Kent Street, Arlington, Virginia 22209, (703) 841-6000, FAX (703) 841-5507.

BDM Technologies, Inc., Systems Integration Tech., Contact: R. R. Preston, 1801 Randolph Road, S.E., Albuquerque, New Mexico 87106-4295, (505) 848-5324, FAX (505) 848-4144.

Booz-Allen & Hamilton, Inc., Contact: Frederick Slems, 8283 Greensboro Drive, McLean, Virginia 22101, (301) 951-2200, FAX (301) 951-2383.

Coopers & Lybrand, Contact: Spencer Haddock, 1530 Wilson Blvd., Arlington, Virginia 22209, (703) 908-1625, FAX (703) 908-1695.

Dynamics Research Corporation, Contact: Allan Dushman, 60 Frontage Road, Andover, Massachusetts 01810, (508) 475-9090, FAX (508) 470-0201.

Eclectic Solutions Corporation, Contact: C. A. ("Al") Irvine, 5580 La Jolla Blvd., Suite 130, La Jolla, California 92037-7692, (619) 696-7529, FAX (619) 558-7928.

KPMG Peat Marwick, Contact: Kevin Martin, Executive Office, #3 Chestnut Ridge Road, Montvale, New Jersey 07645-0435, (202) 467-3336, FAX (202) 293-5437.

MicroMatch Limited, Contact: Peter Yeomans, 10 Salamanca, Crowthorne, Berkshire, RG11 6AP England, 44/344-772794, 44/850-319349, FAX 44/344-773114.

New England Business Consultants, Contact: Richard Bevilacqua, 61 Elm Street, Methuem, Massachusetts 01844, (508) 794-0375, FAX (508) 685-3719.

Pierson Applications Development, Inc., Contact: Joy Matthews, 71 Michael Road, Stamford, Connecticut 06903, (203) 322-1606, FAX (203) 329-1287.

Technology Solutions Company, Contact: Kathy Novak, 9 Village Circle, Suite 400, Roanoke, Texas 76262, (817) 430-5900, FAX (817) 430-5901.

NOTE: Many of the software product vendors also provide training support for their IDEF products.

PROCESS MAPPING CONSULTANTS

Technology Research Corporation, **V. Daniel Hunt,** 5716 Jonathan Mitchell Road, Fairfax Station, Virginia 22039, (703) 764-5208, FAX (703) 764-9432.

Northeastern University, **Dr. Thomas P. Cullinane,** 7 Irving Road, Weston, Massachusetts 02193, (617) 899-2739.

Clarence Feldman, (617) 729-6191.

Dr. Harrison D. Green, 3501-B Avenue Q, Lubbock, Texas 79412, (806) 744-3744, FAX (806) 744-3753.

Viable Systems Inc., **Jay Karlin**, 12236 Stoney Bottom Road, Germantown, Maryland 20874.

SofTech, Inc., **Douglas Ross,** 460 Trotten Pond Road, Waltham, Massachusetts 02154-1960, (617) 890-6900, FAX (617) 890-6055.

PROFESSIONAL ASSOCIATIONS/SOCIETIES

Society for Enterprise Engineering (Formerly IDEF Users Group), Contact: Mary Ellen Johnston, 1900 Founders Drive, Kettering, Ohio 45420, (513) 259-4702, FAX (513) 259-4343.

Society for Computer Simulation, 4838 Ronson Court, Suite L, P. O. Box 17900, San Diego, California 92177, (619) 277-3888, FAX (619) 277-3930.

GOVERNMENT PROCESS REENGINEERING CONTACTS

General Services Administration, Federal Systems Integration Center, Contact: Jack W. Rose, 5203 Leesburg Pike, Suite 400, Falls Church, Virginia 22041, (703) 756-4162.

Department of Defense, Deputy Assistant Secretary of Defense/ Information Management, Contact: Michael S. Yoemans, The Pentagon 3E240, Washington, DC 20301, (703) 746-7932.

Defense Information Systems Agency, Functional Process Improvement Program, Contact: Judy Albert, 1951 Kidwell Drive, Suite 603, Vienna, Virginia 22182, (703) 285-5211.

Center for Functional Process Improvement Expertise, c/o Logicon, Contact: David Carter, 2100 Washington Boulevard, Arlington, Virginia 22204, (703) 486-3500.

Glossary

A-0 Activity Diagram: The special case of a one-box Process Map context diagram containing the top-level function being mapped and its inputs, controls, outputs, and mechanisms along with statements of the map's purpose and viewpoint. A single activity that represents the entire process that is mapped.

Activity: A business process, function, or task that occurs over time and has objective, measurable results. Activities transform input transactions into output transactions, operating under some form of external controls, and use resources in the transformation process.

Activity-Based Costing: A form of cost accounting that examines the cost of each business process function as part of process mapping, focusing on identifying non-value-added process functions so they can be eliminated.

Activity Dependence: An activity intermeshed with other activities in such a way that the first dependent activity cannot be executed until one or more outputs of other activities have been received or accomplished.

Activity Process Mapping: A technique used to define the "As-Is" and "To-Be" configuration of a process.

Alternate Path: A path through a process map composed of one or more optional process tasks for the primary process activity. In simple flow charting it may be preceded by a decision diamond.

Approval Level: One of the following four words assigned to a Process Map to indicate its relative degree of review and approval:

Working	(Lowest level)
Draft	(Next to lowest level)
Recommended	(Next to highest level)
Publication	(Highest level)

Arrow: A directed line, composed of one or more arrow segments, that maps an open channel or conduit conveying data or objects from source (no arrowhead) to use (with arrowhead). There are four arrow classes: Input Arrow, Output Arrow, Control Arrow, and Mechanism Arrow (includes Call Arrow). See Arrow Segment, Boundary Arrow, Internal Arrow.

Arrow Label: A noun or noun phrase associated with a Process Map arrow or arrow segment, specifying its meaning.

Arrow Segment: A line segment that originates or terminates at a box side, a branch (fork or join), or a boundary (unconnected end).

"As-Is" Process Map: A Process Map that represents the current state of the operation that has been mapped, without any specific improvements or changes to existing processes.

Author: The person who prepares and is responsible for any specific Process Map or diagram.

Block Diagram: An alternative form to a linear flow chart.

Boundary Arrow: An arrow with one end (source or use) not connected to any box on a diagram.

Box: A rectangle, containing a name and number, used to represent a Process Map function.

Box Name: The verb or verb phrase placed inside a Process Map box to describe the mapped function.

Box Number: The number (0 to 6) placed inside the lower right corner of a Process Map box to uniquely identify the box on a diagram.

Branch: A junction (fork or join) of two or more arrow segments.

Business Process Reengineering: Refer to Reengineering.

Bundling/Unbundling: The combining of arrow meanings into a composite meaning (bundling), or the separation of arrow meanings (Unbundling), expressed by arrow join and fork syntax.

C-Number: A chronological creation number that may be used to uniquely identify a Process Map diagram and to trace its history; it may be used as a Detail Reference Expression to specify a particular version of a Process Map diagram.

Call Arrow: A type of mechanism arrow that enables the sharing of detail between Process Maps (linking them together) or within a Process Map.

Characteristic: Attributes that are unique to a particular product or service.

Child Box: A Process Map box on a Child diagram. One of the subactivities delineated by the decomposition of a higher-level process activity.

Child Entity: The Process Map entity that is dependent in a specific hierarchical process relationship. It is the entity that receives the migrating key from the other entity in the Parent-Child Process Mapping relationship.

Commenter: A Process Map reader/analyst with sufficient training in Process Mapping techniques who can offer specific comments using the reader note numbering system. The Commenter may also identify flaws in the application of the Process Mapping technique itself. An assigned reader who shares responsibility with the author for the quality of the Process Mapping kit, diagram, or other Process Mapping results.

Context: The immediate environment in which a function (or set of functions on a Process Map diagram) operates.

Context Diagram: A Process Map diagram that presents the context of the map, whose node number is A-n (n greater than or equal to zero). The single box A-0 diagram is a required context diagram; those with node numbers A-1, A-2, . . . are optional context diagrams.

Control Arrow: The class of arrows that express Process Map Control—that is, conditions required to produce correct output. Data or objects modeled as controls may be transformed by the function, creating output. Control arrows are associated with the topside of a Process Map box.

Clustering: Boxes are split and clustered in diagramming. Clustering is the grouping of two or more boxes to form a single box. Its goal is to combine multiple functions into a single more general function.

Customer: The recipient or beneficiary of the outputs of your work efforts or the purchaser of your products or services. May be either internal or external to the organization. The recipient that must be satisfied with the output.

Decision Diamond: A diamond-shaped figure in a flow chart that poses a question and suggests either an alternative path or an inspection point.

Decomposition: The partitioning of a Process Map function into its component functions.

Detail Reference Expression (DRE): A reference (e.g., node number, C-number, page number) written beneath the lower right corner of a Process Map box to show that it is detailed and to indicate which Process Map diagram details it.

Diagram: A single unit of a Process Map that presents the details of a box.

Diagram Node Number: That part of a Process Map diagram's node reference that corresponds to its Parent box node number.

Do-over Loop: A result of a failed inspection point. Requires the process mapping step to be done over again or repeated.

Draft: See Approval Level.

Expert: A person familiar with a part of the real-world system (or subject) being mapped. May serve as a source of information or as a reviewer of part of the Process Map.

For Exposition Only (FEO) Diagram: A graphic description used to expose or highlight specific facts about a Process Map diagram. Unlike a Process Map graphic diagram, a FEO diagram need not comply with Process Mapping rules.

Fork: The junction at which a Process Map arrow segment (going from source to use) divides into two or more arrow segments. May denote unbundling of meaning.

Function: An activity, process, or transformation identified by a verb or verb phrase that describes what must be accomplished.

Function Name: Same as Box Name.

Glossary: A listing of definitions for key words, phrases, and acronyms used in conjunction with a Process Map node or Process Map as a whole.

ICOM Code: The acronym describing Input, Control, Output, Mechanism. A code that associates the boundary arrows of a Child diagram with the arrows of its Parent box; also used for reference purposes.

IDEF Modeling Techniques: A combination of graphic and narrative symbols and rules designed to capture the processes and structures of an enterprise. IDEF0 (pronounced "eye-deaf-zero") is an activity, or behavior, process mapping technique. IDEF techniques were derived from the Integrated Computer-Aided Manufacturing (ICAM) program sponsored by the U. S. Air Force. The acronym IDEF was formed from the term ICAM **DEF**inition Language. Today, it has been renamed and stands for Integrated **DEF**inition Language.

Input: The materials, equipment, information, people, money, or conditions that are needed to carry out the process.

Input Arrow: The class of arrows that express Process Map Input—that is, the data or objects that are transformed by the function into output. Input arrows are associated with the left side of a Process Map box.

Inspection Point: A pass/fail decision point in a flow chart.

Interface: A shared boundary across which data or objects are passed; the connection between two or more Process Map components for the purpose of passing data or objects from one to the other.

Internal Arrow: An input, control, or output arrow connected at both ends (source and use) to a box on a diagram. Contrast with Boundary Arrow.

Join: The junction at which a Process Map arrow segment (going from source to use) merges with one or more other arrow segments to form a single arrow segment. May denote bundling of arrow segment meanings.

Kit: A standardized package of diagrams containing portions of or complete-to-date Process Maps that are to be reviewed. See Kit Cycle.

Kit Cover Sheet: A special form used to control the routing of a Process Map kit through the kit cycle.

Kit Cycle: A formal Reader/Author Cycle procedure that uses kits to obtain peer or expert review during Process Map development.

Librarian: The person responsible for routing and tracking of Process Map kits and keeping orderly project files and archives.

Mapping: The activity of creating a detailed flow chart or process map of a work process showing its inputs, tasks, and activities, in a structured sequence.

Mechanism Arrow: The class of arrows that express the Process Map mechanism—that is, the means used to perform a function; includes the special case of Call Arrow. Mechanism arrows are associated with the bottom side of a Process Map box.

Model Note: A textual comment that is part of a Process Map diagram, used to record a fact not otherwise depicted.

Node: A box from which child boxes originate; a parent box. See Node Index, Node Tree, Node Number, Node Reference, Diagram Node Number.

Node Index: A listing, often indented, showing nodes in a Process Map in "outline" order. Same meaning and content as Node Tree.

Node Number: A code assigned to a box to specify its position in the Process Map hierarchy; may be used as a Detail Reference Expression.

Node Reference: A code assigned to a Process Map diagram to identify it and specify its position in the Process Map hierarchy; composed of the Process Map name (abbreviated) and the diagram node number, with optional extensions.

Node Tree: The graphical representation of the Parent-Child relationships between the nodes of a Process Map model, in the form of a graphical tree. Same meaning and content as Node Index. A node tree is a type of activity map. An activity and its decomposition are displayed in a hierarchical manner. A node tree can be used to provide an overview of a Process Map. They may also be useful for trying out different decomposition strategies before drafting Process Maps.

Output: The tangible product or intangible service that is created by the process, that is passed on to the customer.

Output Arrow: The class of arrows that express Process Map Output—that is, the data or objects produced by a function. Output arrows are associated with the right side of a Process Map box.

Parent Activity: A single activity that decomposes into one or more component activities.

Parent Box: A Process Map box that is detailed by a Child diagram.

Parent Diagram: A Process Map diagram that contains a parent box.

Parent Entity: The entity that is not existence dependent in a specific Process Map relationship. The key of the Parent migrates through the relationship to the Child entity.

Primary Process: The basic steps or activities that will produce the desired output.

Process: A sequence of steps, tasks, or activities that converts inputs from suppliers to an output. A work process should add value to the inputs by changing them or using them to produce something new.

Process Boundaries: The first and last steps of the process.

Process Diagram: A single unit of a Process Map that presents the details of a box.

Process Map: A graphic description of a process, showing the sequence of process tasks, that is developed for a specific purpose and from a selected viewpoint. A set of one or more Process Map diagrams that depict the functions of a system or subject area with graphics, and text.

Process Map Role: A position in a Process Mapping project. See Author, Expert, Commenter, Reader, Librarian.

Process Owner: A designated person within the business process who has authority to manage the process and responsibility for its overall output performance.

Project Field: The field on the Process Map diagram form that records the name of the organized task for which a Process Map is prepared.

Publication: See Approval Level.

Purpose: A brief statement of the reason for a Process Map's existence.

Reader: A person with (limited) training in the Process Mapping technique sufficient to accurately interpret syntax and basic meanings and to read and write reader notes who sees part or all of a Process Map.

Reader/Author Cycle: A procedure using reader notes to obtain peer or expert review during Process Map development.

Reader Note: A textual comment by a reader about a Process Map diagram. Reader notes are not published as part of the Process Map diagram but rather are used for communication during the Reader/Author Cycle.

Recommended: See Approval Level.

Reengineering: Dr. Michael Hammer defines reengineering as "the fundamental and radical redesign of business processes to achieve dramatic improvements in critical, contemporary measures of performance, such as cost, quality, service, and speed.

Requirements: What your customer needs, wants, and expects of your services.

Reviewer: A reviewer shares accountability for the utility of the Process Mapping kit, diagram, or other Process Mapping result. Some reviewers lack Readership training but participate in guided walk-throughs.

Role: Same as Process Map Role.

Semantics: The meaning of the syntactic components of a language.

Split: Boxes are split and clustered while diagramming the Process Map. When a Parent box is detailed on a Child diagram, the Parent box is split into pieces, some of which may then be clustered, to form the three to six boxes on the Child diagram.

Squiggle: A small, jagged line that may be used to associate a label with a particular arrow segment or to associate a Process Map note with a component of a Process Map diagram.

Structured Analysis and Design Technique: The structured analysis and design technique (SADT) was originally developed in

1972 by Douglas T. Ross, of SofTech Corporation. It was selected by the U. S. Air Force as "The Architecture Method" for their Integrated Computer Aided Manufacturing (ICAM) program. The major subset of the SADT technique was latter renamed "IDEFO."

Syntax: Structural components or features of a language and the rules that define relationships among them.

Text: An overall textual (nongraphical) comment about a Process Map graphic diagram.

Theoretical Cycle Time: The sum of the times required to perform each step in the process. Does not account for hand-off or in-process waiting time. It is in theory the shortest time possible to complete a process.

Title: A verb or verb phrase that describes the overall function presented on a Process Map diagram; the title of a Child diagram corresponds to its Parent box name.

"To-Be" Process Map: Process Map that show the results of applying change improvement opportunities to the current (As-Is) process operation.

Total Cycle Time: The total amount of time required to complete a process.

Tunneled Arrow: An arrow (with special notation) that does not follow the normal requirement that each arrow on a diagram must correspond to arrows on related Parent and Child diagrams.

Value-Added Process Step: A process step that directly contributes to customer satisfaction.

Viewpoint: A brief statement of the single perspective from which the Process Map is constructed.

Working: See Approval Level.

Index

ABOUT THE AUTHOR

V. Daniel Hunt is the president of Technology Research Corporation, located in Fairfax Station, Virginia. He is an internationally known management consultant, emerging technology analyst, and author on the topics of productivity (quality, change management, teamwork), systems engineering (concurrent engineering, and product and process improvement), integrated product development (reengineering, business process redesign, and process mapping), and advanced manufacturing technology (CAD, CAM, CIM).

Mr. Hunt has 32 years of management and advanced technology analytical experience as part of the professional staffs of Technology Research Corporation, TRW Inc., The John Hopkins University/ Applied Physics Laboratory, and the Bendix Corporation.

He has served as consultant on projects for the Electric Power Research Institute, the U.S. Department of Defense, the U.S. Department of Justice, the Advanced Research Project Agency, James Martin and Company, Hitachi, Pacific Gas & Electric, Science Applications International Corporation, Professional Services International, the Pymatuning Group, Maxim Technologies, Arthur Andersen/Andersen Consulting, the Dole Foundation, and many commercial and industrial firms. Mr. Hunt is also the author of *The Survival Factor, Reengineering—Leveraging the Power of Integrated Product Development, Quality in America, Quality Management for Government, Managing Quality, The Enterprise Integration Sourcebook, Understanding Robotics, Computer Integrated Manufacturing Handbook, Robotics Sourcebook, Mechatronics: Japan's Newest Threat, Dictionary of Advanced Manufacturing Technology, Artificial Intelligence and Expert System Sourcebook, Smart Robots,* and the *Industrial Robotics Handbook.*

A holder of degrees in electronic engineering and management, Mr. Hunt maintains an active schedule as author and international lecturer on business survival, change management, strategic process improvement, quality improvement, and productivity while serving various industrial companies, government agencies, and other institutions as a management consultant.

Technology Research Corporation provides consulting, planning, implementation, and executive presentation services to assist organizations in improving their profitability, performance, and survival by applying reengineering, strategic process improvement, and quality management tools and techniques to meet their unique needs.

For additional information, contact:

Technology Research Corporation
5716 Jonathan Mitchell Road
Fairfax Station, Virginia 22039
Attn.: Mr. V. Daniel Hunt
(703) 764-5208
FAX (703) 764-9432